African Adventurer's Guide To

ZAMBIA

African Adventurer's Guide To
ZAMBIA

Brendan Dooley &
Nicholas Plewman

SOUTHERN
BOOK PUBLISHERS

ISBN 1 86812 789 3
First edition 1999
2 4 6 8 10 9 7 5 3 1

Published by
Southern Book Publishers
(A division of the New Holland Struik Group)
PO Box 5563, Rivonia 2128

Cover design by Micha McKerr
Maps by Michael Thayer
Set in Optima 10/12
Reproduction by Creda Communications, Eliot Avenue, Eppindust II, Cape Town.
Printed and bound by Creda Communications, Eliot Avenue, Eppindust II, Cape Town.

CONTENTS

ACKNOWLEDGEMENTS

It would not have been possible to research and write this book without the assistance of a great number of people in many and varied ways and to them the authors owe a debt of gratitude. In the first instance we still owe thanks to all those who assisted us in producing the original edition of this book: The Director of the Zambia National Tourist Board, Mr George Lewis and his staff in Lusaka and Donald Pelekamoyo of ZNTB, Johannesburg; Moira Smith and Zambia Airways; the Managing Director of BP Zambia, Mr Peter Knoedel, for his generous sponsorship of a large part of our fuel requirements; the Director of The National Heritage Conservation Commission, Mr Nicholas Katanekwa, for historical advice; the Chairman of the Hotel and Catering Association, Mr Gaudenzio Rossi, for help with accommodation; all the lodge and hotel owners throughout the country who opened their establishments to us and all the organisations who provided information to us. To the numerous Samaritans who helped keep 'the antichrist', our Land Rover, on the road against all odds and to all those who took us in along the way – especially the missionaries at Chavuma, Likulu, Kalabo, Sioma and Serenje, Sheila Siddle at Chimfunshi and Pete and Lynn Fisher at Hillwood Farm – thank you all. In addition, very special thanks to David and Mark Harvey, Ron and Megan Landless, and David and Joan Littleford for their tireless hospitality and encouragement.

Rewriting the book for this edition required the help, not only of some of the above again, but also particularly of Bruce Chapman of the Ridgeway Holiday Inn, Agnes at ZNTB, and Morag Lanzendorf at Aero Zambia. Reworking the material required a great deal of effort on the part of Reneé Ferreira at Southern Books and our editor Danya Ristic and proofreader David Pearson. Thank you.

Lastly, with love and thanks we dedicate this book to the best and most companionable of fellow travellers, Louise and Kathy, without whom we would never have crossed the Zambezi.

HOW TO USE THIS GUIDE

Chapter 1 introduces Zambia and explains how it came to be the country that it is. **Chapter 2** broadly outlines the activities available to visitors, special considerations in Zambia affecting those activities and where best to pursue them. **Chapters 3, 4 and 5** outline the options for getting to and around the country and preparations you should make beforehand.

Once you have a broad idea of what you want to see and do on your visit to Zambia, the best times for visiting, and how to get around, you are ready to tackle the more detailed information in the second part of the book. **Chapters 6 to 11** tell where to go and how to get there in more detail. Zambia is divided into eight administrative provinces (see section on geography, chapter 1). However, other than for certain bureaucratic functions this division is of little consequence to the visitor. For the purpose of describing routes and destinations in the country, the map of Zambia can be divided into six regions of interest (see pages 54–55) and they are described by chapter as follows:

Chapter 6: The Central Region; including Central and Lusaka provinces, west to the Kafue National Park, as far north as Kapiri Mposhi and south to Chirundu and the Lower Zambezi National Park.

Chapter 7: The Southern Region; between the lower Zambezi River and the Kafue River Flats and between Victoria Falls and the Kariba Dam.

Chapter 8: The Western Region; including both sides of the upper Zambezi between its source right up in the north-west corner of the country and the Victoria Falls.

Chapter 9: The Copperbelt; including all the mining towns north of Kapiri Mposhi.

Chapter 10: The Northern Region; includes the Congo watershed between the Great North Road, Democratic Republic of Congo and the lakes.

Chapter 11: The Eastern Region; the Luangwa Valley between the Great North Road watershed and the Malawi border.

Each chapter starts with a brief introduction to the specific region, followed by detailed information on its attractions and in-depth descriptions of the main tourist routes. The main tourist attractions are clearly cross-referenced to the route(s) by means of a route symbol in the margin. In addition, symbols alongside the text have been used to draw the reader's attention immediately to different activities, attractions and accommodation options available. For ease of reference, a list of these symbols can be found on the front cover flap.

Routes 1 to 11, shown on the tourist regions map on pages 54–55, are described at the end of each regional chapter. Each route description is preceded by the direct distance, time, road conditions, the availability of fuel and recommended stops. Distances and times are estimates only and exclude detours and lengthy stops. In addition, details that may make the journey interesting or diverting are included in these routes.

Most places to stay are mentioned in the regional chapters, but there is a detailed directory of addresses and telephone numbers in **chapter 12**.

Chapter 13 gives further directories as well as useful tips and information.

Authors' notes
Distances given in the routes are only approximate. Note that distance measurement tends to vary from vehicle to vehicle. Zambia's tourist industry is expanding rapidly and tourist operations are being established all the time. Consult travel agents for further information.

While all possible care has been taken to ensure that the information is up to date and correct, information does change. This is especially the case with telephone numbers.

The authors and publishers would welcome any information or comments which would assist in updating and improving future editions. Please contact: The Editor, *African Adventurer's Guide to Zambia*, Southern Book Publishers, PO Box 5563, Rivonia 2128, South Africa.

INTRODUCTION TO ZAMBIA

History

Pre-colonial history

From the Victoria Falls on the Zambezi to the shores of Lake Tanganyika, Zambia has a great variety of archaeological sites that provide evidence of human occupation dating back to the Stone Age. Many of these sites have been documented and preserved by the National Heritage Conservation Commission of Zambia, although hitherto most have been neglected as a source of tourist interest.

Tools found in the Zambezi Valley below Victoria Falls are comparable with those from East Africa dated up to 2,5 million years ago. There is evidence at the same sites of hominid advancement and a gradual improvement in tool-making until 70 000 years ago. At Kalambo Falls above Lake Tanganyika there is evidence of fire-making from the same time and at the Broken Hill mine, now Kabwe, perhaps Zambia's most famous archaeological discovery was made – Homo rhodesiensis, a skull that became known as Broken Hill Man and also dates from this period. Perhaps under the influence of environmental change, these early Stone Age hominids began to spread out from the river valleys and occupy caves on the open plateau about 50 000 years ago.

The steady evolution of the species can be traced in Zambia by the refinements of tool-making until the appearance of modern man – evidenced in another discovery at Broken Hill of a jawbone that more closely resembles our own than that of the previously discovered skull.

The Stone Age progressed through further environmental changes and an increase in population until most of the region was occupied. While tradition holds that these Stone Age dwellers in caves and rock shelters were Khoisan people, or Bushmen, there is some evidence to suggest that they were rather of Negroid stock. But Bushmen Stone Age cultures did survive until comparatively recently, particularly in south-western Zambia.

Excavations near Sesheke on the upper Zambezi have unearthed pottery shards of an Iron Age culture as young as 310 BC; no longer simply hunter-gatherers, the people practised agriculture, kept stock and settled in villages of wattle and daub. Iron-working appears to coincide with the immigration of large numbers of Bantu-language speaking people.

This Bantu colonisation seems to have occurred in three waves coming from three directions. The first movement edged up the Zambezi Valley from the east, moving as far as Sesheke three centuries before Christ. In the 6th century AD another wave migrated down the Zambezi from the north. Both of these migrations brought cattle with them. Then in the 9th century a large group moved down from the Congo Basin. These people did not own cattle but began to assimilate the peoples who had preceded them, and by the 11th century they found themselves in the majority. Smelting of both iron and copper was well under way and with the development of wealth and power nation-states emerged in the kingdoms of the Kazembe, Lunda, Lozi and Chewa.

Colonial history

A fairly substantial trade, carried out mainly by the Arabs, existed between central Africa and lands across the Indian Ocean before the arrival of the Europeans. Then in the 15th century the Portuguese, lured by rumours of fabulous wealth in the kingdom of Mwene Mutapa south of the Zambezi, began exploring the valley and establishing bases on the Mozambique coast. They made little effort at real colonisation, instead spending their resources on ill-conceived expeditions of plunder, but over the succeeding centuries trader-adventurers began to penetrate the interior.

In 1793 a Goanese, Goncalo Pereira, became the first European to substantially explore what is today Zambia, venturing as far as the kingdom of Kazembe, south of Lake Mweru. At approximately the same time Portuguese traders from Angola made journeys as far as the headwaters of the Zambezi and in 1795 reached the Barotse floodplains.

At the beginning of the 19th century events took place in southern Africa that would dramatically affect the future of the territory. Under the dual pressure of slavery practised by Portuguese and Arabs on the east coast and European settler advance from the Cape, an extraordinary and terrible chain of events was set in motion by the rise of the Zulu nation and their systematic conquering and destruction of tribes around them. The only escape was flight and the plunder of new lands, which gave rise to a domino effect that spread right up into central Africa and was known as the *Difaqane*.

Cutting a swathe of destruction as they went, the Ngoni people moved eastwards through Zimbabwe to eventually settle in Zambia, Malawi and Tanzania. The Kololo, who were Basotho people, fled westwards across the Kalahari Desert as far as the Zambezi. After conquering the Batonga, the Kololo settled in what is today southern Zambia. Fearful of attack by the Matabele, who had fought their way into Zimbabwe under a dissident Zulu general, Mzilikazi, the Kololo leader Sebitoane took advantage of the recent death of the Lozi king to annex Barotseland as well. David Livingstone was present when Sebitoane died in 1851 on the threshold of a new era in central Africa.

When Livingstone returned in 1855 Sekeletu, Sebitoane's son, showed him the falls, which he named the Victoria Falls on 16 November 1855. Thereafter the passage of European pioneers increased. Two of the most prominent were George Westbeech, an ivory hunter and trader, and François Coillard, a missionary, both of whom had a profound effect on future developments in the region. Livingstone, of course, went on to explore what is now north-eastern Zambia and the lake region, bringing to the world's attention the enormous Arab-controlled slave trade that had blossomed there, before he eventually died on the eastern side of Lake Bangweulu (see page 147).

The exploits of Livingstone and other missionaries and traders put the region north of the Zambezi on the map. Cecil John Rhodes's British South Africa Company expressed interest in the territory's potential mineral wealth, while the British Crown was interested in stamping out the slave trade as well as securing land ahead of its European rivals. By the 1880s the scramble for possession of Africa became intense. Anxious to prevent the Portuguese from pursuing their plans of joining Angola with Mozambique, Rhodes sent one Frank Lochner to Lealui, the Barotseland capital. Deceitfully proclaiming himself an emissary of the British queen, Lochner persuaded the king, Lewanika, to sign over all mineral rights to the British South Africa Company.

At the same time British officials from British Central Africa (Malawi) made administrative forays into what is today northern Zambia to seek alliances with local chiefs and eliminate the ongoing Arab slave trade and gradually bring the region under British control. It became known as North-eastern Rhodesia and had its capital at Fort Jameson, today called Chipata. Barotseland and the west was incorporated into North-western Rhodesia with a capital at Kalomo, before it was moved to Livingstone in 1907. Although formally part of the British Empire, both territories were controlled under Royal Charter by the British South Africa Company. In 1911 the territories were joined to become simply Northern Rhodesia with Livingstone still the capital. Between 1911 and 1914 an Anglo-

Belgian boundary commission established the position of the territory's northern border. Having made little effort to settle and develop the region, the British South Africa Company handed over Northern Rhodesia to the British Government in 1924.

With the beginning of large-scale copper mining in the north and gradual settlement in the rest of the country, a more centralised administrative centre was required and in 1930 the capital was moved to the hitherto rather underdeveloped railway town of Lusaka. In 1953 agitation by settler communities led to the amalgamation of Northern Rhodesia with Southern Rhodesia and Nyasaland to form the Central African Federation. Ill-conceived, the Federation could not withstand the growing tide of African nationalism and the desire for majority rule and self-government in each territory. Short lived as the Federation was, it had a staggering effect on Zambia. The book *Africa on a Shoestring* (Lonely Planet, 1989) quotes some devastating statistics. During Federation some US$200 million created in Northern Rhodesia was spent in Southern Rhodesia. By the time the colonial era drew to a close the British South Africa Company had extracted about $160 million in mining 'royalties'. The British Treasury had collected $80 million in taxes but spent only $10 million on the territory. Subsequent abuse notwithstanding, that imbalance between exploitation and investment is written bold across every mile of Zambian infrastructure.

There is a rather jaded permanent exhibition in the Lusaka Museum, (see chapter 6, page 65) which details the struggle for independence. Zambia was saved from the devastation wreaked upon so many of her neighbours because the struggle was conceded before its relatively minor strikes and demonstrations and the countermeasures of police action and imprisonment could develop into full-scale civil war. The Federation was dissolved in 1963 and on 24 October 1964 Northern Rhodesia became the independent Republic of Zambia with Dr Kenneth David Kaunda as president. Although the country was at first nominally a democracy it was ill served by a turning toward the Communist Bloc for role models and advice. In 1972 the constitution was amended to make it a one-party state with Kaunda's United Independence Party (UNIP) as that party. Obsessed with an African socialist philosophy that he called 'Humanism', Kenneth Kaunda, or KK as he became known, nationalised almost every sector of the economy. In doing so he bound the country's fortunes even more tightly to the copper mines and when the bottom fell out of the copper market Zambia plunged with it (see the section on Economy in this chapter).

At the same time KK's African socialist ideals led him to support a string of liberation armies fighting in neighbouring countries. In return the Rhodesians and South Africans laid waste to road and rail infrastructure in a long campaign of sabotage and intimidation. Subsequent food and commodity shortages provoked widespread instability and produced the violent paranoia about national security that made travel in the country so unpleasant. To this day it is extraordinary how little Zambians know about their country as a whole.

Popular dissatisfaction grew until in 1990 Kaunda capitulated and agreed to a multi-party election under the misconception that he would be returned to power. Instead the winner of the first democratic election in nearly 30 years was the liberal capitalist Movement for Multiparty Democracy, born, perhaps ironically, out of the trade union movement, under Frederick Chiluba who became president. The MMD returned to power in the following election with Chiluba as president again. The new constitution does not allow Chiluba to remain president for more than two terms and at the time of writing he has pledged that he will not follow the deplorable example of certain neighbours by seeking to amend the constitution to allow him to do so.

The progress and fortunes of Zambia's 'third republic' are very much bound to the dire economic straits into which its earlier history plunged it. The commitment of the government to pulling Zambia out of debt by playing by the rules of the IMF, though laudable, has had dire consequences for the currency, inflation and consequently the population, most of whom are desperately poor and have had to watch the price of basic foodstuffs multiply exponentially. This is covered in more detail under the section on the economy. In the mid-nineties it seemed almost impossible that the country would survive these hardships. But, from what we have seen during our latest visits of the imminent rejuvenation of the Copperbelt and the steady rise of tourism, Zambia appears set on a road to greater prosperity.

Geography

The 750 000 square kilometres that is Zambia, landlocked in south-central Africa, forms a vast, kidney-shaped plateau, most of which drains gently southward to the great Zambezi River. Its shape may seem absurd but its boundaries conform to geographical features such as watersheds and rivers. Although well within the tropics, between 10 and 18 degrees south of the Equator, it has a relatively high altitude of 1 300 m above sea level on average and therefore has a surprisingly temperate climate. It is well watered with large rivers, swamps and lakes. It is generally flat and well wooded. Being such a large country it is bound by no fewer than eight other countries, whose borders are divided along major rivers and watersheds. Zambia is immediately surrounded by the Democratic Republic of

Congo (formerly Zaïre), Tanzania, Malawi, Mozambique, Zimbabwe, Botswana, Namibia and Angola.

The country is divided into eight provinces, the divisions corresponding roughly with the changing topography. The Zambezi River rises from its forested upland watershed in North-western Province, just kilometres away from the Democratic Republic of Congo (DRC) border where the land tips northward and begins emptying its rivers into the Congo Basin. Thence it flows into Angola and out again, southward into Western Province and Barotseland, a flat region of vast grass plains, floodplain and dry woodland. Southern Province extends from the flat lands around the hook of the Kafue River southwards to where the Zambezi divides Zambia from Namibia, Botswana and Zimbabwe and plummets over the Victoria Falls into the valleys of the Batoka Gorge and Kariba.

Between the tributaries of the Kafue and Luangwa rivers lies hilly Lusaka Province. Central Province, between Lusaka and Kapiri Mposhi where the Great North Road turns east, is the developed farming heartland of the country. North of Lusaka lies rich farmland and north of that again, Copperbelt Province with its towns and cities close strung along the seams of ore from which it gets its name. Here a narrow strip of the DRC known as the Congo pedicle cuts Zambia almost in two.

The two halves are connected by the Great North Road which runs into Northern Province along an undulating escarpment. To one side of the road lies the basin of the Bangweulu Swamp, from where the Luapula River ultimately runs into the Congo River. On the other side the plateau collapses down the Muchinga Escarpment into the Luangwa Valley, which runs eventually into the Zambezi on the border with Mozambique. Northern Province straddles the watershed up to Lake Tanganyika. To its west lies Luapula Province, mostly flat country stretching westwards to the DRC border along the Luapula River and Lake Mweru. On the other side of the Luangwa lies Eastern Province, rising up to the Nyika Plateau and forming the highest point in the land at 2 148 m on the border with Malawi.

Population

Zambia's eight million people are mostly Africans of Bantu origin (see the section on History in this chapter) belonging to a large number of tribes which speak 73 dialects, although the *lingua franca* is English (see the section on Language, chapter 3).

From its colonial history Zambia has inherited a thriving expatriate community, largely British in origin interspersed with Asians, who settled under the British and now live and work in the major business centres.

Recently other nationalities have come to work on aid projects and even to settle, all making for an extremely diverse society. About 40 per cent of Zambia's population is urbanised, the most densely settled areas being Lusaka and the Copperbelt.

There are seven major tribes in Zambia. Some have lived in the country for centuries whilst others are more recent settlers.

The Tonga and Ila tribes inhabit Southern Province where they have lived for almost 1 000 years. Their relatively peaceful existence was first greatly disrupted in the 19th century by raids carried out by their Matabele and Lozi neighbours and then shattered in the 1950s by the flooding of their traditional lands in the Zambezi Valley under the waters of Lake Kariba which forced them to move to higher ground.

The Lozi are the traditional inhabitants of Barotseland and base themselves on the Barotse floodplain, which they claim extends from the Kafue to west of the Zambezi. Fiercely independent, the Lozi pledge allegiance to their king, the *Litunga*, and have a colourful agrarian culture that centres on the annual *Kuomboka* ceremony. The issue of Lozi independence from the rest of Zambia is still hotly debated.

The Luvale hail originally from the region around Lake Tanganyika whence they migrated centuries ago through the Congo Basin to the Zambezi watershed, conquering and assimilating smaller tribes *en route*. In North-western Province they are made up of the smaller Valuvale, Valuchaze, Vambunda, Vachokwe and Vaviye tribes.

The Kaonde live north and west of the Kafue River between the towns of Kaoma, Mumbwa and Solwezi. They are descended from the central African Empire of the Lunda-Luba and associated with some of the earliest mining of copper.

The Lunda tribe, descended from the same empire, live in Luapula Province and North-western Province.

The Bemba are by far the most numerous people in the northern provinces and also predominate in the Copperbelt, having migrated there to work when the first mines were opened. They too have origins in the Lunda-Luba Empire. They were the last tribe to make any serious stand against colonial encroachment before submitting to the British at the turn of this century.

The Ngoni, who live in Eastern Province, originated in South Africa, having fled that region during the great upheavals of the early 19th century. Arriving in what is today eastern Zambia and Malawi, they conquered and assimilated existing tribes. After their own subjugation to the British Crown they declined during the 20th century and the Chewa and Tumbuka tribes gradually reasserted themselves. Although still called the Ngoni they now speak Nyanja – a language of Chewa origin.

Economy

In 1990, when the Movement for Multiparty Democracy (MMD) took power in the first post-colonial election, the economy of Zambia was in a dreadful state. The section on History on page 2 outlines the causes of this. Briefly, only a tiny fraction of the money generated during the colonial period from resources such as mining was reinvested in the territory. The quasi-socialist, one-party state of the post-independence government sought redress for this by centralising economic power and nationalising all major commerce and industry.

Zambia's economy is heavily reliant on copper, the mining of which is the largest provider of formal employment and the biggest earner of foreign exchange. When Kenneth Kaunda's government nationalised the copper mines the economy developed rapidly for the first 10 years after independence, riding on the back of a high world copper price. Then in 1974 the value of copper collapsed and the whole country fell with it. Failure to free the economy from its dependence on copper has left the country in a state of economic stagnation ever since. Despite this, on the strength of these copper reserves Kaunda borrowed extensively to carry out the socialist programme he called Humanism. However high minded this philosophy, its practical outcome was the inflation of an enormous bureaucracy, in which as much as 40 per cent of Zambia's employed were paid by the government. His support for a string of southern African liberation movements dragged Zambia into turmoil and further into debt.

When Frederick Chiluba and the MMD acceded to power in 1990 they inherited a colossal foreign debt of US$6,6 billion, the heaviest per capita debt in the world.

The new government promised a radical change by decentralisation and re-privatisation of almost all sectors of the economy and entered into agreements with the IMF and the World Bank on what became known as the Structural Adjustment Programme. But unbundling the economy from the bureaucracy with which it had become enmeshed has proved to be politically complex and several years after the lugubrious process began, effective results have been disappointing. In consequence the country's growth rate remained negative for much of the last decade.

The Structural Adjustment Programme brought its own problems. One of the first acts in dismantling state control was to lift the subsidies on maize and fertilisers. Simultaneous relaxation of exchange controls saw the artificially enhanced value of the Kwacha spiral downwards, inflation surge as high as 200 per cent, interest rates become so high that commercial farmers could not plant on borrowed money and consequently basic food prices sky-rocketed. To the average rural Zambian, less interested in balances of payment than staying alive, the process has been mystifying and demoralising. Scarce wonder that many even began to turn back towards the UNIP party and Kaunda.

The 1990s have been extraordinarily difficult, but, as perhaps no other country on the continent has done, Zambia has stuck to its guns of tight monetary policies and in 1999, after years of struggle, it appears the policy is beginning to bear fruit. A recent article in a financial newspaper projected a Gross Domestic Product for the year of 4 per cent, a resounding improvement on the negative growth of preceding years; this encouraged a massive boosting of aid and loans as donors are reassured that economic reforms and privatisation of parastatals will continue. Projected inflation rates of 15 per cent are a strong improvement on 27 per cent in 1998 and vastly different to 138 per cent in 1993 and 208 per cent in 1992.

The structure of the Zambian economy

Mining products are still Zambia's principal exports with copper followed to a much lesser degree by zinc, lead and cobalt. Other exports include agricultural and horticultural products, gemstones, timber and cement. The biggest imports are crude oil, chemicals, machinery and manufactured goods.

Copper accounts for almost 80 per cent of Zambia's export earnings and the mining of it has hitherto been the preserve of Zambia's biggest parastatal, Zambia Consolidated Copper Mines (ZCCM). It is fair to say that most Zambians believe that the privatisation of ZCCM will alter the entire economic fortune of the country for the better. At the time of writing this process is far advanced, accounting for much current optimism.

By African standards Zambia is relatively industrialised – industry employs 60 per cent of the workforce and accounts for 24 per cent of the GDP. Agriculture accounts for another 20 per cent of the GDP. As mentioned above the removal of maize price controls and massively high interest rates made planting this staple non-viable and many commercial farmers have switched to export crops like soya and sunflowers, making it necessary for the government to import maize. Over 60 per cent of Zambia's maize yield is produced by small-scale or subsistence farmers. This points to one of the most important features of Zambian agriculture: that a relatively high percentage of agricultural produce comes from the surplus of subsistence farmers. Tobacco, maize, wheat, groundnuts and beef are produced mainly by a small number of commercial farmers, the balance being the surplus produce of subsistence farmers.

Exploitation of Zambia's gemstones remains underdeveloped although the quality of Zambian emeralds is still rumoured to be unsurpassed.

Another legacy of the machinations of the previous government is that tourism remains a rather small contributor to the economy. As this book will show, the potential for tourism in Zambia is enormous and there is no reason why this and the agricultural sector should not be able to put Zambia back on its feet.

Heavy reliance on depressed copper prices, which are set to fall even further, extremely high inflation, rapid population growth, corruption in many levels of the bureaucracy and a tardy conversion to the free market hold the formal sector helpless between the old system and the new. It is a bleak outlook. But on the positive side, Zambia today is perhaps the most stable and pro-business country in the region. Vast, untapped resources together with its central position, cheap labour and electricity, and the economic reforms to which it has tenaciously committed itself may still make Zambia a shining example on the continent.

WHY VISIT ZAMBIA?

Zambia offers an unexpected variety of destinations and experiences to the visitor. Although there are many package tours available, there is no doubt that driving in your own, preferably four-wheel-drive, vehicle is the best way to see the country. This is really what this book is about and will be dealt with in chapters 6 to 11 on the various regions. Please note the section on 'In your own Vehicle' in chapter 5 and read the section on driving tips and motor spares in chapter 13.

National Parks and Game Viewing

Most tourists to Zambia will be coming to visit the country's game reserves. From the early days of European exploration the African interior north of the Zambezi was known for its vast herds of game, particularly elephant, and ivory trading has been practised for many, many years. In some areas, particularly the Lozi Kingdom of Barotseland, traditional law controlled exploitation of wildlife resources. However, increasing trade competition toward the end of the 19th century precipitated alarming over-exploitation, especially of ivory, and at the beginning of this century the newly arrived colonial administrations introduced regulations to control hunting.

From these regulations emerged the first game reserves as well as elephant control officers whose job it was to shoot marauding animals, but who became in fact the proto-conservationists who began to set aside wilderness areas for game preservation. At first such reserves were used for hunting safaris, followed by the introduction of photographic and walking safaris. The walking safari, which is so popular in Africa today, may be said to have been pioneered in the Luangwa Valley (see page 50). Due to protection in the first three-quarters of the century game numbers increased enormously. For example, in the Luangwa Valley where they had been practically wiped out at the beginning of the century, there were almost 100 000 elephants and several thousand black rhino by 1970.

Like almost everything else under the Kaunda government these reserves, some amongst the most famous big-game areas on the continent, were nationalised and the majority proclaimed 'National Parks' in the

1970s. Sadly, with the introduction of vast quantities of automatic rifles into the country as that government took several of the sub-continent's liberation movements under its wing, poaching assumed greater proportions than ever before.

An abandonment of responsibility coupled with the prevalence of downright corruption by the government led to wholesale slaughter that in little more than a decade wiped out 80 per cent of the country's game populations. The hundreds of thousands of elephants were reduced to a total population of perhaps 25 000. It is unlikely that a single black rhino remains alive in the whole country today.

That said, all is not lost and visitors can still be assured of seeing game, sometimes even in spectacular proportions, in game reserves that are among the most magnificent wildernesses on the continent. (Consult the chapters on the various regions for detailed descriptions of specific national parks and their game.)

Conservationists can take heart from the precedents set earlier in the century. If it is protected it will not take long for game in depleted reserves to return to its former numbers. The vital thing is that in Zambia, unlike so many African countries, the environment remains largely intact. Today the parks are run by the National Parks and Wildlife Service of Zambia (NPWS) which falls under the Ministry of Tourism. In addition to national parks, enormous areas around the parks and places of environmental importance called Game Management Areas, or GMAs, have been declared. Together these areas amount to nearly 30 per cent of the whole country. (The map office in Lusaka publishes a map of these areas, which should be studied if you wish to fully understand conservation in Zambia.)

In principle the Game Management Areas act as buffer zones in which people may live and controlled harvesting of natural resources is permitted. Some have plenty of game and safari hunters operate their tours here. A proportion of the money generated by hunting is then fed back into local communities under what is called the Administrative Management Design (Admade) Programme. This is an attempt to give local populations a stake in conservation.

The infrastructure in Zambian national parks varies tremendously and their means of travel will determine which parks particular travellers will want to visit. Some can be seen only through specialised safari operators, while others have no infrastructure for visitors at all. Details and recommendations that may affect your choice are given in the regional chapters.

Permits are required to enter national parks and the fees are expensive. These are arranged by safari companies if you visit the parks under their aegis, otherwise permits can be bought at park gates. Fees differ between the major parks and those that are more remote.

At the moment the South Luangwa National Park costs US$15 per person per day. The Kafue, Lochinvar, Sumbu and Lower Zambezi cost $10 and the rest $5 per person per day. In addition vehicles are charged $10 per entry and camping in a national park costs $15 per adult per night. An angling permit can be bought for $10.

For all remote parks it is recommended that permits be bought at Chilanga or regional NPWS offices. For further enquiries contact the Chief Warden, National Parks and Wildlife Service, Private Bag 1, Chilanga. A personal visit will prove far more effective. Drive south from Lusaka toward Kafue and Chirundu for about 18 km and the head offices are located in bungalows on the left-hand side of the road just as it passes through a stand of tall eucalyptus trees.

Almost all national parks which visitors can tour self-sufficiently require four-wheel-drive vehicles. In some it is wise even to take two vehicles as a precaution against being stranded by mechanical failure extremely far from help.

When travelling into remote parks with no facilities it is recommended that you enquire at the nearest NPWS office for a guide. The local scouts have the only detailed knowledge of the areas and you will save yourself an enormous amount of frustration by negotiating a scout's services for the duration of your visit. You will have to feed him, but he will bring his own bedding and – sometimes no small comfort – a rifle. In remote parks where there may still be poachers, you should consider that they are well armed and seldom friendly, although they are more likely to try to slip away unnoticed than provoke an encounter.

The lack of control in some parks places a great onus on visitors to act responsibly. The wilderness is a precious thing, and in many ways its fate in Zambia lies in tourists' hands. Treat it as you would anything ancient and venerable – with the greatest respect. Where camping for example, although not yet formally required by law, it is environmentally friendly to remove and not simply bury all non-biodegradable waste. Four-wheel-drive vehicles can cause great damage to sensitive environments. Remember that game reserves were created to protect these environments and their inhabitants, not entertain tourists. Please travel carefully, ensuring that you and your vehicle leave as little trace of your presence as possible.

Being in the bush requires common sense. In Zambia, where help will not always be at hand, it may save lives. Almost all wild animals can be dangerous. Avoid surprising animals – some may attack as a form of defence. Be extremely wary when walking along riverbanks; coming between hippos and water is a recipe for disaster. Please don't consider swimming, and take the utmost care when drawing water. Crocodiles abound in even the most benign looking of Zambian lakes, swamps and rivers. In any other encounter with dangerous game don't run, especially from lions. Remember they are cats and by comparison human beings are slow-footed mice. Retreat slowly, avoiding eye contact. In the possible, but unlikely, event of being charged by an animal, you are more likely to survive if you stand your ground. The number of tourists who are eaten or trampled is increasing. Again, the presence of an armed scout may be a comfort as well as a sensible precaution.

The national parks and important game areas are described in the following chapters on the regions within which they fall. A summary then follows of location, why and how to go there, and what precautions are advised. For more information contact the National Parks and Wildlife Service, Private Bag 1, Chilanga; or the Wildlife Conservation Society of Zambia, Box 30255, Lusaka, tel. (01) 25-4226.

Canoeing and Rafting

Despite the attractions of many other rivers in Zambia, the Zambezi is the only waterway in which canoeing and rafting are done commercially. Rafting is essentially restricted to the Victoria Falls where several companies on either side of the river vie for the privilege of offering you 'the most exciting stretch of white-water rafting in the world'. (For a more detailed description see page 91.) Recently a company operating at the Ngonye Falls at Sioma has proposed rafting there (see chapter 8).

Canoeing is a more leisurely pursuit and several companies offer canoeing safaris either above the Victoria Falls (see pages 82 and 91) or down the lower Zambezi (see page 75). A list of canoeing safari companies can be found in chapter 13. As opposed to the rafting, which is a hair-raising, one-day affair, the canoe trips are spread across several days and the emphasis is on game- and birdwatching. Close encounters with big game on the shores and islands of the Zambezi during the silent passage of the canoes make this a unique way to see wildlife.

Hiking and Backpacking

Alas, this is very underdeveloped in Zambia and suitable hiking environments are limited. Certain safari operators offer guided backpacking walking safaris in the Kafue and the Luangwa Valley national parks, which is the most exciting way of seeing big-game country (see chapters 6, 11 and 13). But there are no hiking trails that backpackers can follow on their own. At the moment the best on offer is the Nyika Plateau (see page 160) where you can walk alone for miles or take a guided hike of several days, but that is essentially a Malawian experience.

Birdwatching

Many parts of Zambia remain sparsely-populated areas of pristine wilderness and therefore excellent locations for birdwatching. Diverse habitats from Kalahari sandveld to lakes and forests host numerous species found nowhere else. There are a number of books available for identification. A new field guide to Zambian birds has recently been published by the Ornithological Society of Zambia. Southern African guides like Roberts or Newman's *Birds of Southern Africa* combined with a guide to the birds of East and Central Africa will cover most species. The Zambian National Tourist Board publishes bird checklists for Zambia.

Below are listed the principal birding areas and some of the birds that are special within them.

The Kafue Flats

Possibly the best-known locations for birdwatching in the country are the floodplains of the Blue Lagoon National Park (see page 78) and Lochinvar National Park (see page 97), north and south respectively of the Kafue River. A wide variety of local and migratory birds are to be found – over 430 species have been recorded. Local fig trees may conceal the rare and endemic Chaplin's barbet.

The Zambezi below Victoria Falls

The river between the falls and the lower Zambezi Valley (see chapter 7) covers a wide range of habitat preferred by thicket and riparian forest birds. Kariba itself is rather disappointing, although it hosts a vast number of fish eagles. The Zambezi marks the southern limit of the presence of many central African species and so well defined is the valley barrier that many species found on the Zambian side do not occur in Zimbabwe. These include Fülleborn's longclaw, pale-billed hornbills, the miombo pied barbet, the central bearded scrub robin, Böhm's flycatcher and the white-tailed blue flycatcher. Unfortunately the damming of Kariba destroyed the flood cycle on which some species, such as the African skimmers and rock pratincoles, depended for breeding.

The Zambezi Valley hosts a great variety of birds of prey and the Batoka Gorge is a particularly remarkable area for nesting raptors. Although the gorge is difficult to access, the avid birdwatcher will be rewarded by the possibility of some 36 species, including the rare taita falcon, bat hawks, peregrine falcons, ospreys and black and crowned eagles.

Below the Kariba wall the roads to Chirundu, Mbendele and Mutulanganga pass through excellent areas for birdwatching with the hot summer months producing such special finds as Narina trogons, barred cuckoos, Livingstone's flycatcher, white-spotted nicator and the mottled and batlike spinetails. And perhaps most prized of all the beautiful Angola pitta can be found in surrounding thickets.

The Upper Zambezi, the Kafue National Park and the Busanga floodplains

Habitats in this region are large and varied, from floodplain and grassland to riparian woodland, 'miombo' woodland, Kalahari sandveld and mopane forest. Special birds include Chaplin's barbet, a Zambian endemic found in fig savanna, black-cheeked lovebirds (which are a Red Data species) and Pel's fishing owl in the riverine woodlands. Denham's bustard can be found west of the Zambezi. The Busanga plains (see page 71) host vast flocks of wattled cranes, pelicans and pratincoles as well as Böhm's bee-eaters and African skimmers. Carmine bee-eaters nest in magnificent colonies along the main rivers.

Mwinilunga and the north-west

High rainfall in this area produces equatorial forest and well-developed riparian forest which together with large grassy 'dambos' and pans make for excellent birding. Many rare and interesting birds are to be found here, including white-spotted flufftails, olive long-tailed cuckoos, Grimwood's longclaw and thrush babblers. The West Lunga National Park (see page 112) is a particularly good area for such species although the park itself is difficult to access.

The Nyika Plateau and north-eastern montane forests

Visitors to this area should be equipped with a field guide to the birds of East and central Africa and should be on the lookout for Angolan and red-rumped swallows, pink-breasted turtle doves, bartailed trogons, Sharpe's akalat and scarlet-tufted malachite sunbirds. The habitat is unique and has many species not found anywhere else in Zambia. In order to spot the birds, you need to walk very slowly and quietly or simply sit and wait in likely areas as forest birds are wary and often feed in travelling bird parties 'on the hop'.

The Bangweulu Swamps

This area is unfortunately most difficult to access during the best birding season after the rains but a visit at any time of the year is worthwhile, with most wetland species being found here. It is particularly well-known as the most southerly locale of that extraordinary bird, the shoebill (see pages 135 and 137). On Shoebill Island these can be seen at particularly close quarters. Other species include coppery-tailed coucals, white-rumped barbets and marsh tchagras, endemic to northern Zambia.

Northern Zambia and the Great Lakes

Population density in much of northern Zambia has resulted in habitat degradation in some areas. However, many species can still be found that do not occur further south. Shoebills occur in several marshes. Lake Mweru has some interesting localised species such as the Payn's yellow warbler, slender-billed weaver, orange-cheeked waxbill and spotted thrush babbler. Red and blue sunbirds are beautiful creatures found over much of northern Zambia and a very localised monotypic genus of white-winged starling occurs only in the upper Luangwa and on Lake Mweru Wantipa. The spectacular Lady Ross's tauraco, more mundanely known as Ross's lourie, is common in the northern provinces. Palmnut vultures can be found in the phoenix palms along the tributaries of the Chambeshi. The Kapishya hot springs near Shiwa Ngandu (see pages 139 to 141) are a particularly good location for these last two species.

The Luangwa Valley

This extensive and pristine wilderness is a prime location for both game- and birdwatching. Most of the species found here are similar to those in the Zambezi Valley, but they have been more extensively recorded, particularly in the region around Mfuwe. A local speciality is Pel's fishing owl. There are large numbers of African skimmers along the sandbanks of the Luangwa. In the miombo woodlands the elusive African broadbill can be seen performing its delightful aerial display and the bar-winged weaver, a miombo endemic, may also be spotted here.

Zambia has a small but active ornithological society, ZOS, from whom more extensive information on the country's birdlife can be obtained. Their address is Box 33944, Lusaka 10101; e-mail at zos@zamnet.zm. ZOS has published the first Zambia Bird Report and intends to update it annually. For philatelists Zambia has produced a collection of stamps of exquisitely painted, specially selected Zambian birds.

Angling

Zambia is estimated to have 45 per cent of the total water resources of southern Africa. So it's little wonder that the multitude of rivers, lakes and swamps host an enormous and varied fish population. While only a fraction of these will interest anglers, many species that occur here are not found elsewhere in southern Africa. Despite its enormous potential, sport fishing is relatively underdeveloped in Zambia, so it presents keen anglers with all sorts of exciting possibilities.

The premier fishing destinations are the Zambezi and Kafue rivers, Lake Kariba and Lake Tanganyika, but that should not deter those keen to try other areas. Angling is even allowed in national parks as long as a permit has been obtained beforehand.

For the most part the hot summer months provide the best fishing season except in the Barotse floodplains of the upper Zambezi where June through to August are said to be the most worthwhile. Anglers are advised to take their own equipment and paraphernalia as there are no stores selling tackle anywhere in the country. Boats are available only at certain lodges. Remember that strict regulations control the movement of boats between the waters of different countries in southern Africa. Fishing from banks is often difficult and even dangerous with few waters free of crocodiles and some positively infested with the reptiles.

Some of the better known destinations, their angling possibilities and, where necessary, particular fishing techniques are described here.

The Zambezi and its tributaries

One of the longest rivers in the world, with diverse habitats as well as huge waterfalls and rapids that form obstacles to the passage of different species, the Zambezi naturally provides a wealth of fishing opportunities. The river is probably most famous for tigerfish. These are caught on a variety of spinners, spoons or baits and methods vary from place to place. There are numerous bream species including yellow-bellied, three-spot, redbreasted, Kariba and Mozambique breams. Then there are a host of others worth catching, some with quite ludicrous names such as vundu, thin-faced largemouth, pink happy, green happy, cheesa, nkupi, bottlenose and Cornish jack.

The upper Zambezi and Barotse floodplains (see page 105) are an excellent destination in the dry season when the floodwaters recede from the surrounding floodplains, concentrating food sources and improving visibility on the river.

Popular fishing spots are Senanga, Mongu and the Ngonye Falls and Sesheke or Katima Mulilo. There are several professional angling safari operations. **Barotse Fishing Safaris** operate out of Senanga. The **Senanga Lodge** has a few boats and some equipment for hire. **Tiger Fishing Tours Ltd** has a tented camp about 35 km north of Mongu.

Below the Ngonye Falls at Sioma where the Zambezi narrows, fishing from the banks is said to be good. There are a number of new camps downstream of the Ngonye Falls which cater for fishermen. These lodges and safari companies are described in chapters 8, 12 and 13.

Lake Kariba itself is an angling haven. There is little commercial development on the Zambian side and indeed it is accessible only at Sinazongwe and Siavonga. Some lodges at Siavonga provide boats. The best time to fish at Kariba is between October and March. The lower Zambezi is a fine fishing location although of the few camps on this stretch of the river (see page 76), most are closed during the wet season when fishing is at its best.

The Kafue River presents an anomaly to anglers because certain species such as the tigerfish, which are present in all the other tributaries of the Zambezi, are not found above the Kafue Gorge. This is explained by the Kafue Gorge rapids and a fascinating theory which indicates that the upper and lower Zambezi were once different rivers altogether. For more details see Mike Main's book *Zambezi, Journey of a River*. The Kafue is famous for its yellow-bellied bream which are caught along its entire length. Lafupa and Chunga camps in the Kafue National Park have motorised launches. Accommodation is available at **Lechwe Lodge** not far from Lusaka and **Gwabi Lodge** close to where the Kafue joins the Zambezi near Chirundu.

Lake Tanganyika

This enormous lake (see page 142) has so many fish species that many have not yet been named. But there are several well known to anglers which make this a premier destination. There are kupi, salmon, Goliath tigerfish and the redoubtable Nile perch, for which these are the most southern waters. The lake is crystal clear and extremely deep with an obstruction-free bottom. This has led to a curious type of angling in which special enlarged 'lips' are added to deep diving lures, then trolled on thin (2 to 4 kg) line up to 200 m behind the boat. A downrigger would probably work just as well.

The kupi is arguably the most sought-after fish. Swallow-tailed and gold in colour, it can weigh 4 kg and is usually caught on small, deep diving lures or fillet baits fished near the bottom. Once hooked it is a tenacious fighter and once cooked quite the most delicious fish from the lake.

This Rift Valley lake is renowned for its Nile perch, although this species does not attain the gargantuan proportions of its Lake Victoria relative. But specimens up to 50 kg are landed, often while fishing for nkupi with artificial deep-diving lures at depths of over 30 m. They are not especially strong fighters but their slightly oily flesh can be tasty.

Perhaps the most exciting fish to hook in the lake is the Goliath tigerfish, which is much larger, more fearsome and every bit as good a fighter as its smaller southern cousin. This monster really belongs to the Congo River drainage system but can be found here in the estuaries of major rivers entering the lake. Generally the Zambian shores are not the best areas on the lake for fishing, because they are shallower than others but in February each year the Zambian National Angling Championship is contested out of Kasaba Bay. For more details about the tournament write to Regg Hueys at Box 90669, Luanshya. He has organised the tournament since its inception over 20 years ago.

Although the potential for sport angling is only beginning to be realised in Zambia, the local population have of course been fishing the waters for years. Unregulated use of gill nets and the like has depleted resources on some rivers, especially in heavily populated areas. Despite this, the fishing remains excellent and angling locations are often as wild and pristine as you could wish for. For visitors particularly interested in fish and fishing, Paul Skelton's *A Complete Guide to the Freshwater Fishes of Southern Africa* (Southern Books, 1993) is highly recommended.

Hunting Safaris

Zambia is renowned for offering some of the finest big-game hunting in Africa. Game management areas have been described earlier, and it is in these vast wildernesses surrounding, unfenced, the major national parks that safari hunting takes place. Swamps and savanna, deciduous woodland, Kalahari sandveld, forests and plains provide habitats for a diverse game population, with several species endemic to Zambia. Heavy poaching in the last decade has considerably reduced game populations. In an effort to reverse this tendency the government has introduced the Admade programme for Zambia's game management areas. The principle underlying Admade is that local residents will derive financial benefit from hunting and thereby be motivated to care for and manage their environments with the help of the National Parks and Wildlife Service. Ideally game will thus be protected and returns accruing to local communities can be used to upgrade their services and facilities.

The hunting coincides with the dry season between May and October or November. Temperatures are low through to September when they start rising rapidly. Hunting in the Luangwa in October can be a hot business indeed. During these months hunters in Zambia can hunt three of the 'big five', namely lion, buffalo and leopard. There is a moratorium on shooting elephants and there are no rhino left at all. Zambian 'specialities' include sitatunga, red lechwe, Lichtenstein's hartebeest, sable and roan antelope and the endemic species of black lechwe, Kafue lechwe, Cooksons's wildebeest and Defassa waterbuck. The chosen prey will determine the area of the country in which you are likely to hunt and the appropriate safari company with which you travel.

All hunters are required to purchase hunting licences and further to abide by the rules and regulations laid down by the NPWS. There are a number of regulations regarding hunting with hand guns or bows and arrows. Temporary importation of firearms and ammunition is possible, as is the export of trophies, but all sorts of regulations must be observed; before coming to the country to hunt you are advised to contact the Professional Hunters Association of Zambia at Box 30106, Lusaka, or telephone them on Lusaka 21-1644, fax 22-6736 or telex ZA44460. They will also provide a list of professional hunters and safari companies.

Festivals and Cultural Events

Not surprisingly in a country with such a diverse cultural heritage, many Zambian tribes have special events or festivals that celebrate their particular culture. Most of these are well worth seeing if your trip coincides with them and the very grandest, such as the *Kuomboka*, are worth travelling to see in their own right. Major tourist centres such as Livingstone and some of the biggest hotels have displays of traditional dancing, but these are a poor imitation of the genuine performance.

The *Kuomboka* ceremony of Barotseland is perhaps the most remarkable and exciting traditional ceremony left in Africa. The name means 'to get out of the water onto dry ground'. The heart of Barotseland is the vast Barotse floodplain that lies on either side of the Zambezi River.

The Lozi, a proud and beautiful people, live on the plain. Lozi traditions and agrarian culture are tied to the annual flood cycle of the river. Barotseland is no longer the independent kingdom it once was but the Lozi remain loyal to their traditional ruler, the Lozi King or *Litunga*. The present *Litunga* is King Yeta IV. He is the representative of Western Province in government.

At the end of the annual rainy season the Zambezi overflows its banks in Barotseland and the surrounding grasslands are suddenly turned into a vast and shimmering lake of green and azure. As the waters begin to rise, usually in April, the Lozi people (and an increasing number of other Zambians and world media) wait in excited anticipation. Then, at a time of his choosing, preferably on a Thursday immediately prior to the full moon, and not in the least affected by all the outside attention, the *Litunga* beats the royal war drums to signal his readiness to move from the lowland palace at Lealui to his high ground residence at Limulunga.

Three massive drums named the *Kanaona, Munanga* and *Mundili*, each said to be over 170 years old, are brought into the royal courtyard.

These drums are over a metre wide and deep and resonate far over Barotseland telling everyone that the king will not sleep at Lealui that night and summoning his subjects to the *Kuomboka* ceremony. Once the king has started the drumming, the royal drummers will keep up the beat continuously until they are taken onto the *Litunga's* barge, the *Nalikwanda*.

The *Nalikwanda*, depicted in paintings and tourist magazines across the country, is an enormous wooden canoe built by a German carpenter at the beginning of the century and painted with broad black and white stripes. In it, a large half-dome of reeds and canvas protects the king from the sun. Surmounting it is a big black *papier maché* elephant and above it flies the *Litunga's* flag, with the silhouette of an elephant set on a brilliant red background.

Enthroned on the barge, the *Litunga* is powered from Lealui to Limulunga by over 100 paddlers. It is a great honour to be a paddler. Each paddler wears a knee-length skirt of various animal skins and a scarlet beret or turban topped by a tuft of lion's mane hair as a headdress. They row with great vigour, but if the *Macabula* drum is sounded, it signals that one paddler is not exerting himself enough and the unfortunate is immediately and unceremoniously thrown overboard by the other paddlers. Throughout the day-long journey the royal orchestra of xylophones and drums proclaim the passage of the king. Following behind in a slightly smaller but equally resplendent barge, the *Nalola*, comes the queen and behind her a flotilla of attendants, dignitaries and onlookers. Three white-painted dugouts scout ahead for suitable channels for the *Nalikwanda* and the procession to pass through. At the end of the day the royal harbour, Nyayuma, at Limulunga is reached and the king is enticed ashore by women dancing in traditional dress.

When the king steps forth from the *Nalikwanda* he is no longer in traditional dress but is splendidly attired in the full uniform of a British admiral, complete with gold-braided jacket and ostrich feather hat, all tailor-made in London at the time of his ascendancy to the Lozi throne. As he steps ashore his subjects chant and give the royal salute or *kushowelela* by kneeling, raising their hands above their heads and then bowing until their foreheads touch the ground. The ceremony ends when the king is taken into the winter capital. Then all Barotseland feasts and celebrates so enthusiastically that many a reveller passes the remainder of the night, if not the week, in a state of somewhat intoxicated sensibility.

During the ceremony, accommodation in nearby Mongu or even Senanga is all but impossible to find. Most hotels in Mongu hold special *Kuomboka* functions. One should try to book early although this is made rather difficult by the unpredictability of the event. The Zambian National

Tourist Board always attempts to give the earliest possible confirmation of the date.

Seemingly rather similar, but in fact quite different, is the *Umutomboko*, a colourful ceremony held in Luapula Province. In a specially prepared arena on the banks of the Ng'ona River, Senior Chief Kazembe celebrates the heritage of one of the great old central African empires by dancing the ancestral war dance, the *Mutomboko*. It takes place on the weekend nearest to the end of July.

The *Likumbi lya Mize* is held by the Luvale people of north-western Zambia when they come together to display their traditional crafts – a process accompanied by much traditional dancing and singing. It takes place every July at Mize, some 7 km west of the town of Zambezi, where the senior Luvale chief, Chief Ndungu, has his palace.

Shimunenga is a tradition of the Ila or Ba-Ila of southern Zambia. It is a ceremony of devotion to the divine ancestors of the tribe and it is usually celebrated either in September or October on a weekend closest to the full moon at Maala, which is about 35 km west of Namwala.

The Ngoni of eastern Zambia have a religious ceremony of thanksgiving for the harvest in which Chief Mpenzi samples the first fruits. It takes place at Mutenguleni village near Chipata on February 24. Like most traditional ceremonies this is accompanied by the consumption of vast quantities of beer and lots of dancing, with Ngoni dancing being something of a local speciality. The traditional *Vimbuza* dancer, bedecked in vivid, gaudy colours dances for many special occasions. Then there are the masked dancers, the Nyau, who are rather more difficult for the public to see, being associated with tribal cults and rituals.

Buying Crafts and Souvenirs

Crafts and curios are not as readily available in Zambia as, for example, in Zimbabwe where vast quantities are flogged along the roadside. There are craft shops in the major centres, the biggest hotels and at Lusaka Airport. But generally the quality of goods is questionable and the shops are full of kitsch curios and trinkets that could have been made anywhere.

In Lusaka, the **Kabwata Cultural Village**, is being revamped and is definitely worth checking out. **Cafe d'Afrique,** in Luanshya Road, has interesting contemporary crafts and both the **Pamodzi** and **Holiday Inn** have curio shops (see page 63).

In Livingstone some vendors flog carvings just off the main road near the Tourist Information offices. Rather better quality wood carving is to be found in the craft shop next to the Falls themselves. An essential stop for curio buyers who are travelling that way is the **Tonga Craft Museum** in

Choma, which not only exhibits some of the finest authentic crafts from all over Zambia but has a shop selling articles of excellent quality. Also do visit **Kubu Crafts** in the town centre and **African Visions Arts and Crafts** next to Faulty Towers (see page 88).

Crafts in the Copperbelt seem restricted to articles carved in malachite which are not to everybody's taste.

Along the road to Siavonga villagers will try to sell enormous hunks of amethyst and other semi-precious stones. People buying jewellery would do well to be cautious of the young men vending precious stones and articles made from them at petrol stations and other outlets. Most of these offerings are worthless. It is possible that genuine precious stones and diamonds are brought to Zambia from the Democratic Republic of Congo and Angola, but this trade is illegal, and besides you have to be an expert to determine whether or not the pieces are authentic.

By far the best way to find genuine crafts is to buy them from rural villages, where you can be sure the articles are authentic and your money goes directly to the craftsman or owner. Beautiful reed and papyrus mats are made in Western Province. Here you will see locals walking along with genuine spears and bows and arrows, and good furniture is made in the region too.

The Lunda in North-western Province make masks as well as extraordinary arrowheads with symbolic and ritualistic significance. Basketware seems better in eastern Zambia. Different kinds of fishing baskets and traps are made all over the country and every village has one or two old maize stampers.

Remember that in Zimbabwe the tourist preference for huge rough wooden carvings poses a serious environmental threat and it would be as well not to encourage the trend in Zambia.

Photography

The writer Shiva Naipaul wrote of his brief visit to Zambia in his otherwise riveting book *North of South*:

'The Zambian landscape is one note endlessly repeated ... unending woodland, a featureless wilderness of spindly trees ... [that] for mile after mile, hour after hour remains the same.'

To some extent that is true of many stretches of road in Zambia, but whether the landscape will provoke such boredom in most visitors is another question. Certainly Naipaul spared little imagination to find the beauty in such enormous tracts of unspoiled environment and had no time to see the many splendid variations on the theme; from the spectacular vastness of the western plains to the ineffable might of the Zambezi, Kafue and Luapula rivers, from green rushes shuddering with life on lake and swamp shore to the endless azure of the horizon, from sombre forests and mesmerising waterfalls to the riotous *laissez-faire* atmosphere of contemporary Zambian towns.

Except in South Luangwa wildlife has grown wary from years of poaching, but this is sometimes made up for by sheer numbers. However telephotos are essential, with 200 mm lenses being the minimum size necessary. It is a case of the bigger the better. Because stability becomes a problem with big lenses, take a bean cushion, drape it over the window and support the camera on it – raising or lowering the window as desired. If you will be in an open vehicle take a tripod, but unless you are in a private party these can be cumbersome on game drives. It is not the sort of country where you will be able to take quality game shots on foot. Zambia has wide, wide horizons for which a corresponding wide-angle lens is indispensable.

Most people in Zambia will not object to having their photograph taken. But a few, particularly old rural women, object on superstitious grounds and an increasing number feel they are being exploited by photographers. Always ask before you 'shoot'. Some subjects will demand money but they can usually be won over with a few minutes of idle banter. Markets are always a source of life and colour.

Cultural events, such as the *Kuomboka* ceremony (see page 21), particularly lend themselves to photography. Snotty and trachoma-riddled children will swarm around you and young men are quite happy to take up your entire film on a series of the most contrived and outlandish poses.

In contrast to Naipaul's disenchantment, the authors' experience is that no amount of camera film is enough. Estimate what you think you will need and double it. Take everything with you, especially spare batteries – which are extremely difficult to find even in the main centres. Video enthusiasts should have an ample supply of charged batteries because opportunities to recharge them will be few and far between. Many lodges and camps do not have electricity and many hotel rooms do not have usable plugs.

Pack your equipment in robust, well-cushioned and dustproof bags or cases. The irregularity of the Zambian road surfaces causes possessions to be roughly treated and dust seeps into everything, so take lens cleaning cloths and brushes. Remember to take a waterproof bag for photographing the Victoria Falls as the spray tends to be pervasive.

Daylight is usually harsh, so early mornings and evenings are best. Film ratings of 50 or 100 ASA are recommended.

When photographing the local people, use a fill-in flash to avoid high contrast. For wide-angle scenic shots a polarising filter is strongly recommended to bring out depth and reduce glare.

PLANNING YOUR TRIP

Climate: When to Visit

Although Zambia lies well within tropical latitudes its reasonably high altitude moderates both heat and humidity, ensuring a generally pleasant climate. The year can be divided into three seasons that determine when it is appropriate to visit the country. Between November and April, the rainy season, it is hot and wet and travel is impossible in many areas, particularly many national parks where untarred roads become impassable even to four-wheel-drive vehicles. Annual rainfall varies from 700 mm in the south to over 1 200 mm (40 inches) in the north.

The rains cease in May and between then and the end of August the days are mild, but nights can be surprisingly cold. Water levels in the river valleys and floodplains recede and remote roads gradually become negotiable again.

Between September and November temperatures start rising. October is 'suicide' month in the Zambezi and Luangwa valleys, being extremely hot and dry, and the air is torpid and heavy with the expectancy of the coming rains.

Obviously the best visiting time depends to some extent on the visitor's intentions. Generally the cool, dry season between May and October is best. The country is most beautiful early in the season when the deciduous woodland is still green. Alas, Zambians are a nation of pyromaniacs who ritually set fire to the whole country every dry season, rendering much of the land black and ugly during the peak visiting time. Even in national parks there is a policy of burning early in the dry season to prevent the possibility of bush fires later when they would be far more destructive.

Many remote places become accessible only as the dry season progresses, with several game lodges and safari companies closing between November and April. Game viewing improves as the bush dries and thins, peaking in October when food and water resources are most limited. Fishing on the upper Zambezi is best in the dry season but on the lakes it is better in the hot months. April is a good time to visit Barotseland when the floodwaters are at their most spectacular and there's the possibility of seeing the *Kuomboka* ceremony (see page 21). For bird enthusiasts the summer months offer the greatest variety although many destinations are inaccessible. It must be said, however, that the country is far, far more beautiful in the summer with vegetation so luxuriant and green that the winter months seem to belong to a different country altogether. Enterprising travellers will find much to compensate for some of the impediments to travel at this time and tour operators are trying to find more activities and destinations for tourists in the 'green season'. Certain activities and specific destinations are best at particular times, as explained in the regional descriptions in the following chapters.

What to Pack

Clothing

Bearing in mind the climatic conditions described above, summer visitors should definitely pack rain gear. Anyone planning to visit the Victoria Falls, particularly between April and June, would do well to pack a water-proof garment of some sort. For all seasons you should combine light cotton clothes for warm days with a windcheater or bush jacket for evenings, which can be surprisingly cool.

Camping in winter certainly requires provision against cold nights in the form of woollens and tracksuits. There is always plenty of sunshine, so wide-brimmed hats and loose, long sleeves are a good idea. For any bush travel and game viewing neutral-coloured clothes are recommended. Some safari operators frown on bright clothes as they make it very difficult to approach wildlife. Bear in mind that if you wear them it will disadvantage everyone else in the party as well as yourself.

Tsetse flies are endemic to most national parks and they are attracted to dark colours, especially black or blue. You wear these colours on game drives and walks at the risk of considerable discomfort as these pernicious little creatures can bite through all but the thickest clothing. Fortunately they are active only in daylight and such considerations need not affect your choice of evening wear.

Shoes should be stout and provide protection against thorns and other hazards. After a day in boots, light 'strops' or sandals will be a relief indeed, but never walk around barefoot, especially at night, as this is the preferred time for snake and scorpion activity. If camping or otherwise adventuring on your own, take a comprehensive medical kit (see the section on Health precautions in this chapter).

Photographic equipment

Take everything you need, with spares and plenty of film as very little can be bought locally. Binoculars are essential for game viewing as Zambian game, with the possible exception of animals in the South Luangwa, tends to be a little more wary and reserved than elsewhere. For the same reason big lenses are necessary for any serious game photography. Sturdy, well-cushioned camera bags are recommended to protect equipment from the inevitable dust and bumping. Seal all film in plastic canisters to prevent damage by dust and grit during processing. Also remember that excessive sun and heat can ruin film and damage equipment. Take plenty of spare batteries as you are unlikely to find replacements anywhere in Zambia. Ordinary 35 mm print film can be bought in the major centres but slide film is much more difficult to obtain.

Although there are developing studios in Lusaka and Ndola it is suggested that you process film after returning home. (See the section on Photography in chapter 2.)

Personal items

Outside Lusaka, Livingstone and the Copperbelt many toiletries and personal items such as sanitary towels or tampons, and even insect repellents, sunscreens and skin creams may be difficult to find, although these items are more widely available today than a few years ago. If planning to use small-town hotels or rest houses you would be well advised to take your own bath plug and toilet paper.

Sporting equipment

The general rule is to take your own. Fishing safari companies generally supply tackle but specialist items are often unavailable. Importing firearms for hunting requires special permits and an endorsement from the safari company involved.

Food and supplies

There are supermarkets with a fairly wide selection of foodstuffs in the big cities. The South African chain 'Shoprite Checkers' has opened in Lusaka, Livingstone, Mongu, Mazabuka and no doubt other major regional centres where travellers from the south can expect familiar fare. Specialist items are unavailable outside major centres, if at all. Do not expect to find frozen meat packed in cling-wrap. However, when it comes to vegetables and staples the local markets are remarkably good – depending on the season you can expect to find onions, sweet potatoes, tomatoes, wild spinach and rape, as well as a wide variety of fruit such as bananas, mangoes, papaws, apples, oranges and lemons. Wild berries and fruit are worth tasting although many are tart. Groundnuts are abundant. All markets sell dried and sometimes fresh fish. The dried sardines or kapenta can be good as a relish if lightly fried but it is recommended that fresh fish be bought directly from the water's edge. Be careful to wash all fruit and vegetables thoroughly. Hepatitis A is common and dysentery endemic. Most Zambian water is beautifully clear and potable, but it is advisable to boil it before drinking, particularly if you are near human settlements.

In most villages you will be able to buy delicious, fresh bread, baked locally and sold in portioned loaves. Cold-drinks are available in most towns but you are usually required to drink them immediately and return the bottle. A local fruit juice in a plastic bottle is vendored almost everywhere, being singly responsible for the vast increase of litter in populated areas.

Mosi, the Zambian lager, deserves a special mention. Zambia is one of the largest per capita beer-consuming nations in the world. Today many canned South African brands are available in major centres and are the preferred status drink but Mosi, in its brown, over-recycled and sometimes unlabelled bottles, is cheaper and just as good. In the past, the liquid in every fifth bottle was flat but a copious survey by the authors reveals this to be a problem no longer. Zambian Breweries was recently taken over by South African Breweries, which may have influenced the matter.

Small restaurants are ubiquitous and offer a standard meal of maize meal – nshima – and relish of kapenta or rape, sometimes with meat or chicken in addition. Try them. Such meals can be excellent. Chicken is usually offered in two varieties: frozen chicken from the supermarket which, although still held in gastronomic awe by local chefs, obviously has more cholesterol and less taste than its poor relation, the much despised 'villagy' chicken which just lost its head in the backyard.

Camping equipment

A few supplies are available in Lusaka, but they can be expensive so it is advised that all equipment should be brought from home. Camping facilities in Zambia are unsophisticated. It is definitely not a country for caravans. Facilities for backpackers are becoming increasingly available although national parks and most other places of interest outside Livingstone do not specifically cater for them in the same way as Zimbabwe does, for example. Tents are a good idea although not essential in the dry season. A mosquito net is recommended and simply sleeping beneath one rigged to a tree can be more comfortable than a tent on hot nights. Also, not all of the hostels and small hotels have such nets so one of your own could be valuable. In most national parks, even those with big game, the campsites are not enclosed, so sleeping in a tent tends to make you feel more secure during nocturnal encounters of the heavy breathing and growling kind.

If travelling into remote areas, especially in the west of the country, take plenty of water, a small medical kit (see the section on Health precautions in this chapter and the sensible precautions covered in chapter 13).

Entry and Customs Regulations

Citizens of most countries in the world will have no difficulty getting into Zambia provided they have a valid passport. It is not necessary for tourists to apply for visas in advance, as they can be bought on arrival at any port of entry for a nominal sum, currently US$10. Regulations have recently been relaxed for South Africans and a visa is no longer required for entry into the country. Visitors from other Commonwealth countries, the Irish Republic and states with which Zambia has visa abolition agreements, such as the Scandinavian countries and Pakistan, do not need a visa.

Recently, day trippers across the border at Victoria Falls became the victims of a disagreement between the two countries whereby any persons not planning to actually spend the night in the country into which they have crossed are subject to a special 'day visa'. Currently it costs US$10 to cross into Zambia for just the day, and Zimbabwe is about to charge the same or even more to Victoria Falls visitors going in the opposite direction.

Visitors can import into Zambia their personal effects, photographic, sporting and camping gear and a limited quantity of beer, wine and spirits as long as these are declared. Foreign currency may be imported without restriction but should also be declared.

Travellers leaving the country by air should remember that there is an airport tax of US$20.

Motorists arriving in Zambia will have to obtain a customs importation permit at the point of entry and a 'Motor vehicle act policy and certificate of insurance' which costs a nominal sum and is also usually available at the border post. To do this you will have to produce a valid licensing and registration certificate from the vehicle's country of origin showing engine and chassis numbers. In addition you may be required to produce proof of ownership or alternative authorisation. You may also be asked to produce a valid international driver's licence. All this should be carried conveniently at hand so that these papers can be produced when required at the country's numerous roadblocks.

If you are planning to take a pet along, a veterinary import permit must be obtained from the **Director of Veterinary Services**, PO Box 50060, Lusaka, and you are advised to apply a month or two in advance.

Health Precautions

Zambia does not require any specific inoculation certificates unless visitors are coming from countries such as the Democratic Republic of Congo, Tanzania and India where they may have passed through infected areas, in which case certificates for cholera and yellow fever are desirable. However, travellers to Zambia are advised to take certain basic medical precautions. Those whose itinerary is wholly arranged and guided by registered tour operators can expect some assistance from them, but for your own comfort you should pack remedies for headaches, stomach upsets, insect bites and stings. All visitors to any part of the country in all seasons must take a course of malaria prophylactics (see page 33).

A more detailed list of health precautions follows. It is aimed at self-guided travellers, but other visitors would do well to read it and abstract any applicable information.

Generally Zambia's health care facilities are satisfactory but the transport infrastructure, while considerably better than many other African countries, is poorly equipped to deal with life-threatening emergencies in remote places. Distances are great while roads and communication are poor, so considerable delays can be expected between accidents and hospitalisation or treatment.

The major centres have reasonable hospitals and rural clinics are fairly abundant. These are not always adequately staffed, however, and stricken travellers should go straight to the nearest mission hospital, of which a good network exists across the country. Missions often have an expatriate doctor in attendance as well as radio communication and sometimes even their own aircraft to deal with extreme emergencies.

Taking out medical insurance with one of several medical insurance companies who will 'casevac' emergency patients to South Africa or Europe is a sensible, if not wholly necessary, precaution.

A comprehensive medical kit is essential for self-guided travellers going to remote places. This should include at least the following: a few pairs of rubber gloves; scissors; an oral airway (and one of suitable size for children if necessary); alleviants for diarrhoea and vomiting, such as Imodium and Valoid; oral rehydration salts (essential); effective painkillers; a few rolls of crêpe bandage for severe lacerations and to use as a pressure bandage in the case of snakebite; assorted stretch-fabric plasters; paraffin gauze dressing for small burns (the most likely and least pleasant of camping injuries, please note that severe burns should be simply rinsed and cooled with cold, clean, water then wrapped in clear polythene cling-wrap before receiving urgent and proper medical attention); a disinfectant such as Mercurochrome; antiseptic and antihistamine creams; sterile packed syringes and a few needles of different sizes (for administration by appropriately qualified persons).

Some knowledge of first aid is necessary. In addition the wilderness traveller might consider taking a snakebite kit, although antivenom should only be used when all other options for treatment have failed. Generally, the application of a crêpe bandage (wrapping it around the entire affected limb to close down the lymphatic system) and evacuation to hospital should be the preferred option (see page 37).

There is much gossip about the hazards of central African hospitals, but going to the extent of carrying quantities of your own dehydrated blood is recommended only to the utterly paranoid.

Malaria

The threat of malaria cannot be overemphasised. The disease is rampant across Zambia. If you do contract the disease and if you are then incorrectly diagnosed and treated you may die. Chloroquine-resistant mosquitoes, against which some traditional prophylactics are no longer effective, are prevalent in Zambia. Bear in mind that the disease is more likely to occur in populated areas because humans are a necessary part of the organism's life cycle.

Reputable medical advice should be sought before your trip. Generally a combined course of chloroquine and non-chloroquine based pills is advised. There are alternative, 'one-pill' drugs available, including a popular one that shall be nameless, that is prescribed with increasing frequency because it is so powerful. We should point out that it is notorious for causing severe side effects and even disturbing psychological symptoms. It is strictly not advised for epileptics, anyone prone to depression or having a history of any kind of mental or psychological problems. Suffice to say that doctors who work in malaria-prevalent areas prescribe it far less than their urban and overseas colleagues. Whatever you choose, take as prescribed and in particular be sure to complete the full course after leaving the malaria-infected area as the parasite remains in the bloodstream for a considerable length of time.

Summer is a particularly high-risk period, whereas the dry season is less so and visitors might do well to consider this when planning a visit to Zambia. The river valleys and swamp areas carry a greater risk, especially populated ones, but don't take chances; consider the whole country malaria-prone at all times of the year.

The best protection against malaria is to take steps to avoid being bitten at all. Mosquitoes are most active in the early evening and very early morning. Wear long sleeves, long trousers and socks, and apply mosquito repellent to any exposed skin at night. If venturing into swampy terrain, take these precautions during the day as well. Sleep under a mosquito net. Almost all lodges supply them, but many urban hotels do not. Although it might take some ingenuity to suspend it, taking your own might be a good idea. Sleeping under the brisk draft of a fast-turning fan is very effective because mosquitoes cannot land in the wind.

Because prophylactic tablets do have the unfortunate side effect of making diagnosis of malaria more difficult, some veteran travellers advocate not taking prophylactics in favour of rigorous bite prevention and immediate treatment if the slightest symptom arises. We would only advise this to just such veterans and African dwellers whose doctors are unlikely to prevaricate over symptoms, blood samples etc. Time is of the absolute essence in treatment and many an overseas visitor has succumbed due to lugubrious testing by medical care unfamiliar with the symptoms. It is unlikely that you will avoid being bitten entirely, so never consider that such precautions make the taking of malaria tablets unnecessary. Malaria prophylactics are strictly not advised for pregnant women and children. Contracting the disease in both cases may be fatal.

Symptoms: Not all mosquitoes carry malaria. The malaria parasite usually takes two weeks to manifest itself. Symptoms are varied and sometimes difficult to diagnose. Unfortunately prophylactics exacerbate the problem by suppressing the parasite and masking symptoms. Reasons for alarm are severe headaches, diarrhoea and vomiting, and flu-like symptoms progressing to high fever. As the disease takes hold victims become delirious. In the case of cerebral malaria death can follow within a week.

Treatment: If you suspect malaria consult a doctor immediately. In the absence of an alternative diagnosis treat for malaria anyway. Early treatment will ensure a rapid recovery; various medicines are prescribed which should clear the parasite within a week, leaving only mild side-effects. Extreme care should be taken by visitors leaving Africa immediately after being in a malaria area as doctors unaccustomed to tropical diseases may misdiagnose the disease. If in doubt it is wise to tell the doctor that you suspect malaria, and consult a specialist in tropical diseases. If no symptoms have manifested eight weeks after leaving a malaria area you should be safe.

Tickbite fever

Although not usually fatal this is a very unpleasant disease against which there are no prophylactics. Only some ticks carry the disease, so if you are bitten it does not automatically mean you will fall ill. To avoid being bitten wear long trousers and socks and apply an insect repellent to the line of your trouser hem.

After walking in the bush, especially in thick grass, inspect your whole body very carefully. The tiny ticks are the most dangerous. Don't simply pull ticks out as their heads may be left behind and they can eventually cause a nasty wound. Smear them with Vaseline or paraffin which will suffocate them and cause them to loosen their hold, then remove them by grabbing the head, not the body, with tweezers.

Treatment is possible with tetracyclines. Like malaria, the initial symptoms are migraines and high fever. Unpleasant delirium may follow but the disease is readily curable.

Sleeping sickness

Much of Zambia is still inhabited by tsetse flies, the carriers of *trypanasomiasis*, which causes this chronic illness. Wooded escarpments and the major river valleys where there is game harbour hordes of these tenacious creatures which, if attracted by movement, will zoom in and inflict a most painful bite. The insect looks rather like a horsefly. It is extremely tough and will not succumb to even a hard swat. The tsetse fly has an impressive proboscis which can penetrate the toughest clothing and against which repellents are quite ineffectual.

Tsetse flies are active only during daylight hours and are particularly attracted to dark colours and movement. They are incapable of flying far from trees so when totally exasperated by them move into a wide open space and keep still. Wear baggy, light-coloured clothing. We were recently advised of a local remedy: many shops in Zambia stock a local skin cream called 'Zebra Cream'. Apparently it works wonders; heaven knows why, but in the absence of anything else, why not give it a try?

Only the tiniest fraction of bites result in sleeping sickness in human beings. Cattle succumb far more easily. The authors have been bitten by literally thousands to no effect. Inhabitants of infected areas are bitten all the time and few ever contract the disease. Nowadays the illness is readily curable and not life-threatening. Tsetse flies can, however, make walking or driving in heavily infected areas most unpleasant. A wise precaution if planning to drive into these areas is to pack some pieces of fly screen that can then be taped to the vehicle's windows to keep the pests at bay.

Do remember that the tsetse fly has earned a reputation as the single greatest protector of wildlife on the continent because it prevents human encroachment in so many areas.

Rabies

This very nasty and always fatal disease is carried particularly by small carnivores and domestic dogs and cats. Beware of 'tame'-looking wild animals such as jackals and mongooses as well as aggressive dogs and cats. If bitten by an animal which you suspect carries the disease consult a doctor immediately. It is possible to be inoculated against rabies but once the disease has taken hold a dreadful death is certain. If you are going to be travelling rough for some length of time in Africa a rabies inoculation is a good idea.

Bilharzia

This parasite is carried by a snail that inhabits still water at the edges of lakes and rivers, particularly near human settlements. Few rivers in Zambia can be guaranteed free of bilharzia, so care should be taken when swimming. If you do swim, you stand a much better chance of being eaten by a crocodile than of catching bilharzia, so there's every good reason to remain on dry land. However, if you still decide to take the plunge and emerge alive, dry yourself vigorously to remove any larvae that may have remained on your skin.

Symptoms of bilharzia include drowsiness, loss of vigour and eventually blood in both urine and stools. The disease is easily cured.

Hepatitis

This is a viral disease that causes jaundice and liver complaints. The more common form is hepatitis A, which is carried by water and food contaminated with human excrement. Avoid drinking water from streams and ponds near human settlements without boiling it vigorously for 10 minutes beforehand. Wash vegetables very thoroughly and preferably peel and cook them before eating.

Hepatitis B is lethal and transferred by blood contact, so safe sex and sterile needles are precautions against it.

Diarrhoea, dysentery and ghiardia

Dysentery is an amoebic infection of the intestine. Its primary symptom is severe diarrhoea.

Few things ruin a holiday as quickly as a case of this illness. The cause is usually contaminated water and food. Be sure to wash food bought in local markets. If it looks excessively dirty or rotten avoid it. Zambia is fortunate to be amply coursed with rivers of wonderful clear water, but be careful. As a rule, always boil drinking water thoroughly. Do not take it for granted that water in the major centres is drinkable. Lusaka water particularly is considered unpotable and unless you have a cast-iron stomach you would do better to drink bottled or boiled liquids.

At the same time travellers should consider that the greater the resistance built up by the body, the less the likelihood of falling ill. Those who painstakingly avoid anything but the most sterilised of foods are bound to slip up somewhere and then infection is all the more likely. Eat and drink with caution but, particularly if your visit is a lengthy one, let your system get as used to local conditions as possible.

Have a supply of anti-diarrhoea tablets at hand and, most importantly, after a diarrhoea attack drink plenty of liquids and take oral rehydration salts. Diarrhoea causes dehydration and this can end in death. If one or two tablets do not stop diarrhoea, do not continue with them – rather consult a doctor as soon as possible. If such symptoms persist months after your trip you may have ghiardia and should be treated accordingly.

Other possibilities

Putsi fly is a horrible little creature that lays its eggs on wet fabric. After washing clothes be sure to iron them thoroughly – this usually destroys the eggs. If the eggs survive in clothes the larvae hatch in contact with warm skin and immediately burrow into it, causing a small, boil-like bump with a black centre. If left alone they eventually re-emerge as flies. To remove the maggots once infected, apply grease to the affected area which will prevent the larvae from breathing. If they do not come out on their own, apply pressure to force them out.

The flies resemble tsetse flies and inflict an unpleasant and stinging bite by diving down shirt fronts or other openings in clothing. However, they are not all that common and even less prevalent in the dry season.

Scorpions can be divided into two kinds. The large black ones have comparatively big pincers, and a sting from one of these is not terribly serious. Small brown scorpions have correspondingly small pincers. These are more poisonous and their sting can cause severe swelling and discomfort but very rarely death. If you shake out your shoes before putting them on each morning a scorpion sting is unlikely.

If the victim starts showing severe symptoms seek medical attention and treat accordingly.

Snakes are common all over the country, but only a small number of species are poisonous. Generally they bite only under extreme provocation. Few people are bitten and of those fewer die. Nevertheless snakebite is extremely traumatic and you should take every precaution against it. Proceed warily when walking in the bush. Wear long trousers and boots. Be careful particularly after sunset when most snakes are active and especially when collecting firewood. Wear shoes all the time. In a close encounter with a snake don't panic – walk away quietly. Don't pick up seemingly dead snakes.

Although not all bites, even from poisonous snakes, result in poisoning, it is natural to fear the worst. Different snakes provoke different symptoms; an adder or cobra bite causes immediate burning pain followed by swelling. Mamba bites quickly result in dizziness and difficulty in breathing. Tree snakes and twig snakes provoke terrible headaches some hours after the bite, followed by bleeding from cuts and mucous membranes, then internal haemorrhaging.

Unaccompanied travellers into the bush would do well to carry a snake guidebook and find out in advance how to deal with snakebite. The following are just a few first aid tips: don't panic but move quickly to calm the victim, who should move as little as possible to try to prevent the poison from circulating too quickly in the bloodstream. Immediately apply a pressure bandage to the bitten area and preferably wind it firmly round the entire limb. The aim of this is to immobilise the lymphatic system. Cutting off the blood supply with a tourniquet can do irreparable tissue damage. Suction on the bite wound may help if it is done immediately, preferably with a suction device.

Unprotected suction by mouth may poison the sucker if they have any mouth lesions. Don't try to kill the snake as this may well lead to another bite, but if it's definitely dead take it with you to aid identification. Rush the victim to hospital, while trying to keep them as still as possible.

Do not inject serum without proper medical supervision unless help is not at hand and it is clear that death will otherwise result.

Certain cobras spit venom, some as far as 2,5 m. Venom that lands on skin will do no harm but if any reaches your eyes terrible burning and swelling will result, which if untreated may cause blindness. Rinse the eyes immediately with whatever harmless liquid comes to hand: water, milk, cold-drink or beer. If you have absolutely nothing else available even urine will help. It may be necessary to rinse the eyes with serum diluted 1:9 in water. Then get medical attention as soon as possible.

Crocodiles abound in Zambian rivers and lakes and even the shallowest and most peaceful-looking stretch of water may conceal a hungry reptile. So be careful when drawing water and we advise that you don't swim. The locals usually know whether or not waters are safe. There are many stories, some of which must be true, about people who thought there wasn't a croc for miles around, only to be gobbled up five minutes later!

AIDS today is a bigger killer by far than all of the above combined. AIDS is absolutely rife in Zambia, especially along the trucking routes. Typical of the rather mordant sense of humour often produced by adversity, the disease is known in Zambia as 'having a slow puncture'. A drive out to the main cemetery on Leopard's Hill Road in Lusaka to count the number of funerals a day serves as a sobering reminder that sexual contact with anyone you do not know well is stupid, but if you insist please **do** use condoms. Today even in Zambia AIDS awareness is widespread so it needs little elaboration.

Special AIDS kits with plasma, syringes, needles and such are available. It is probably sensible to pack your own syringes and needles and for self-guided travellers to take surgical gloves. In the event of involvement in a trauma case involving blood be very cautious about assisting anyone if you do not have gloves.

Currency and Banks

The Zambian monetary unit is the *kwacha* and 1 kwacha is officially divided into 100 *ngwee*, but recent inflation has so diminished the value of the kwacha that the smaller currency unit has fallen away. It is possible, but unlikely, that some public telephones still require ngwee coins, which are best purchased in the local post office and then fed into the phone in large quantities for just a few seconds of call time.

Kwacha are issued in K10 000, K5 000, K1 000, K500, K100, K50 and K20 notes. A K10 coin has also recently been minted. Even the largest units have to be carried around in great wads to buy anything. In 1994 one US dollar was worth 600 kwacha. In November 1998 it was worth K2 000 – a steep, but not precipitous, decline. At the same time the exchange rate against the South African rand fell from R1 to K185 in 1994 to R1 to K385 at the end of 1998. Prices generally are not outrageous. A beer in a hotel bar, for example, cost about K2 000 in 1998. Inflation is still high and the kwacha can be expected to continue to decline in value for some time yet.

All restrictions on foreign currency dealing have been lifted. You can change currency over the counter in any bank. Some years ago the black market was legalised and made official by the creation of *bureaux de change*. These are reliable places to change money, but it is in the streets as you leave them that caution must be taken against mugging.

Changing money on the street is not illegal, but it is unwise as you are likely to be ripped off. If banks are closed try shops, hotels or even petrol station attendants, who will not run away when you have handed over your side of the bargain. Banks are open between 08:15 and 14:30 or 15:00 on weekdays and until 11:00 on Saturdays. Almost every town will have at least one bank where money can be changed during those hours. In some rural banks the process, however, can be tedious.

Public Holidays

1 January – New Year's Day
12 March – Youth Day
March/April – Good Friday
March/April – Holy Saturday
1 May – Labour Day
25 May – African Freedom Day
First Monday in July – Heroes' Day
First Tuesday in July – Unity Day
First Monday in August – Farmers' Day
24 October – Independence Day
25 December – Christmas Day

Time

It is worth noting that Zambians unilaterally use the 24-hour clock. To refer, for example, to two o'clock in the afternoon will cause confusion if not total incomprehension. Rather say, '14 hours' or simply, 'I will meet you at 14'.

Language

No less than 73 different dialects are spoken in Zambia. Thankfully, though, English is the official language and is spoken throughout the country. Even in remote areas it is rare to find a village where no one speaks any English. But for those situations where communication without recourse to English is necessary, such as asking directions, and indeed simply as a politeness, it may be helpful to know a few ice-breaking or emergency phrases in the major local languages. There are seven of these in the country; they are classified as semi-official languages and they are generally spoken in the different regions outlined below.

- *Bemba* is possibly the largest indigenous language and is spoken both on the Copperbelt and throughout Northern Province.
- *Kaonde* is spoken widely in the region north-west of Lusaka, particularly around northern Kafue and in the districts of Kasempa and Solwezi.
- *Lozi* is a Sotho-based language and it is spoken all over Western Province, especially around Mongu.
- *Lunda* is spoken predominantly in north-western Zambia around Mwinilunga.

- *Luvale* is spoken in north-western Zambia, particularly between Lukulu, Kabompo and Chavuma.
- *Nyanja*, the language of the Ngoni people, is spoken generally from Lusaka eastwards, particularly in the eastern region. The Ngoni still speak their original Ndebele-like language on ceremonial occasions.
- *Tonga* is spoken in Southern Province between Chirundu and the Victoria Falls.

Here is a brief guide to greetings and emergency phrases in each language:

Bemba

Good morning sir/madam. *Mwashibukeru mukwai.*
(Pronounced m'kwai.)
Reply: *Eya mukwai.*

Good afternoon. *Mutende mukwai.*
Reply: *Endita mukwai.*

Good evening. *Cungulopo mukwai.*
Reply: *Eya mukwai.*

If greeting a child or close friend you may use the greeting *Uli shani?* (How are you?)
Reply: *Ndifye bwino.* (I am alright/ok.)

I need a doctor. *Ndefwaya dokota.*

He/she is over there. *Ulya ali palya.*

Where is the bus station? *Nga basi sitesheni ilikwi?* (note anglicism.)

It is over there. *Ili apo.*

Kaonde

Good morning sir/madam. (How are you?) *Mwabuuka mwane.*
Reply: *Ee mwane kana nweba.* (I am fine — and you?)

If greeting a child or friend: *Wabuuka.*

I need a doctor. *Mbena kukeba dokota.*

He or she is over there. *Uji kokwa.*

Where is the passport office? *Pasipoti ofesi ijipi?*
It is on Cairo Road. *Pasipoti ofesi iji ma Cairo road.*

Where is the bus station? *Nga kitesheyi kya ma basi kijipi?*

Lozi

Good morning sir/madam. *Mwazuha.*

If greeting a child or friend: *Wazuha.*
Reply: *Eni sha.*

How are you? *Muzuhile cwani?*

I am fine – and you? *Batili nizuhile hande; nimina mucwani?*

I am fine too. *Batili nazuha.*

I need a doctor. *Nibata dokota.*

The doctor is over there. *Dokota winzi fo.*

Where is the bus station? *Ikanti sitesheni ya basi ikai?*

It is not far. *Inzi fakaufi.*

It is quite far. *Inzi kwaule.*

Where is the passport office? *Kanti pasipoti ofesi ikai?*

It is on Cairo Road. *Inzi mwa Cairo Road.*

Lunda

Good morning. *Handemi mwani.*

How are you? *Mundi wahi mwani.*

I am looking for a doctor. *Nina kukena kudi ndontolo kudi.*

Where is the bus station? *Bus station idi kundi kuno?*

Which road goes to the passport office? *Jila yakuya ku passport office indi kundi?*

Luvale

Good morning. *Muli ngadu lilu.*

How are you? *Numa yoyo mwane?*

I am looking for a doctor. *Nguna kutonda kuli ndontolo kuli.*

Where is the bus station? *Bus station ya twa mina kuli kuno?*

Which road goes to the passport office? *Ngulweze uko jila yakuya ku passport office?*

Nyanja

How are you this morning? *Mwauka bwanji?*
(again, if spoken to a minor or good friend the respectful prefix can be dropped.)
Mulibwanji? is acceptable as a daily greeting.

I am fine. *Ndili bwino.*

I need a doctor. *Ndifuna Dotolo.*

The doctor is over there. *Dotolo ali kuja.*

Where is the bus station? *Nanga basi sitesheni ilikuti?*

Which road goes to the passport office? *Ndi iti njila yaku pasipoti ofesi?*

It is called Cairo Road. *Icedwa Cairo Road.*

Tonga

Good morning sir/madam. *Mwabuka.* (simply say wabuka to an inferior or a friend.)

I'm fine; and how are you? *Ndi kabolu; muli buti?*

I need a doctor. *Ndiyanda dokota.*

The doctor is over there. *Dokota ali awa.*

Where is the bus station? *Basi siteshoni ili kuli?*

Where is the passport office? *Pasipoti ofesi ili ali?*

It is on Cairo Road. *Mulaijana mu Cairo Road.*

Security

There is a popular misconception that Zambia is a den of thieves with armed thugs and malcontents waiting behind every bush and around every corner to pounce on unsuspecting tourists. Curiously, it is a perception fostered by Zambians themselves; and it is nonsense. Zambia is one of the safest countries on the continent to travel in. That is, of course, a qualified statement and Zambia is far from being crime-free. Armed car theft occurs regularly in Lusaka and along sections of the Congo border in the vicinity of the Copperbelt. However, such incidents are far less common than in Johannesburg, for example. Generally large, new and anonymous-looking four-wheel-drives will be the targets. Always lock your vehicle and in Lusaka or crowded places keep an eye on the car when parking for a length of time. Petty theft will take place if it is invited. Lock hotel rooms and leave valuables in the hotel safe. Don't carry all your money in the same pocket or bag.

Look confident and keep your wits about you. In short, take the same reasonable precautions that you would when travelling anywhere in the world.

Suggested Reading

Zambia has not featured in travel writing or popular fiction in the way that east and southern Africa have. But for those interested in knowing more about the country than this book can provide, here are some suggestions. If you read nothing else, Mike Main's *Zambezi, Journey of a River* (Southern Books, South Africa, 1990) is essential. Used as source material for this book, this is a fascinating combination of detail, anecdote and adventure about the river and the region it passes through. The National Heritage Conservation Commission of Zambia has published a guide book to the national monuments of Zambia by DW Phillipson which is an excellent guide to many places of historical or particularly scenic interest that are otherwise poorly reported. Several have been included in these pages. The booklet can be bought from the commission offices in Livingstone. More recently the Commission has published an interesting booklet for visitors to the Victoria Falls area called *Mosi-oa-tunya, A handbook of the Victoria Falls region* (edited by DW Phillipson, 1994). *Kakuli* was written by the great naturalist Norman Carr shortly before his death and follows his much earlier book *Return to the Wild*. It is about the Luangwa Valley in which he spent the entire latter half of his life. There is a beautiful coffee-table book called simply *Zambia* by Richard Vaughn and Ian Murphy, published by CBC, Zimbabwe, and another, *Luangwa, Zambia's treasure* by Mike Coppinger and Jumbo Williams, published by Inyathi, which just as beautifully describes the Luangwa River as their earlier book on the Zambezi.

Other books on Zambia are less contemporary and more difficult to obtain. *Generation of Men: The European Pioneers of Northern Rhodesia* (Stuart Manning, Salisbury, 1965) by WV Brelsford is an account of some of the pioneers, explorers and downright brigands who came into the territory during the early colonial era. There are bound volumes of *The Occasional Papers of the Rhodes-Livingstone Museum* and *The Northern Rhodesia Journal*, both dating from the pre-independence era and filled with scientific information and interesting esoterica. There are two books on the Fisher family of Kalene Hill which give an account of pioneer missionary days in western Zambia, *Ndotulu* by WS Fisher and J Hoyte, and *Nswana – The Heir* by Monica Fisher. Both now appear to be out of print.

Lastly, don't leave home without good bird books and other wildlife field guides. And remember that for many species found in Zambia southern African books are insufficient, so supplement with central and east African books. *Common Birds of Zambia* is a booklet revised and published by the Zambian Ornithological Society in 1993.

There is now also a great website covering general information on Zambia and up to date bulletins about what's on or happening, so we heartily recommend checking it out at www.africa-insites.com/zambia.

HOW TO GET THERE

By Air

Zambia's main international airport lies just outside Lusaka and most incoming international flights land there. There is an international airport at Livingstone, but direct flights there tend to be erratic and mostly confined to charters.

Aero Zambia flies Lusaka-Johannesburg Mondays, Tuesdays, Fridays and Saturdays; Johannesburg-Lusaka Mondays, Tuesdays, Fridays and Saturdays; Nairobi-Lusaka Tuesdays and Thursdays returning Mondays and Thursdays; to and from Dar-es-Salaam on Thursdays; Harare-Lusaka-Harare Wednesdays, Fridays and Sundays. Aero Zambia does not fly to Livingstone. The airline is planning flights to and from Kinshasa, Luanda, Entebbe, Maputo and Dubai shortly.

A few other airlines land at Lusaka, including **British Airways** and **Air France** from Europe. **South African Airways** flies three times weekly to and from Johannesburg Wednesdays, Thursdays and Sundays. **Aeroflot**, **Angola Airlines**, **Air Namibia**, **Royal Swazi Air**, **Air Tanzania** and **Air Zimbabwe** all land at Lusaka.

Flights direct to Ndola are handled by **Interair**, flying Johannesburg-Ndola Fridays and Sundays. Both Livingstone Airport and Mfuwe Airport in the Luangwa have the capability of handling international flights, but do not do so currently. However it is foreseeable that they will do so in the future.

By Rail

The only regular passenger train service in and out of Zambia is the Tanzania-Zambia Railway, known as the Tazara Express, which runs once a week between Dar-es-Salaam in Tanzania and Kapiri Mposhi in Zambia and back again. Only the express goes the whole way with customs and immigration facilities on board. But it is also possible to catch ordinary trains running twice weekly in either direction that connect at, but do not cross, the border. The border between Tunduma and Nakonde used to be one of the most infamous border crossings in Africa. Today it is not quite trouble-free, but blame for this has shifted from the Zambian side, where officials are courteous, to the Tanzanian side where bribery and corruption are becoming rife. Do not attempt dishonesty or you will face the consequences. The only complication is that Tazara runs to and from Kapiri Mposhi, so a connection must be made with the regular service between Livingstone, Lusaka and Kitwe. The two trains do not connect directly, however. You must either spend a night and the better part of a day in Kapiri, which is not a particularly salubrious town, or hitchhike or take a bus between there and Lusaka. There is a bus service running hourly between the two places.

Theoretically it would also be possible to take trains to the two other border points connected by rail in Zambia: Livingstone opposite Victoria Falls in Zimbabwe, and Ndola which is connected by rail to Lubumbashi in the Democratic Republic of Congo. There do not, however, appear to be regular passenger services connecting the border posts in those countries. A tradition has started of an annual trip on a highly exclusive nostalgic steam train from South Africa through Zimbabwe and Zambia to Dar-es-Salaam. Contact **Rovos Rail** in South Africa for details.

By Bus

There is a regular bus service between Lusaka and Harare in Zimbabwe via Chirundu. The **United Bus Company of Zambia**, UBZ, runs between the two cities every day of the week except Sunday. It is wise to book in advance as this service is extremely popular.

For travellers from South Africa there is an equally regular coach service between Johannesburg and Harare. Or you could take a coach to Bulawayo and a bus from there to Victoria Falls before crossing to Livingstone in Zambia on foot (necessitating a 10-km hitch into town).

From Malawi there is a private bus company that runs all the way between Lilongwe and Lusaka. Or you can take the national bus companies to and from the border through Chipata. From Tanzania there are no direct buses but national buses to and from the border at Tunduma-Nakonde. From the Democratic Republic of Congo there is again no direct coach service but you can take buses or hitchhike with a choice of two borders: either between Chililabombwe and Kasumbelesa or between Mufulira and Mokambo. At the time of writing the whole Congo region is in such turmoil that there can be no certainty about the possibility of travel between the two countries or even along the border so please be most careful. Chingola is fairly safe but you are advised to proceed straight through to Kitwe or Ndola nevertheless.

By Boat

The ferries on Lake Tanganyika connect the Zambian 'port' of Mpulungu with Kigoma in Tanzania and Bujumbura in Burundi. The **Tanzania Railways Corporation** runs two boats, the MV *Liemba* and the MV *Mwongozo*. The *Mwongozo* only serves Tanzanian towns but the *Liemba* runs weekly between the three countries. The *Liemba* is an ancient vessel with an interesting history. It was originally named the *Graf von Goetzn* and saw service under the Germans in the First World War. To avert capture by the British it was eventually scuttled but in 1927 the British raised it and, thanks to the Germans who had greased the boat from top to bottom before sinking it, the renamed *Liemba* has plied the lake ever since. The TRC agents for the ferry in Zambia are **Cosy Enterprises Ltd**, with booking offices in Mpulungu and Lusaka. The *Liemba* has six first-class cabins, each with two beds, 12 second-class with four bunks in each and a third-class lower deck. Expect to pay about US$75 for first class, $60 for second class and $35 for third class.

By Motor Car

There are several ways to enter Zambia in your own vehicle. Visitors coming up from South Africa can choose between three routes through Zimbabwe, one through Botswana and one through Namibia. The most direct route to Lusaka is to travel through Harare and across the border at Chirundu. It is a good tar road with fuel and facilities at regular intervals.

From Harare it is also possible to enter via Kariba, crossing the border over the dam wall. Alternatively take the Bulawayo road past Hwange Game Reserve to Victoria Falls, possibly the nicest stretch of road in all Africa, then cross over the Victoria Falls Bridge which, as a fitting culmination of that road, is surely one of the world's great frontiers.

A popular route from South Africa is to travel through Botswana. But any tourists who intend taking a boat or canoe to Zambia should note that Botswana expressly forbids the transit of any kind of boat through its territory without the authority of the Department of Water Affairs in Gaborone. Proceed via Francistown and Nata, and then up the Pandamatenga road to Kazungula. It's all tar and from Nata onwards forms a beautiful route. A stopover in the spectacular Chobe National Park is possible before you either cross the border by ferry directly at Kazungula or proceed into Zimbabwe to the Victoria Falls to cross the border there. Of course the latter may necessitate buying a Zimbabwe visa (see the section on Entry and Customs Regulations in chapter 3), but affords travellers the chance of seeing game, especially elephant, on the road to the Falls.

Only travellers wanting to reach the upper Zambezi and Barotseland are recommended to take the Namibian route and cross into Zambia at Katima Mulilo. Even coming from central Namibia, if you are heading for Livingstone you are advised to go through Botswana and cross on the Kazungula ferry or proceed all the way into Zimbabwe and over the border at the Falls. The reason for this, as fully described in chapter 8, is that the road from Katima Mulilo to Livingstone in Zambia is extremely difficult to traverse, and in addition you will have to pay R60 to cross on the Sesheke Ferry. The road from Katima to Ngoma Bridge is being tarred at the time of writing, again making the Botswana route the better option.

It is assumed that the route through Mozambique will remain little travelled for a while yet. You have to go through Zimbabwe anyway and into Mozambique at Tete. Once in Zambia, having crossed the border at Mlolo, you join the Great East Road at Katete, within easy distance of the South Luangwa./

From Malawi the only tar route and the usual way is to go from Lilongwe to Chipata, again within striking distance of the South Luangwa and about 570 km from Lusaka. There are three other points of entry in northern Malawi, two off the Nyika Plateau which are described in chapter 11 and only recommended if you particularly want to go from there to the Luangwa Valley or take a shortcut to northern Zambia via Isoka. The third at Chitipa is used usually as a route up to Tanzania, as it runs for about 50 km through Zambia to the Tanzanian border at Tunduma.

From Tanzania and east Africa, motorists can choose between crossing the border at Tunduma, which is the most direct route from Dar-es-Salaam and Dodoma, or boarding the Lake Tanganyika ferry, the MV *Liemba* at Kigoma, possibly the most direct route from Kenya and Uganda, or boarding at Bujumbura in Burundi. The ferry docks at Mpulungu in Zambia.

Travellers coming south from the Democratic Republic of Congo will take the road from Lubumbashi to Chingola and the Copperbelt. It is not a pleasant frontier with bandits on either side of the border although the Zambians tightened security in the region after a spate of car hijackings, including one of a cabinet minister.

At the moment the Angolan frontiers do not really warrant attention, as most fall within territory not controlled by the Angolan government and in any event border relations between the two countries are strained to say the least. Eventually it may be possible to cross at Jimbe Bridge in the north-west corner of Zambia.

GETTING AROUND

It is assumed that tourists to Zambia will fall into one of the following three groups: those travelling by air and under the aegis of organised tours and safaris; those travelling in their own vehicle (preferably, but not necessarily, a four-wheel-drive); and backpackers travelling by means of public transport, hitchhiking or on bicycles.

By Air

Most major towns in Zambia have airstrips but internal commercial air travel is limited. There are regular flights between Lusaka and Ndola in the Copperbelt (see page 126) but at the time of writing there are no routine flights to other airports with airliner capacity. This may change in the future with regards to Livingstone and Mfuwe. In addition to the national airline there are charter companies which will land on any registered strip. Some of these are listed in chapter 13. For details of other towns around the country that can be reached by private charter planes, travellers should contact one of the private charter companies.

Organised Tours and Safaris

For the uninitiated, without their own vehicle and whose interest lies mainly in seeing the country's wildlife, this is the trouble-free option. A number of safari and tour operators conduct business out of Lusaka and Livingstone or have bases in and around the major game reserves. Prices are competitive when compared with those of operators elsewhere in southern or east Africa. Chapter 13 gives a complete list of these operators, their addresses and the regions in which they specialise.

The majority run safaris to either the South Luangwa National Park or the Kafue National Park or specialise in trips and adventures on the Zambezi River. There are companies that run specialist safaris to other areas and some companies will tailor trips to clients' specific interests. Most of the existing tour operators at the time of writing are listed in chapter 13, but it is likely that others will have come into being thereafter, so consult the travel agencies or the Zambian National Tourist Board, or address enquiries to the **Tour Operators Association of Zambia**, Amandra House, Ben Bella Road, Lusaka, Box 36655, Lusaka.

By Rail

Zambia's rail network is limited to a single line from Livingstone to Lusaka and thence north to Kapiri Mposhi where it forks, one branch proceeding through the Copperbelt to the Democratic Republic of Congo and the other, the famous Tanzania-Zambia Railway (Tazara), going north-east via Mpika and Kasama to Tunduma and Tanzania, where it ends ultimately in Dar-es-Salaam. Travellers can choose between sleeper, standard and economy rates on local trains or first, second and third class on Tazara.

There is a daily service that runs from Livingstone through Lusaka to Kitwe via Kapiri Mposhi and in the opposite direction. Slow and a little erratic, the trains take about 12 hours to run between Livingstone and Lusaka and the same again to the Copperbelt. Rates in kwacha are the equivalent of about US$4 for a sleeper or $2 economy between each city.

Travellers wishing to take Tazara to Dar-es-Salaam should note that the train leaves from Kapiri Mposhi and does not connect with the normal north- or southbound service, necessitating an overnight stop and a day's wait in Kapiri. The weekly train normally departs at 18:00, so it would be possible to take a bus to or from Kapiri on the same day. Tazara must be booked at least one week in advance. Rates are approximately US$40 first class, $26 second class and $12 if you have the *sang-froid* to brave third class.

By Bus

Buses are the main means of inter-city transport in Zambia and cover an extensive network throughout the country. The main carrier is the **United Bus Company of Zambia**, UBZ, but there are now also some good coach services operating on several routes. **T/Lux**, for example, has a daily service between Livingstone, Lusaka and the Copperbelt that is inexpensive and offers smart, luxury coaches which you won't have to share with livestock. For backpackers this is much the safest and most inexpensive way of travelling around the country.

General buses cover most routes daily and some major ones several times a day. Coaches and the major inter-city lines depart a scheduled times but other buses tend not to follow strict schedules, rather departing only once they are full. It's as well therefore to arrive early on prospective dates of departure. Buses are reasonably reliable, although subject to many delays *en route* at roadblocks and pick-up points. Be aware of, if not necessarily deterred by, incidents such as one witnessed by the authors in which a bus broke down on a country road and the hapless passengers were still encamped beside the vehicle two weeks later, dependent on nearby villages and foraging in the bush for food. Of course, victims of such a mishap with a little spare cash could simply hitchhike on or flag down the next bus that passes.

A facility that was available between Lusaka and Livingstone on our last visit and probably continues to operate everywhere is the post van. This is a small bus or van operated by the post office to transport the post between towns and cities. It will carry passengers too for a competitive rate. Enquire at the local post office.

By Boat

On certain waterways boat travel is a delightful way of getting around. Lake Kariba has a ferry between Siavonga and Sinazongwe. During the high-water season there's a post boat between major towns in Barotseland (see page 102). Motor launches provide the quickest passage around Lake Tanganyika and there are large ferries operating between countries on the lake (see the section on By Boat in chapter 4).

The slow but regular canoe traffic between villages on all navigable Zambian rivers is used by the locals but is yet to be explored as a means of travel by intrepid tourists. Ferries and pontoons are to be found all over the country. The motorised ferries on the Zambezi charge a fortune to transport foreign vehicles; currently about US$25, but travel in the ubiquitous hand-powered pontoons on smaller rivers is free of charge. See regional routes for more details.

Hitchhiking

Zambia's tourist infrastructure is not well adapted to backpackers, nevertheless it is possible to tour the country in this way. Livingstone would be most backpackers' destination of choice and caters best by way of places to stay and things to do, but there are hostels also in Lusaka and facilities close to Mfuwe in the South Luangwa. As has been mentioned elsewhere Zambians are tremendously courteous and helpful by nature, so offers of transport will be forthcoming, but you should expect to pay something and it may save difficulty later if a fee is agreed on at the outset.

Major routes have regular but certainly not prolific traffic, consisting primarily of old Land Rovers limping along like war veterans under loads of quite grotesque proportions. Overloading is not in the Zambian vocabulary and hikers are assured of plenty of company on their journey. Truckers are usually a reliable source of transport if approached while stationary – these juggernauts stop for nothing once they are on their way. Do not expect much traffic along secondary roads.

The biggest drawback to hitchhiking in Zambia is that there are sometimes large distances to be covered between major roads and destinations in game parks or other attractions, so good walking shoes and/or much patience may be considered essential equipment.

In Your Own Vehicle

In the dry season the majority of Zambia's roads are negotiable in an ordinary car but four-wheel-drive is recommended to cope with the wear and tear of the potholes and bumps on roads which have to date been poorly maintained. However, minor roads, particularly in game parks, will occasionally present obstacles such as gullies and riverbeds that necessitate the use of four-wheel-drive. Roads in western Zambia are sometimes very sandy and four-wheel-drive is certainly recommended for this region. In the rainy season minor roads can be hazardous even in four-wheel-drive and some, consisting of black clay 'cotton soil', simply not negotiable at all.

There's a hoary old chestnut that asks: how do you tell a drunk driver in Zambia? The answer is that he is the one who drives straight down the road. Beware of being complacent and speeding on tar roads, as even apparently good surfaces can suddenly collapse into bone and metal-shattering craters. By way of an example, the authors cracked their Land Rover's chassis in half twice, the extensive damage becoming apparent only later. You should also be aware that buses and trucks negotiate these craters not by slowing down but by swerving all over the road, yielding only to bigger buses or trucks. We cannot recommend strongly enough that, whatever car you drive, drive slowly and even 'crawl' where roads deteriorate if you wish to take your vehicle home in the same condition that it first entered the territory. A good rule of thumb would be to travel less than 300 km per day.

There are a number of car hire companies in Zambia which operate in the main cities. Some also offer chauffeurs and four-wheel-drive vehicles. These are listed in detail in chapter 13. For the majority of readers, whom we expect will be driving their own vehicles, we recommend reading the section on driving tips and motor spares as well as the section on dealing with medical traumas in chapter 13.

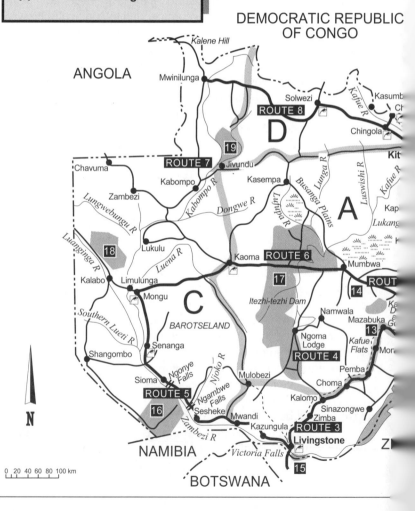

TOURIST REGIONS

A. Central Region

B. The Southern Region

C. The Western Region

D. The Copperbelt

E. The Northern Region

F. The Eastern Region

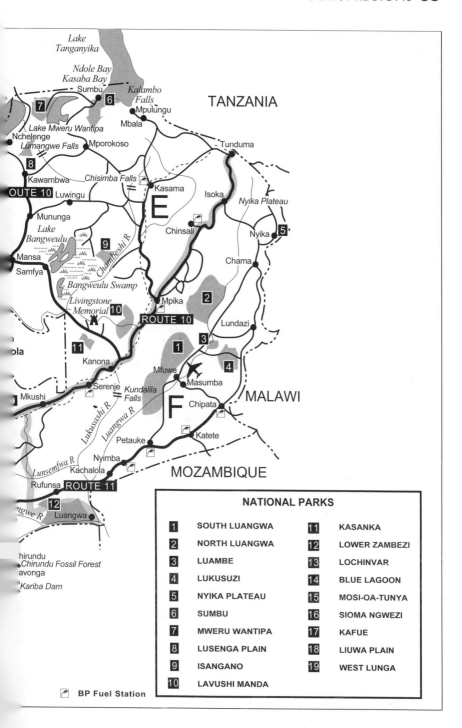

NATIONAL PARKS

1	SOUTH LUANGWA	11	KASANKA
2	NORTH LUANGWA	12	LOWER ZAMBEZI
3	LUAMBE	13	LOCHINVAR
4	LUKUSUZI	14	BLUE LAGOON
5	NYIKA PLATEAU	15	MOSI-OA-TUNYA
6	SUMBU	16	SIOMA NGWEZI
7	MWERU WANTIPA	17	KAFUE
8	LUSENGA PLAIN	18	LIUWA PLAIN
9	ISANGANO	19	WEST LUNGA
10	LAVUSHI MANDA		

BP Fuel Station

Distance Chart

	Chipata	Chirundu	Choma	Kabwe	Kafue	Kapiri Mposhi	Kasama	Kawambwa	Kitwe	Livingstone	Lundazi	Lusaka	Mansa	Mazabuka	Mbala	Mpika	Mporokoso	Mongu	Mumbwa	Mwinilunga	Nakonde	Ndola	Sesheke	Solwezi	Zambezi
Chipata	Chipata																								
Chirundu	705	Chirundu																							
Choma	853	308	Choma																						
Kabwe	707	274	422	Kabwe																					
Kafue	613	92	240	182	Kafue																				
Kapiri Mposhi	775	342	490	68	250	Kapiri Mposhi																			
Kasama	1420	986	1134	712	894	644	Kasama																		
Kawambwa	1298	865	1013	591	773	523	346	Kawambwa																	
Kitwe	927	494	642	220	402	152	796	385	Kitwe																
Livingstone	1041	496	188	610	428	678	1322	1201	830	Livingstone															
Lundazi	186	891	1039	893	799	961	1605	1484	1113	1227	Lundazi														
Lusaka	569	136	284	44	206	163	850	729	358	472	755	Lusaka													
Mansa	1130	697	845	423	605	355	340	163	217	1033	1316	561	Mansa												
Mazabuka	694	148	159	263	81	331	975	854	483	347	880	125	686	Mazabuka											
Mbala	1586	1153	1301	879	1061	812	167	366	964	1489	1772	1017	507	1142	Mbala										
Mpika	1208	775	923	501	683	433	211	557	585	1111	1394	639	559	764	378	Mpika									
Mporokoso	1435	1002	1150	730	910	661	160	138	523	1338	1621	866	307	991	228	371	Mporokoso								
Mongu	1150	717	865	719	625	787	1431	1310	939	525	1336	581	1142	706	1598	1220	1447	Mongu							
Mumbwa	720	287	435	185	195	253	897	776	405	623	906	151	608	276	1064	1086	1192	437	Mumbwa						
Mwinilunga	1428	995	1143	721	903	653	1024	852	501	1331	1614	859	684	984	1192	990	1595	785	906	Mwinilunga					
Nakonde	1583	1150	1298	876	1058	808	243	589	960	1486	1769	1014	583	1192	195	375	902	1595	1061	1461	Nakonde				
Ndola	890	457	605	183	365	115	759	408	58	793	1076	321	240	446	747	548	335	902	547	1061	368	Ndola			
Sesheke	1231	686	378	800	618	868	1512	1391	1020	190	1417	662	1223	537	1528	1301	1676	335	813	1035	1676	813	Sesheke		
Solwezi	1152	719	867	445	627	377	746	574	225	1055	1338	583	409	446	715	810	604	708	625	276	630	276	283	Solwezi	
Zambezi	1338	905	1053	878	813	810	1209	1037	658	1063	1524	769	869	894	1376	1243	1175	538	625	396	1618	716	788	515	Zambezi

6

THE CENTRAL REGION

The central region, being the hub of the country, is well developed and densely populated. But it is quite remarkable how quickly the populated peri-urban area can be left behind. The great wilderness of the lower Zambezi Valley falls away practically from Lusaka's eastern suburbs; the wild Lunsemfwa River valley is barely 100 km away as the crow flies; Blue Lagoon in the Kafue Flats is a similar distance to the west and the Kafue National Park, one of the biggest game reserves in the world, is only four hours travel by road.

The people of the central region embrace several of Zambia's tribes and languages. The predominant language is Nyanja in the city and eastwards, but westwards to the Kafue most people probably speak Kaonde.

Lusaka

The capital of Zambia will be most airborne visitors' first contact with the country and an unavoidable interlude for anyone else on a comprehensive tour. Generally disliked by visitors and residents alike, it's a bustling, energetic city perhaps too gripped by a mercantile and bureaucratic fervour to have ever taken much care of its appearance. Yet it is not without a certain shambolic charm and its people are friendly and cosmopolitan.

The name Lusaka is derived from that of a Lenje headman, Lusaaka, whose village lay nearby at the time of the construction of the railway and siding in 1906. Otherwise relatively uninhabited the area was notorious for lions, and indeed the very night that the siding was laid lions killed several oxen almost beneath the wheels of the shunting engine. Catholic missionaries followed the railway, and then white settlers arrived in the form of Boer families displaced by the Anglo-Boer War in South Africa. The first humble precursor of today's monolithic tower blocks was a wattle and daub store built in 1908. Thereafter expansion followed rap-

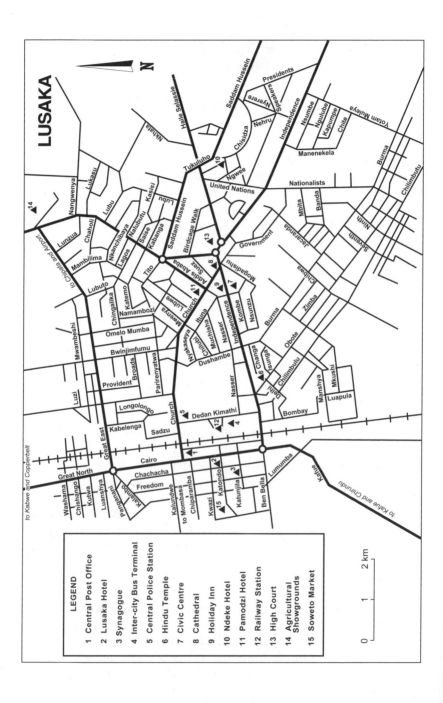

LUSAKA

N

LEGEND
1 Central Post Office
2 Lusaka Hotel
3 Synagogue
4 Inter-city Bus Terminal
5 Central Police Station
6 Hindu Temple
7 Civic Centre
8 Cathedral
9 Holiday Inn
10 Ndeke Hotel
11 Pamodzi Hotel
12 Railway Station
13 High Court
14 Agricultural Showgrounds
15 Soweto Market

0   1   2 km

idly and the town was gazetted in 1913, but when the First World War broke out building stopped and between 1915 and 1929 the town stagnated.

Built on limestone, Lusaka had no surface water supply during the dry season but was annually flooded during the rains. Despite such inadequacies the people of its central location persuaded the colonial administration in 1930 to move the capital here from Livingstone (see page 82), and a minor building boom began on the higher ground to the east of the railway line and Cairo Road. Government House (now State House) and the British South Africa Company offices (now the Ministry of Foreign Affairs) were built in Georgian style and the site and its surroundings became known as 'Snobs' Hill'. In 1933 the governor commented: 'It is ... quite apparent ... that there are the most hideous buildings growing up all over Lusaka'. By 1935 it was officially proclaimed the capital of Northern Rhodesia. After the Second World War thousands of new settlers arrived in the country and development spread to create the vast, incoherent sprawl of mixed suburbia, business and administration that the city comprises today.

Incredibly, by 1960 Lusaka still did not have a waterborne sewerage system and relied solely on night soil wagons. Cairo Road was described by a visiting British peer as 'surely the greatest spectacle since the Calgary stampede'. His reservations did not deter the Queen, who in 1955 conferred by royal charter upon Lusaka the 'style and dignity of a city'.

Independence in 1964 provoked the predictable rush of name changes and another building boom. Before the economy collapsed several new tower blocks were built along Cairo Road, rather throwing 'style and dignity' to the winds with monumental scale taking priority over beauty and imagination.

Today a thoroughly modern skyline rears up to proclaim the city's metropolitan stature over the surrounding bush. During the latter years of socialist rule and the financially difficult years that followed Lusaka slipped with the rest of the country into appalling decay. However, while hardly a *fin de siecle* renaissance, the turn of the millennium finds the city beginning to replace some of its shabbier clothes with new ones. On our last visit we were delighted to find a quiet spirit of renewal at work. Potholes that once seemed capable of swallowing vehicles whole have been filled. Cairo Road has been cleaned up. Buildings are being refurbished. There are new shops and well-stocked supermarkets; new restaurants, pubs and nightclubs. A shopping mall is under construction and there is even a new cinema. Perhaps the only negative development is that the free market has brought the scourge of disposable packaging and the resulting litter in the suburbs is copious and unpleasant.

Access

By air: Zambia's main international airport is located just outside Lusaka on the Great East Road. There are car hire companies at the airport; the Pamodzi and Intercontinental hotels have courtesy buses and there are plenty of taxis in which a ride into the city will cost about US$15. Zambian taxis do not have meters, so be sure to establish the fare beforehand. Generally fares seem to be controlled by some unwritten code applied with surprising honesty, but you may be able to reduce them a few per cent by haggling.

From the airport the Great East Road brings you straight into town via the University of Zambia and the agricultural showgrounds. The junction immediately after the showgrounds is marked by a slightly bizarre new pedestrian bridge. Proceed straight for the CBD, meeting Cairo Road at its north end circle or turn left up Addis Ababa Drive to the administrative and embassy belt and the chief hotels. The Pamodzi Hotel is on the right just before Church Road; the Ridgeway Holiday Inn is on the corner of Church Road and Independence Avenue; and the Intercontinental is found on Haile Selassie Avenue, 100 m beyond the circle in front of the Supreme Court.

By rail: Rail passengers will arrive from either north or south at the main station just east of Cairo Road. The closest hotel is the Lusaka Hotel, directly opposite on the corner of Katondo and Cairo roads.

By bus: The inter-city bus terminal is close to the station, to the east of and opposite the railway line from Cairo Road. UBZ, the national carrier, has several buses coming daily to Lusaka from all corners of the country. Note however that the independent coach services operating between Livingstone, Lusaka and the Copperbelt arrive and depart between Nyanji Commuter Station and the car park behind the Zambia National Tourist Board offices on the Cairo Road side of the railway line.

By car: Travellers coming in their own vehicles will arrive in Lusaka via one of four ways. You may come from the south on the Kafue Road, which runs straight into Cairo Road at its south end circle; from the north at its opposite end; down the Great East Road past the airport as described above, or from the west on the Mumbwa Road. This route, perhaps the most confusing of the four, passes through the chaotic commercial belt and ultimately joins Cairo Road about halfway along its length. If you are arriving from this direction just keep going until Mumbwa Road feeds into Kalundwe Road. Four blocks later Kalundwe road meets Cairo Road, a good first port of call.

Tourist information

Most travel agencies, airline offices and car hire offices are located on Cairo Road. For general information the **Zambian National Tourist Board** has offices in Century House, adjacent to Shoprite Checkers on Lusaka Square, Cairo Road, a good first port of call.

Lusaka can be divided into areas west and east of the railway line. The CBD lies on a narrow grid along Cairo Road, but the greater metropolitan area of Lusaka lies to the east of Cairo Road on the other side of the railway line. It is a confusing sprawl of boulevards, tree-lined avenues and a spidery web of suburban roads laid out according to some unique and incomprehensible logic. Visitors planning to stay in Lusaka for any length of time would do well to buy a map of the city, available from the Zambia National Tourist Board office; the map office in the Department of Survey, Mulungushi House; at bookshops such as the one next to Farmer's House on Cairo Road, the one in the Bancroft Garden Centre on Kabulonga Road or Towerbooks in the Northmead Shopping Centre; or possibly from the gift shops of the big hotels.

Lusaka is known for its petty crime, but if you keep your wits about you it is, like the rest of the country, quite safe. Violent crime is most unlikely but it is unwise to flaunt expensive cameras and the like and drivers of new-looking motor cars should leave someone to watch the vehicle if they park. The Mumbwa Road has the worst reputation for petty theft.

Cairo Road is actually a junction on the Great North Road; the name captures the sense of history and vision that the façades of its blighted buildings have lost. First-time visitors are likely to be rather dismayed by the chaotic stream of traffic that surges up one side of the avenue and washes back down the other at peak hours. If walking on the thronging pavements makes you insecure, the tree-lined avenue in the middle offers more room. In October the trees burst into flower, temporarily garlanding the shabby street in brilliant scarlet. If the paving slabs beneath the trees have a slightly hollow sound it's because beneath them still lies the cesspit that originally ran down the length of the road. At night the street abruptly becomes deserted and dark. Walking around at this time is obviously more dangerous.

Cairo Road is the hub of the retail sector. Although window dressing is limited, most basic shopping requirements will be met and there are several supermarkets that offer a wide range of foodstuffs and beverages. The new **Shoprite Checkers** is probably the best. What was the Wildlife Shop across Church Road from the main post office is now a bookshop called **The Bookhouse** which offers a reasonable range of fiction, maps and information booklets about Lusaka and the rest of the country. Almost all the main banks as well as several *bureaux de change* can be found on Cairo Road.

The area west of Cairo Road is mostly commercial and light industrial. The motor industries particularly are to be found here. The public library and information centre lies just behind the Lusaka Hotel. Be a little wary in this area, it is less than salubrious and a well-known place for black market money changing and other dubious commercial transactions. The notorious **Soweto Market** used to lie a few blocks west of Cairo Road, between Nkwazi and Katondo roads. It defied description beyond that implied by the name, but in its shanty-lined alleyways could be found almost anything you would care to buy if you were not concerned about its origins. It was particularly good for vehicle spare parts. What could not be found could be 'ordered' and usually produced within a day, no questions asked. Now much of the market has been rehoused in smart, roofed premises off Freedom Way. Almost certainly the market's reputation will still stand.

Do not be shy of asking strangers for advice; the search for what you need could be an enjoyable and illuminating experience. But be cautious about prices; while Zambians will not engage in protracted bargaining, as is the practice in some other countries, initial prices are always high and cheaper deals are only arrived at by making a reasonable counter-offer.

Only three roads connect the CBD on Cairo Road with the government sector and embassy belt of the eastern suburbs on the other side of the railway line. The Great East Road runs from the north end circle, Church Road is next to the post office midway along Cairo Road, and Independence Avenue runs from the south end circle. Of these Independence Avenue gives most direct access to the government buildings, embassies, hotels and suburbs. Cathedral Hill is the centre of this area, but it is something of a misnomer, as it is situated only marginally higher than the rest of the city. It is composed primarily of a great traffic circle with the new Anglican Cathedral at one end, the Supreme Court opposite the intersection of Independence Avenue and the secretariat at the other end. Don't try to photograph government buildings – for all the openness enjoyed under the present government Zambians still are strict about security.

Accommodation

Lusaka has a range of hotels and other places to stay, none of them particularly cheap. Visitors can choose between something in the city or one of the 'game lodges' to be found not far from town. The main city hotels are located in the suburbs a few kilometres east of the CBD. Possibly the most popular and predictably comfortable is the **Ridgeway Holiday Inn** on the corner of Church Road and Independence Avenue. If the arrival court lulls you into thinking you are in the northern suburbs of Johannesburg, the crocodiles in the courtyard pond may remind you that you are not. Close by on Addis Abbaba stands the **Pamodzi** which is the most luxurious and expensive hotel in Lusaka. The **Intercontinental** is not much further away on Haile Selassie Avenue. Slightly more downmarket, but in some ways more charming and uniquely Zambian, is the **Ndeke Hotel** on the corner of Haile Selassie Avenue and Saddam Hussein Boulevard. The only one right in the CBD is the **Lusaka Hotel**, the oldest in the city, rather claustrophobic although reasonably priced.

A little more downmarket is the **Hillview** which is small and quiet, and **Andrews Motel** which is rather the opposite. On the Great East Road between the city and the airport there is the **Chainama Motel** and on the Mumbwa Road is the **Garden House Hotel**. Guesthouses are just beginning to present themselves as alternatives to the big hotels and lodges and are certain to be quieter and more personal. Try **Jules' Guesthouse, Kaingo Guesthouse** or the **Vineyard Guesthouse.** For more details see chapter 12.

Typically Zambian humour would have you believe that the best view of Lusaka is the one in your rear view mirror as you drive away, and there are several other options a few kilometres out of town which will provide relief from the bustle of the city. **Chisamba Safari Lodge** is located about forty minutes

north of the city and 7 km from the Great North Road. Not far from there lies the **Chaminuka Private Game Reserve** boasting a luxury lodge and plenty of game, including lion, in an unspoiled wilderness. In the opposite direction about 20 km south of the city down the Kafue Road lies **Lilayi Lodge.** A little further, but not more than an hour's drive from Lusaka is **Lechwe Lodge** on the Kafue Flats which is smaller, older and simpler. All these farms are well stocked with game and offer an easily accessible wildlife experience.

For campers there is the **Eureka Camping Park**. It is well signposted 10 km south of the city on the east side of the Kafue Road. Popular with South Africans, it proclaims itself to have the best showers in Africa, shady campsites and a great atmosphere. Alternatively, **Fringilla Farm** is about 50 km up the Great North Road. In addition to camping and simple, pleasant accommodation it offers riding, fishing and even hunting. **The Pioneer campsite**, east of Lusaka, is a good place to stay if you are coming from or heading to the Luangwa Valley (see page 151) down the Great East Road. The first backpackers hostel opened recently and is called **Cha Cha Cha Backpackers**.

See chapter 12 for more details. Remember that foreign visitors are required to settle their bills in foreign currency in almost all hotels. If you are spending several days in town it is worth asking your hotel for special rates which may offer as much as a 20 per cent discount.

Places of interest in Lusaka

Lusaka isn't brimming with exciting sites for tourists. Tours of the city can be arranged through the major travel agencies. However, if you want to absorb the atmosphere you would do better to stroll down **Cairo Road**, and visit the markets or the museum. There is an excellent little publication called *Lusaka Lowdown* available free from most bookstores which details the events offered by the city and advertises restaurants.

Cairo Road has been described above and so has the Soweto Market. The other market is worth a visit if atmosphere and classic African mercantile hubbub is to your preference. It is visible immediately south-east of the Independence Avenue Bridge. Although much of it is taken up with *Salaula*, the slightly controversial trade in Western 'hand-me-down' clothes that collapsed the local textile industry, there's also loads of colourful Indian and East African cloth, reed mats, local foods and such.

The **Lusaka National Museum** on Independence Avenue deserves a visit. The ground floor has a permanent exhibition of contemporary Zambian art and as this is one of few venues where visitors are likely to be exposed to this kind of art, some of which is quite beautiful, it is worth seeing. Upstairs there is a jaded exhibition extolling the independence struggle. This so resembles the one in Maputo, Mozambique, that you can't help feeling the implication of a common 'eastern bloc' origin. More interesting than the massive but naive canvases glorifying epic moments of the struggle are photographs and artefacts from the time including one notable casualty, the now rather desiccated tip of a man's finger, shot off during some or other confrontation!

On the scale of the bizarre this pales when compared with the exhibits on the other side of the hall –an enormous collection of fetishes and objects of witchcraft. Anyone travelling at all widely in Zambia is likely to hear about witchcraft which, to the dismay of the proselytising churches, is much practised and believed in. One example should testify to the exhibit's curiosity value: an assemblage of fur, string, old torch batteries and a dried out human placenta, comprising apparently a flying machine for witches' midnight sorties – now isn't that more spectacular than a simple broom?

The **Kabwata Cultural Centre** in Burma Road was, at the time of writing, about to undergo a spectacular facelift. The authors were shown the plans which, if realised, suggest it will be first on the visitor's list of priorities. Check the latest edition of *Lusaka Lowdown* for details. Currently it remains a good place in which to find locally crafted carvings and curios and where you can see the craftsmen at work and then try to match their bargaining talent. If you particularly like contemporary crafts then definitely visit **Cafe d'Afrique** (described under Restaurants on page 67) which, as well as serving good food, sells a range of local art and works, many produced in an HIV support scheme, and is therefore additionally worth patronising.

Another place in which to see contemporary Zambian Art is the **Namwandwe Gallery**. Here in a considerably more inspiring setting than the museum a private collector, John Kapotwe, has built a wonderful gallery to house his collection of twenty years as well as temporary exhibitions of Zambian painters, sculptors and ceramicists. Check the *Lusaka Lowdown* or a telephone directory for details. The **Henry Tayali Visual Arts Centre** at the showgrounds also exhibits Zambian artists and the **Bente Lorens Ceramic Studio** in Longacres has a good selection of plates, bowls and ornaments.

If still at your wits end for something to do, try the following:

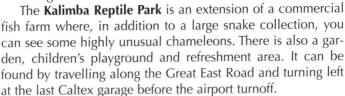

The **Kalimba Reptile Park** is an extension of a commercial fish farm where, in addition to a large snake collection, you can see some highly unusual chameleons. There is also a garden, children's playground and refreshment area. It can be found by travelling along the Great East Road and turning left at the last Caltex garage before the airport turnoff.

The **Mulungushi Convention Centre** is adjacent to the museum. It was built by Kenneth Kaunda to host a summit of the so-called non-aligned states in 1970. The centre is located just off the Great East Road about 1,5 km east of the intersection with Addis Ababa Drive.

The **Anglican Cathedral of the Holy Cross** is up the road from the museum on the corner of Independence Avenue and Chikwa Road and displays a good example of seventies architecture.

The **National Archives** is to be found in Government Road. Open during regular government hours, it houses an African Library and photo exhibits. Maps may be for sale there.

The **National Assembly** is in Nanquenya Road off Addis Ababa Drive. Tours of this, the Zambian parliament building, are conducted on the last Thursday of each month.

The **Civic Centre** is in Independence Avenue and contains Lusaka's municipal offices. The adjoining Nakatindi Hall is used for large official functions.

The **Moore Pottery Factory** in Kabelenga Road is easily accessed from Cairo Road. Take Church Road over the bridge then turn second left; it's about a kilometre down on the right.

The **Munda Wanga Botanical Gardens** are 16 km down the Kafue Road and although the zoo is dismal the gardens may still be worth a visit. But we have not visited the gardens in many years and cannot vouch for what you might find. There are swimming pools and picnic areas.

The **University of Zambia** is set in highly attractive grounds off the Great East Road. It is a modern campus and has some of Zambia's better modern architecture.

Picnic places

Munda Wanga, described above.

Chongwe River, 42 km further down the Great East Road from the university.

The **Kafue Marina** is located on the Kafue River about 50 km from Lusaka. Turn left just before the bridge. Boats may be hired here.

Restaurants and bars

One sure sign of change in the city is the growth in the number of pubs and good restaurants. In addition to several in the main hotels, the following are popular:

Arabian Nights, a Pakistani restaurant and steakhouse, Kabompo Close, tel: 75-0102, closed Sundays.

Bar-B-Que, terrace at the Hotel Intercontinental, tel: 25-0600.

Brasserie, Hotel Intercontinental, tel: 25-0600.

Cafe d'Afrique, coffee shop and lunches but is sometimes open for dinner, Luanshya Road, tel: 23-7745, closed Sundays. This is highly recommended, offering indubitably the best coffee and some of the nicest food in Lusaka.

Café Mon Cheri, daytime coffee shop, showgrounds.

Chantals, lunch and dinner, United Nations Avenue, tel: 25-2163, closed Sunday and Monday evenings.

Chasers, pub, serves snacks, burgers, pasta, Rhodes Park, tel: 75-2659.

Danny's, Indian food and steakhouse, Woodlands, tel: 26-1335, closed Sundays.

Dil, Indian restaurant, Ibex Hill, Kabulonga, tel: 26-2391.

Fra Gigi, Italian restaurant, Lubu Road (where Gringo's used to be), tel: 70-3472, closed Tuesdays, Saturday lunches.

Giant Dragon, Chinese restaurant, Northmead, tel: 29-0776, closed Sundays.

Golden Spur, chain steakhouse, Holiday Inn, tel: 25-4571.

Hibiscus, continental restaurant, Jesmondine, tel: 29-5011, closed Tuesdays.

Jacaranda, continental food, Pamodzi Hotel, tel: 25-4455.

Jaylin, steakhouse and Creole food, Longacres, tel: 25-2206, closed Mondays.

Jungle Pub, pub lunches and suppers, Panganini Road, tel: 70-2261, closed Mondays.

Lilayi, buffet or à la carte at Lilayi Lodge, tel: 23-0611.

Marco Polo, restaurant with European and Californian dishes, showgrounds, tel: 25-0111, closed Mondays.

Memories of China, Chinese restaurant, Suez Road, tel: 25-3787, closed Sundays.

Mr Pete's, steak, ribs and tandoori, Panganini Road, tel: 22-3428, closed Sundays.

Pizza Island, pizza and halaal Middle Eastern food, Castle, tel: 27-3616.

Rendezvous, continental food, Pamodzi Hotel, tel: 25-4455.

Shehnai, Indian and Chinese dishes, Northmead, tel: 29-5420, closed Mondays.

Sichuan, Chinese food, showgrounds, tel: 25-3842.

The Continental, Chinese, Nangwenya Road, tel: 25-2303.

Yugo Club, Yugoslav, Ridgeway, closed Mondays.

Nightclubs

If you enjoy nightclubbing you could try either the **Moon City** nightclub or **Valentino's**, both of which are located in Indeco House on Buteko Place off Cairo Road. The only place recommended to the authors was called **Mike's Car Wash**, situated on the right-hand side of the Kafue Road as you head south out of town. Apparently it is the place to see and hear local bands.

Sporting facilities

Sports facilities for tourists in Lusaka are fairly limited. The Lusaka municipal sports club and Lusaka central sports club are located just off Alick Nkata Avenue.

There are three golf courses in and around Lusaka. Most central is the **Lusaka golf course**, which is on Saddam Hussein Boulevard, tel: 25-1598/25-0244/25-0831. The **Chainama Hills golf course** is on Kalingalinga Road, tel: 25-1010/29-1300. The **Chilanga club** is clearly signposted off the Kafue Road at Chilanga, tel: 27-8417/27-8323. Non-members are usually charged a fee of US$10 to play at these clubs. The **Intercontinental** has tennis courts which can be hired for about 1 000 kwacha. Both the Intercontinental and the **Pamodzi** have squash courts and several hotels have swimming pools. In addition the Pamodzi Hotel has a fully equipped gymnasium, available to non-guests at a membership fee of $400 a year!

Polo is a popular sport in Zambia, particularly among expatriates, and there are often matches at weekends at the Polo Club in the Lusaka showgrounds.

Soccer is far and away Zambia's most popular sport. Watch the press for details of matches in and around the city.

Places of worship

The **Anglican Cathedral of the Holy Cross** is on the corner of Independence Avenue and Chikwa Road.

Northmead Assembly of God is located at the Northmead shopping centre off the Great East Road.

There is a **Baptist Church** in Lubu Road, between Addis Ababa Drive and Saddam Hussein Boulevard.

St Ignatius Catholic Church is located on Addis Ababa Drive near the showgrounds.

The **Presbyterian Church of St Columbus** is on Addis Ababa Drive.

There is a **Seventh Day Adventist Church** in Burma Road, just off Independence Avenue.

There are several **United Churches of Zambia** (UCZ). St Paul's is in Burma Road, just beyond Chibwa Road.

There is a **synagogue** in Katunjila Road between Freedom Way and Chachacha Road.

The **Lusaka Muslim Society Mosque** is on the corner of Burma and Changa roads, just off Independence Avenue.

The **Hindu temple** is easy to find off Independence Avenue, also on Changa Road.

The **Sikh temple** is in Mumana Road, off Katima Mulilo Road off the Great East Road.

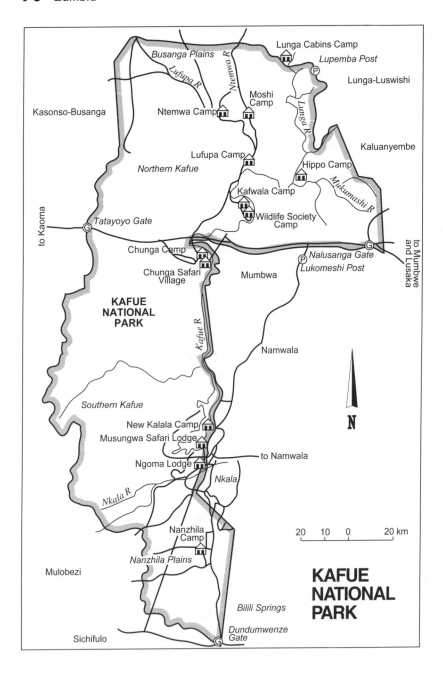

Kasonso-Busanga

Busanga Plains

Lufupa R

Ntemwa R

Lunga Cabins Camp

Lupemba Post

Lunga-Luswishi

Moshi Camp

Ntemwa Camp

Lunga R

Kaluanyembe

Lufupa Camp

Northern Kafue

Hippo Camp

Mukumashi R

Kafwala Camp

Wildlife Society Camp

to Kaoma

Tatayoyo Gate

Chunga Camp

Nalusanga Gate

Lukomeshi Post

to Mumbwe and Lusaka

Chunga Safari Village

Mumbwa

KAFUE NATIONAL PARK

Kafue R

Namwala

N

Southern Kafue

New Kalala Camp

Musungwa Safari Lodge

Ngoma Lodge

to Namwala

Nkala

Nkala R

20 10 0 20 km

Nanzhila Camp

Mulobezi

Nanzhila Plains

KAFUE NATIONAL PARK

Bilili Springs

Dundumwenze Gate

Sichifulo

Kafue National Park

Established in 1924, the park is situated in central-western Zambia, north and south of the Lusaka-Mongu road. It is the oldest and by far the largest park in the country (22 400 km^2) and one of the largest on the continent.

From Lusaka follow the main road west to Mumbwa (see route 2, page 80). Here visitors can either turn north if planning to visit camps right in the north, such as Hippo Camp, and camps such as Leopard Lodge and Lunga Cabins in the Lunga-Luswishi Game Management Area. Alternatively proceed straight down the main road, which bisects the park. Sixty-six kilometres from Mumbwa on the left is the turnoff to the Itezhi-Tezhi Dam, Musungwa Lodge, Ngoma and the southern Kafue. This is a positively dreadful road, consisting of 115 km of broken tar. The road is being improved by grading away the original tarred surface. Or again continue along the Mumbwa-Mongu road through the park until the Kafue River bridge. Roads before the bridge go to new camps on this river. Shortly after the bridge a gate on the north side of the road marks the entry point for Kafwala and Lufupa camps, the road to which proceeds north all the way to the Busanga Plains. A few kilometres further on the tar road, a secondary road turns sharply back south and east to Chunga.

Four-wheel-drive vehicles are not necessary to reach Chunga and Lufupa camps in the dry season, but be very cautious if it rains. A four-wheel-drive is necessary to visit the Busanga Plains and the Southern Kafue around Nanzhila.

Most of the interior of the park is inaccessible between November and April or May. Note particularly that many maps show a road from Chunga to Ngoma on the west side of the Kafue River. This is now impassable to even the stoutest of four-wheel-drive vehicles and should not be attempted. The only route between the northern and southern sections of the park is the deplorable Musungwa Road.

An alternative route to the Kafue that is attractive and adventurous is to come down from the Copperbelt, taking the road that runs from Kitwe (see chapter 9) to Kasempa via Ingwe. The road from Kitwe to Ingwe is good. Ingwe itself is no more than a village but just beyond it the road crosses the main Solwezi-Kasempa road, at which you turn left to follow a good dirt road to Kasempa. The total distance from Kitwe to

Kasempa is about 330 km. From Kasempa there is a reasonable graded track for 98 km to the Lunga pontoon. Just 16 km before the pontoon turn right down a poor track and 19 km further on is the northernmost gate of the Kafue National Park. Neither fuel nor supplies are available along this route.

This northern gate can also be reached via a remote and difficult road from Mumbwa. About 160 km from Lusaka the road into Mumbwa is easily found. Having turned onto it and proceeding north you will see a Total garage on the left as you reach the town. Turn left. This is the last refuelling station in the entire region of the Northern Kafue, so be sure to fill up with a sufficient supply. Proceed down the road in front of the garage and across a stream or gully; continue up to the crest of the hill where a turnoff on the right is marked by a barely legible sign to Hippo Mine. If you cannot find it ask for the road to the mine or to Chieftainess Kaindu. Follow this track for 31 km then take a left fork to the Reform School 9 km beyond that.

Be warned that this part of the country is absolutely infested with tsetse flies. Proceed for 21 km to the Kabalushi gate. Don't be surprised if the scouts are tardy about approaching the car – they are staying out of reach of the enormous cloud of tsetses that you will undoubtedly have brought with you. After the gate it is 19 km to the Lubungu pontoon on the Kafue River. The pontoon is usually in operation, but when the water is very low in October or November you have to ford the river on a drift about 2 km upstream. Ask at the village for a guide. The ford is deep but firm and can safely be negotiated in a four-wheel-drive. **Leopard Lodge** is located on the north bank of the Lubungu River 1 km above the drift. It was closed and for sale at the time of writing.

It is 80 km from the drift to the Lunga pontoon. Turn left 16 km beyond that and continue for 19 km to the gate. Alternatively, keep left after the pontoon and then left again at the next fork; this road leads eventually to **Lunga Cabins** from where it is possible to proceed to Kabalushi gate.

This reserve takes in a considerable portion of the Kafue River drainage basin. Along the perennial rivers there is beautiful riparian forest, but for the most part it is a flat or at the most gently undulating landscape of miombo woodland and grassy savanna. For the sake of clarity the park has been divided along the tarred Lusaka-Mongu road into the north Kafue and south Kafue in the description below.

In the south there's miombo, tall mopane forest and Kalahari sandveld as well as the wonderful, wide **Nanzhila Plains** of grassland dotted with termite mounds surmounted by baobabs, euphorbias and *diaspyros* trees. The **Itezhi-Tezhi Dam** is a 370 km² expanse of water along the eastern border of the southern section on which boat cruises offer a game viewing experience different from almost anywhere else in the country.

Vegetation in the northern section of the park is dominated by miombo woodland, termitaria zones and the enormous Busanga floodplains. During the rains the Lufupa River overflows its banks and then as the plains dry massive herds of game are attracted to the grasslands. The ecological diversity of the park as a whole has resulted in probably the widest range of mammal species of any park in the country. Game is reasonably abundant in both north and south although poaching in recent years has, as elsewhere, taken its toll. The area around **Lufupa Camp** is well known for its predators. Elephants are most likely to be seen near Ngoma in the south, and at Chunga or outside the park in the vicinity of the Lunga pontoon, but it will be some time before they lose their fear and suspicion of people and vehicles.

The park is one of the best reserves for antelope in Africa. Roan, sable, Lichtenstein's hartebeest, eland and wildebeest abound on open dambos particularly on the Nanzhila Plains. Impala are prolific in the south as are puku in the north. Oribi abound on the Nanzhila Plains. Sitatunga and red lechwe are confined to the Busanga floodplains and there are said to be yellow-backed duiker in the Ngoma forests. A point of interest is that the waterbuck found in the park are a sub-species, Defassa waterbuck, which lack the distinct white ring on the rump belonging to waterbuck elsewhere. There are plenty of predators, especially lions, which are frequently seen on the Busanga, around Lufupa and on the Nanzhila Plains. Lufupa Camp has a reputation for leopard sightings.

Cheetah can be seen on the Nanzhila Plains. Cape hunting or wild dogs are found in the miombo woodlands and the park is considered an important refuge for these threatened animals. Buffalo are more secretive than elsewhere but there are large herds around the Nanzhila and Busanga Plains. The Kafue River has an enormous hippo population. Birding is excellent, especially along the river. Pel's fishing owls are a local speciality. Over 400 species of birds have been recorded in the park. For further details see the section on Birdwatching in chapter 2.

The previous government's policy of favouring the Luangwa and allowing other parks, particularly the Kafue, to slide into chaos has meant that the tourist development of the park lags some way behind that of the Luangwa Valley. Poaching was rampant here and the armed forces were themselves responsible for destroying the old established camps like Nanzhila, Ntemwa and Moshi. Nevertheless some established camps remain and a number of new ones are being developed in the surrounding Game Management Areas, and between them there is a number of possibilities for accommodation to suit most budgets and tastes. It may be possible to camp in the abandoned lodges, but they are due to be put out to tender for renovation and their status will change, so permission should first be sought from the local NPWS headquarters at Chunga or Ngoma.

The first camp reached from the main road in the North Kafue is **Kafwala Camp**, which is beautifully situated above a stretch of rapids on the Kafue River and is open only to members of the Wildlife Conservation Society. Temporary membership can be obtained from the society (the address is given in the section on National Parks in chapter 2).

Also on the river, a little further northward and some 87 km by road from the tar road, is Lufupa Camp located above a wide and deep stretch of water at the confluence of the Kafue and Lufupa rivers. Lufupa provides fairly basic full board and chalets or camping facilities. Game drives, walks, boating and fishing are optional extras. The camp is justly famous for lion and leopard viewing. **Lufupa** and **Lunga Cabins** operate fly camps in the Busanga Plains which are open in the latter part of the dry season. Accommodation can be booked through **Busanga Trails**. Most maps show Moshi and Ntemwa camps in the northern part of the park. However, these were destroyed by the para-military and are currently derelict. There are plans to renovate them.

Hippo Camp is an exclusive tented camp on the national park side of the Kafue River in the north-east.

Leopard Lodge is a rather rundown camp on the other bank and outside the park, a few kilometres north of the Lubungu pontoon.

Further north, just where the Lunga River flows into the park, is **Lunga Cabins**, an extremely pleasant lodge run by Ed Smythe of African Experience (Pty) Ltd. They offer walking safaris in the Busanga Plains with accommodation in typical Zambian bush camps, game drives and boating, canoe adventures and fishing trips. They have an air shuttle company which will transfer people to or from Lusaka, Livingstone or Mfuwe.

In the southern section of the park accommodation may be divided again into that immediately south of and accessed from the Lusaka-Mongu road and that in the vicinity of Itezhi-Tezhi Dam. **Chunga Camp**, next door to the local NPWS headquarters, is the most easily accessible camp in the Kafue, being only 17 km south of the Lusaka-Mongu road. It is a small, old-style camp sitting picturesquely on a wide bend in the Kafue River – a reasonably good area for game. The proximity of the NPWS headquarters detracts a little from its tranquillity and beauty. It consists of six rondavels, and camping facilities with very helpful staff who will bring hot water for baths if it is not on tap and even do your cooking. **Mukambi Safari Lodge** is located on the eastern bank of the river overlooking the park a few kilometres from Chunga. It is signposted shortly before the Kafue bridge about 270 km from Lusaka. At the time of writing the lodge was being renovated and therefore only offering self-catering accommodation in its rondavel chalets.

Then in the south-eastern region of the park the old **Ngoma Lodge** remains in disrepair. It is also in the midst of the local NPWS headquarters. **Musungwa Lodge** is the most established lodge in the area, located on a hill with a spectacular view out over the Itezhi-Tezhi Dam. Fuel is available to residents. Nearby is the David Shepherd Camp, which is open only to members of the Wildlife Conservation Society of Zambia or temporary membership holders. **Puku Pan** is situated on the eastern side of the GMA between Ngoma and Itezhi-Tezhi.

Nanzhila Camp is right in the heart of the Nanzhila Plains. The old derelict lodge is being replaced by a new permanent camp built by Chundukwa Safaris. Chundukwa specialise in walking trails through this remote and unique area.

Lower Zambezi National Park

The Lower Zambezi is an extraordinarily beautiful and wild wilderness more or less opposite Zimbabwe's famous Mana

Pools. The western upper river section has seen some development in recent years, but further downriver and in the rolling hills of the escarpment it is underdeveloped.

Located south-east of Lusaka, the park covers an enormous area between the Zambezi River and the escarpment.

Access to lodges is probably best arranged by air charter although some of the camps can be reached with four-wheel-drive vehicles. The commercial operators (see below and chapter 13) who currently venture into the park itself are either based in the vicinity of the Chongwe River – which demarcates the park's western boundary – or enter the park by canoe. The Chongwe River can be accessed from Chirundu along a road for which four-wheel-drive is recommended, crossing the Kafue River by pontoon just beyond Gwabi Lodge. This is the most direct and commonly used route into the park. There is another route which is not used by safari operators as yet and requires special permission from the NPWS at Chilanga and is recommended only to the most intrepid of adventurers in sturdy and reliable four-wheel-drive vehicles. This is to descend the escarpment from the Great East Road via the old Chakwenga mine. The warning above is not given lightly: the going is tough, it is easy to get lost and vehicle failure could more than spoil the holiday. A wildlife scout guide and a second vehicle are advised. Please don't consider going down here during or just after the rainy season. In times past this route was connected to Chirundu via Jecki but that road has been reclaimed by the bush.

But if you still insist, take the Great East Road from Lusaka for 106 km till you reach the tsetse fly barrier. About 100 m beyond it a small track turns to the right. It is 22 km to the park gate and there a road left leads to the scout camp where you are advised to pick up a scout. Return to the gate and proceed down the escarpment. The distance is 80 km and takes four to five hours. The road is good at first but after the first river crossing begins to wind steeply up and down. After the last steep descent a fork indicates a right turn to the now difficult-to-decipher way through to the Chongwe River and Chirundu; keep left, turning past a pan and through a tall mopane forest. About 5 km further on at another fork turn right. The left turn here goes all the way to Fira. The right fork leads eventually to an abandoned camp on the banks of the river. Just before the camp a barely visible track leads past the old airfield through a river. After this keep right, beware of huge dongas and gullies and make for the river. *A last word of warning is that the remote corners of the park are said to be still landmined from the Zimbabwe war.* This park is a magnificent wilderness. Topographically it ranges from the river's edge overhung with huge *diaspyros, ficus* and other riverine species through a floodplain of treacherous 'cotton soil' fringed by mopane forest and interspersed with *Acacia albida* (winterthorn) to the endlessly climbing hills covered in broad-leafed woodland.

Unfortunately it has been and continues to be poached, particularly for ivory. However, elephants, being the wise creatures that they are, frequent the area around the Chongwe River where the presence of safari operators has lessened the poaching risk. There are big herds of buffalo and plenty of lion as well as waterbuck and impala. The river, of course, has lots of hippo and enormous crocodiles. Birdlife is incredible, specialities being trumpeter hornbills, Meyer's parrot, Lilian's lovebird, and, in summer, Narina trogon.

The **Royal Zambezi Lodge** just west of the Chongwe River can accommodate 12 guests in 'luxury' tented chalets and offers game drives and walking safaris in the park. **Gwabi Lodge**, more of a stopover between Zimbabwe and Lusaka, is located on the Kafue River, close to its confluence with the Zambezi. The longest standing camp inside the park itself is Chiawa Camp, a 16-bed luxury tented camp. Tongabezi has opened **Chifungulu** comprising Sausage Tree and Potato Bush camps. If the names sound like 'bangers and mash', be assured that the camps have all the finesse visitors would expect from the company and are to our minds the most appropriate and beautiful in the country.

In addition to small bush camps deep in the park that are used on canoe safaris, Safari Par Excellance has developed **Kayila Lodge**, a conventional, permanent, luxury lodge on 10 000 acres of private land upstream of the park, **Chongwe Canoe Camp** on the Chongwe River comprising simple thatched huts with outdoor *en suite* facilities and **Mwambashi River Lodge**, luxury safari tents on platforms deep in the park itself. **Mvuu Lodge** comprises wood and thatch chalets and lies about 15 km from the park in the Chiawa Game Management Area. See chapter 13 for a full list of operators.

Blue Lagoon National Park

The park lies west of Lusaka, on the northern side of the Kafue Flats. Although very close to Lusaka, until recently the park was not open to visitors as it fell under the preserve of the Defence Ministry. So it is poorly signposted. Take the Mumbwa Road from Lusaka (route 2, on page 80), then turn left at a faded blue ZCCM sign approximately 27 km from Lusaka and just opposite a store called the Bancroft Supermarket.

This road leads eventually to the park gate. The gate does not itself mark the real entrance to the park, but you can sign in here before being escorted back the way you have come and down un-signposted roads to the edge of the Kafue Flats.

This park lies directly opposite Lochinvar National Park on the Kafue Flats (see page 97). It was conceived by two doyens of conservation in Zambia, the Critchleys, who farmed here. Although at first the topography seems less attractive than that of Lochinvar, the view when one eventually reaches the flats is quite astounding. A vast, watery plain as level as a billiard table stretches to the horizon and as far as the eye can see it is covered with tens of thousands of Kafue lechwe, some buffalo and myriad waterbirds. In the bush behind there are also zebra and other antelope.

Although strictly speaking it is not yet open to the public, do ask to be shown the old Critchley farmhouse. With an unremarkable exterior, it has been the special retreat of cabinet ministers and generals and the interior is immaculately preserved to the extent that all the old family furniture, silver and photographs remain just as they were when the Critchleys lived there. There are plans to convert this into a tourist lodge. Then ask to see the extraordinary causeway that Mr Critchley built way out into the swamp so that his wife could watch birds. If your vehicle has a tight turning circle drive out along it for a splendid view, but mind the incredible number of huge monitor lizards that live on it. You will marvel at the spirit of endeavour in a bygone age.

There are no facilities or organised safaris that we are aware of at the moment.

The camp that once existed here was destroyed. Visitors signing in will probably be told to camp at the gate. Don't take up this invitation. Ask to be guided down to the abandoned camp at the water's edge. There is a large fig tree nearby which makes for a splendid campsite surrounded by all manner of wildlife. There is no dangerous game.

Contact the Wildlife Conservation Society of Zambia (see page 14 for the address) or the Zambian Ornithological Society (see page 17 for the address) for more information.

ROUTE 1
LUSAKA TO CHIRUNDU

DISTANCE: 137 km **TIME:** 1,5 hours **ROAD CONDITIONS:** Generally good tar **FUEL:** Kafue and Chirundu
RECOMMENDED STOPS: None

The road leaves Lusaka straight from Cairo Road at its south-end circle, but the section out of town is under reconstruction. Until this stretch is finished it will remain rather chaotic.

The distance from Lusaka to the Kafue Bridge is 44 km. There is a good **textile market** on the right-hand side of the road as you pass through Kafue town. Keep your eyes open for police roadblocks.

From Kafue Bridge the road is good but becomes hilly and winding. Here it is advisable to drive with caution because the huge trucks frequenting the route tend to have faulty brakes and career recklessly down the pass, often with disastrous results. About 4 km from the Siavonga turnoff on the Lusaka side and immediately south of the road lies the **Chirundu Fossil Forest**, a petrified forest dating back 150 million years. Petrified tree trunks up to 3 m long have become exposed by erosion over millennia. Sporadic finds have also indicated that Middle and Late Stone Age inhabitants of the area used the petrified wood to make tools. It is, of course, strictly against the law to remove fossils or artefacts.

ROUTE 2
LUSAKA TO KAFUE NATIONAL PARK, THE M9

DISTANCE: 276 km **TIME:** 3,5 hours **ROAD CONDITIONS:**
Fair with some potholed sections **FUEL:** Mumbwa
RECOMMENDED STOPS: None, other than Blue Lagoon, a
detour for which an overnight is recommended

This road is scheduled for a major upgrade so look out for
detours and beware of potholes before then. Leave Lusaka by
taking Kalundwe Road west from Cairo Road past the Soweto
market on your left and out through a rather chaotic commercial and industrial area. As you pass the Hindu crematorium
on the left the surroundings open out. Shortly thereafter you
pass the Garden House Motel on the right.

About 27 km from town on the left-hand side there is a
turnoff to **Blue Lagoon National Park** (see page 78), marked by
a rather faded blue ZCCM sign. The road is potholed in places,
and particularly badly so in the region before Mumbwa. Keep
a lookout for military roadblocks, tsetse fly and African swine
fever control barriers.

The distance is 151 km from Lusaka to Mumbwa. The town
lies about 4 km north of the road and is of little consequence
other than as the last refuelling stop en route to the Kafue.
Mumbwa also marks the turnoff to Hippo Camp, lodges in the
Lunga-Luswishi GMA and the road to Kasempa. For these turn
left at the Total garage, go down the hill, over a gully and up
the next hill at the crest of which the road leads off to the
north. If you absolutely must stay in Mumbwa there is the **La
Hacienda Hotel**. Once run by National Hotels, it does not
appear to belong to anyone at the moment and although the
rooms are reasonably clean, with hot water, don't expect the
food and drink supplied to match the grand pretensions of the
menu.

Shortly after Mumbwa a barrier on the road tells you that
the Kafue National Park lies to the right of the road and on the
left is the clearly signposted road to Musungwa, Itezhi-Tezhi
and the south Kafue. The boldness of the signs belies the
appalling condition of that road. But from here on the Lusaka-
Mongu road is satisfactory. It is 58 km to the Kafue River

bridge, where there is usually a military roadblock. The guard, with his RPG missile launcher, will persuade you to stop, but thereafter you can marvel unhindered at the view of this enormous river. Shortly after the bridge the road into the northern Kafue is marked by a barrier on the right. The main road proceeds straight on, bisecting the national park, and it is not uncommon to see game from here, especially early in the morning. The road to Chunga is signposted some way on. It is 53 km through the park and the end of the reserve is marked again by a picket. For the rest of the road to Mongu see route 6 in chapter 8.

7

THE SOUTHERN REGION

This is Tongaland. The Tonga people have been living on the northern banks of the Zambezi for almost 1 000 years and their culture is a venerable one, although it was considerably disturbed by the construction of Lake Kariba. The people who follow the most traditional Tonga way of life exist in the hilly region between the lake and the Livingstone-Lusaka road. North of that road until the Kafue Flats Game Management Area the land is fairly developed, particularly in the region of Mazabuka which is rich farming country. The Kafue Flats is, as its name suggests, a vast, almost completely flat area which prior to the building of the Itezhi-Tezhi Dam was annually flooded by the Kafue River, resulting in an enormous wetland habitat and wildlife paradise. Farming interests have seen the eradication of big game but it remains a sanctuary for many antelope, in particular the unique Kafue lechwe, which roam the plains on either side of the Kafue River in tens of thousands – or certainly did so until very recently, although continued uncontrolled hunting has been reducing numbers drastically in recent years. It is one of the greatest birding areas in the sub-continent. One of the best places to see wildlife in the southern region is the Lochinvar National Park. The Kafue National Park extends down into the southern region and can be accessed from Kalomo (see Route 4 in this chapter), but is dealt with under Central Region (see chapter 6). The other attractions in the southern region are Livingstone, the Victoria Falls and the Zambezi, and Lake Kariba itself. The Zambian shore of the lake does not have the game that Zimbabwe boasts and the only development has taken place near the dam wall on the eastern side of the lake at Siavonga and at the fishing town of Sinazongwe.

Livingstone and the Victoria Falls

The **Victoria Falls** is arguably the most famous tourist attraction in southern Africa, unquestionably one of the great wonders of the world and reason alone to visit Zambia. (The view up the gorge from the Zambian bank is considered by many to be more spectacular than that seen from Zimbabwe.) It is 1 690 m

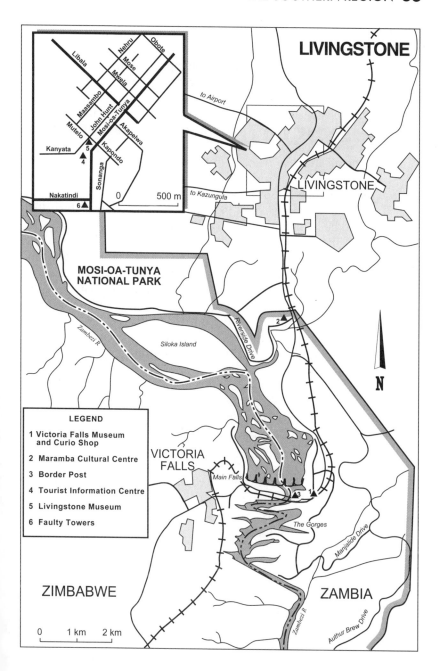

LIVINGSTONE

Libala
Nehru
Obote
Mose
Mutela
Maasambo
John Hunt
Mosi-oa-Tunya
Akapelwa
Mutelo
Kapondo
Kanyata
Sonanga
Nakatindi

to Airport

to Kazungula

0   500 m

LIVINGSTONE

**MOSI-OA-TUNYA
NATIONAL PARK**

Zambezi R.

Riverside Drive

Siloka Island

N

LEGEND

1 Victoria Falls Museum
  and Curio Shop

2 Maramba Cultural Centre

3 Border Post

4 Tourist Information Centre

5 Livingstone Museum

6 Faulty Towers

VICTORIA
FALLS

Main Falls

The Gorges

Manjalide Drive

ZIMBABWE

ZAMBIA

Zambezi R.

Authur Brew Drive

0   1 km   2 km

from left to right, has an average height of 92 m, and when in flood discharges as much as 546 million litres of water a minute. But the statistics are unimportant: the mighty cascade of the Zambezi River as it plunges into the Batoka Gorge in the widest curtain of falling water on the planet remains, even to frequent visitors, a spectacle of epiphanic proportions.

The force of the water as it pours with a roar into the chasm causes great gusts of air to shoot a curtain of spray high into the air that can be seen from up to 30 km away, which gave rise to the Falls' original name of *Mosi-oa-tunya*, 'the smoke that thunders'. So it was called when David Livingstone was led to it by Sekeletu of the Makokolo on 16 November 1854, and he named it after his queen.

The first European settlement at the falls was located a mile upstream on the north bank at the old drift where people and goods crossed the Zambezi prior to the building of the railway and bridge (see the section on What to see and do in this chapter). In 1904 a new township was laid out and the town of Livingstone established on its present site.

Livingstone is, to our minds, one of the most attractive towns in this part of Africa and has in the last few years suddenly awoken from the recumbent torpor into which it had fallen. It still has a soporific atmosphere; colonial houses with corrugated iron roofs and deep verandas recline and decay beneath the deep shade of mango trees; the central business area, spaciously set astride the wide Mosi-oa-tunya Road still snores rather than hums. Two highly attractive buildings from the art-deco era hold their own against more recent and ugly architecture and the back streets such as Kuta Way are a living memorial to African commerce of an earlier era. But, from a tourist perspective, winds of change are whistling down the boulevard, ruffling the papers on bureaucratic desks, banging shop doors and throwing back the shutters on new enterprises one after another.

A pioneer spirit prevails and if a whiff of the tourist dollar floats on that wind, a very different spirit of commerce prevails on the north bank of the river from that on the other side. While upmarket travellers are more likely to find their preferred accommodation at one of the lodges along the river, adventurous travellers would do well to consider the options in town and partake, while it remains possible, of an old African charm altogether lost in Victoria Falls across the river.

There is not the same degree of hustling by money chang-
ers and car washers in Livingstone as there was a few years
ago, although some may still try their luck. An instant, firm and
smiling refusal is the best policy. Changing money from the
black market vendors, although legal, is likely to leave you
with considerably less than you originally had so rather use the
bureaux de change or banks. Car theft is not the problem that
it is in Lusaka and the Copperbelt (see page 43), nevertheless
don't leave a packed car unattended.

Access

By air: Livingstone International Airport is located close to
town off Libala Drive. Although an international airport, no
scheduled commercial flights were landing at Livingstone at
the time of writing and the airstrip was in need of upgrading.
However, regular charter flights continue to use the airport.
Improvement of the airport and strip is apparently set to coincide with the Sun International developments, so check with
the airlines. Charter flight passengers can land and clear
customs at Livingstone. Most of the Zambian lodges recommend using the Victoria Falls Airport in Zimbabwe and will
collect and deliver their clients there. If you are planning a
cheaper, backpacker holiday consider the option of flying to
Victoria Falls in Zimbabwe and hitching a ride to the border.

By train: The railway station is located close to Mosi-oa-tunya
Road, just south of the CBD. Trains run to and from Lusaka,
19:00 to 07:00. and you can book an overnight sleeper. First-
class carriages, a *couchette* and bedding are available in two-
or four-bedded compartments. Contact the **Zambian Railways
Passenger Services** in Livingstone, tel: 32-1001/6. Goods trains
come from south of the border, but in the unlikely event of
arriving this way, you will probably not have the patience to
actually wait and cross the border by train rather than on foot.
Highly exclusive package train journeys designed to recall the
splendour of the colonial era run regularly from South Africa
to Victoria Falls and very occasionally proceed across the
Zambezi *en route* to East Africa.

By bus: The general bus station is below the informal market
behind Kuta Way in the old part of town. However coaches
tend to disembark just off the main road in the centre of town
and some do so outside the New Fairmount Hotel.

By car: Livingstone is 480 km from Lusaka on a reasonable tar road. The main road passes through Livingstone as Mosi-oa-tunya Road, linking Zambia with Zimbabwe over the famous Victoria Falls Bridge. The bridge marks the border and a more spectacular frontier would be difficult to find. Clearing customs at this border post is less tiresome and tedious than it was in the past. Precise advice is difficult here because a new customs clearance house is being built and procedures are likely to change when it is completed. It used to be necessary to proceed from the border to the customs office and then to the State Insurance offices to get third party insurance. Now these functions occur at the border. Ask the immigration officers for advice. Remember that day visitors are currently levied US$10 for a special day visa.

Access from Botswana is accomplished by crossing the pontoon at Kazungula, whence one approaches town on a good tar road from Mambova. The road becomes Nakatindi Road when it reaches town.

From Namibia the conventional route from Katima Mulilo is to cross the Zambezi by ferry to Sesheke and then proceed via Mambova to join the route described above. The tar road between Sesheke and Mambova, having collapsed into an appalling succession of potholes, has had the tar graded from it. Its condition is now variable but very unlikely to be quicker than the alternate route via Botswana and the Kazungula ferry. Previously, the only hazardous stretch on that route was the road to Ngoma Bridge, but this is being tarred, which will make it more quickly traversable. If you can bear the thought of so many borders then proceeding through Zimbabwe to Victoria Falls offers substantially better roads and even the chance of seeing game.

Tourist information

The Zambian National Tourist Board has an office that is easily spotted between the museum and the civic centre just where the main road, Mosi-oa-tunya Road, bends into the CBD. Its staff are friendly and reasonably informed. The ZNTB and the National Heritage Commission publish a range of literature that could be useful. The tourist map of Livingstone and Victoria Falls is a useful if dated guide. If they don't have one it may be available from the map office at the Department of Surveys, located across the road in a grimy corridor between the bank and the travel agent. For further information on Livingstone try the *Livingstone Visitor's Guide*, published by the Livingstone Cultural and Arts Festival Organising Committee (editor: Lawrence Sumpa). We highly recommend the *Historical Guide to Livingstone* by Kristin Ese, published by the Livingstone Tourism Association.

Many of the lodges and adventure tour groups have offices in a distinctively renovated block of offices and shops in what was once known as the second class trading area on the corner of Nakatindi Road – the Kazungula road – and Mosi-oatunya Road several hundred metres down the hill from the town centre. It is a good place to begin most enquiries. You cannot miss the Faulty Towers sign for the backpacker accommodation upstairs. There is an Internet café called the Cyberian Outpost. In addition to Internet facilities, Cyberian Outpost offers telephone and fax message forwarding and receiving services and are agents for Mercury Mail, a reliable private mailing agent for global mail via the British postal service. Or, if suffering from urban withdrawal and an excess of outdoor adventure, you could just sit and play computer games and sample arguably the best coffee available in the country.

A note for cell phone users: Zambia has its own cell phone network, but in Livingstone use can be made of the South African cell in Victoria Falls, providing users have cleared their cell phones for international use.

Accommodation

Options for accommodation in and around Livingstone and the Falls have expanded exponentially in recent years. The town of Livingstone is 11 km from Victoria Falls and most lodges, hotels or hostels currently available north of the river are some way from the Falls themselves, being either in town or located up and down the river. This will change dramatically when Sun International complete the hotels they are building on the sites formerly occupied by the Intercontinental Hotel and Rainbow Lodge, apparently set to offer over 600 beds within spitting distance of the Falls.

Nevertheless, a wide choice to suit most budgets is already available. Comprehensively detailed in chapter 12, the following outlines some, but by no means all, of the possibilities. Beginning in the lower budget spectrum, there are now a number of backpacker or budget traveller hostels in Livingstone. **Faulty Towers** is the easiest to find, being described above, right on the main road, corner Nakatindi Road (the road to Kazungula) and gaudily painted. Inside, it is quite small but immaculate.

For latter-day frugality in the seat of past opulence, **Grubby's Grotto** occupies the old governor's house and both **Jolly Boys** and **Gecko's** hostels occupy old houses. Mosquito nets are a prerequisite for a decent night's sleep and not every hostel has them so we suggest that you take your own.

There are various camping possibilities from the lawns of **Gecko's** and **Jolly Boys** in town to upstream riverside options such as **Kubu Cabins** and **Jungle Junction**. The former two might be the preferred options for backpackers in search of adventure, the latter two are most suited to those getting away from all that, although they do have daily shuttles in and out of town, thus offering the best of both worlds. Jungle Junction, on a palm-treed island way up river is so relaxed that were it not for the beady-eyed presence of Stevie the crocodile, it might have blown in on a hurricane from some lazy Caribbean isle. **Nyala Lodge**, close to the gate to the Mosi-oa-tunya Park, has accommodation in the lower to medium budget range and camping facilities.

There are several mid- and up-market riverside lodges from which to choose. All have shuttles to and from town and most across the border to and from Victoria Falls Airport. Most are upstream, but strikingly different and precariously perched on the lip of the **Batoka Gorge** are **Songwe Point** and **Taita Falcon Lodge.** Taita balances old fashioned South African hospitality with a breathtaking eagle's eye view over rapid 17 and, at the right time of year, offers a rare chance of seeing the raptor from which it takes its name. Some 17 km upstream of the Falls,

Tongabezi is one of the most established luxury lodges, as gently eccentric as ever; accommodation like the 'bird house' or 'dog house' is hard to better anywhere for its particular and peculiar combination of rusticity and luxury. The associated company, **Sindabezi**, has a tented camp on an island at the lip

of the Falls and provides a range of river activities. Safari Par Excellence has opened **Thorntree Lodge** about 15 km up river from town. **The River Club** was rated by one group of travel agents as the most luxurious on the Zambian side of the river. Further upstream from Tongabezi are **Chundukwa Tree Lodge** and **Kubu Cabins**. Both have been established for a number of years and offer good, middle-of-the-range accommodation and river activities on superb stretches of river.

Further upstream, almost at Katambora is **Royal Chundu Fishing Lodge** which would appeal primarily (but not exclusively) to fishermen.

What to see and do

Today the tourist industry has styled Livingstone and the Victoria Falls as the 'Adventure Capital' of Africa and the emphasis on adventure sports such as rafting, bungee jumping, microlighting and so on threatens to eclipse the primary reason for being there, seeing the falls themselves. But the title is not unjustified and the many ways to get the adrenalin pumping are listed below.

Top priority, of course, should be to see the **Victoria Falls,** which is now possible from almost every vantage point imaginable. The best time of year is probably not during the high-water period of March to May. Awesome as the sheer volume of the deluge is then, the spray that falls like rain from a height of almost a kilometre all but masks from sight the Falls themselves. Likewise the spectacle is somewhat lessened at lowest water during November or December. Generally, but especially when the water is high, it's advisable to take a raincoat, waterproof bags for cameras and waterproof shoes or sandals. The spray can drench you in minutes. The spray or 'rain' has created a wonderful rainforest along the Falls' edge which – particularly on the Zimbabwean side where it is somewhat better preserved – hosts plant species that would not otherwise survive in the surrounding dry climate, as well as bushbuck, monkeys and baboons and a plethora of birds and insects.

There are numerous points from which you can view the Falls. On the Zambian side they are reached by a small road that turns off just above the customs post. Paved paths lead to various lookout points at which the absence of barriers or protective railing adds to both scenic and thrill value. Ideally, try to see the Falls from both sides of the border, bearing in mind the tit-for-tat day visa levies required by both countries. Zambia offers views of the **Eastern Cataract**, a great view up the main gorge (especially at sunset) and terrific views from the Knife Edge Bridge of both the Falls and down the gorge below the magnificent railway bridge. The bridge was completed in

1905 as part of the grand design of a railway line from Cape Town to Cairo.

Crossing the **Victoria Falls Bridge** is an experience in itself. This is surely one of the world's great frontiers; the Zimbabwean side offers the rainforest and a walk to precipitous **Danger Point** and the deluge over **Devil's Cataract**, above which stands Livingstone's statue and monument. Incidentally the statue is incorrectly placed for the explorer first saw the falls from the opposite bank. Do go and look at the Falls at different times of day, as they are never quite the same. Try to go at night as well (but not alone), especially if there is a moon when you might see a lunar rainbow and the Falls assume a powerful and primordial mystique.

Other viewing points on the Zambian side are from down in the **Boiling Pot** or from the ancient baobab, the **Lookout Tree**, that stands beyond the railway line opposite where Rainbow Lodge stood and some of the Sun International development is taking place.

The **Batoka Gorge** is well worth seeing. It is the beginning of the huge Zambezi Valley, which stretches all the way to the gorge at Cahora Basa in Mozambique and remains one of the wildest and most beautiful places in Africa. Sadly, although the Batoka Gorge is scenically spectacular and a wildlife paradise, it is threatened by the building of another dam. Not only will this destroy a unique habitat and breeding ground for many raptors, including some very rare species, it will certainly wreck some of the activities listed below. Protests have been lodged from many quarters but the Zimbabwean authorities have become increasingly hard of hearing in recent years. The status of the project is uncertain but appears currently shelved due to a lack of Zambian enthusiasm.

Certainly well known, if not notorious by now, the **bungee jumping** venue will come as no surprise – the middle of the bridge. Just imagine the consternation of Victorian engineer, HF Varian if he could see the thrill seekers on a glorified elastic band leaping into the chasm that divided the continent from the masterpiece of rivets and steel that he constructed to unite it. Rated the most spectacular bungee jump in the world the operation is more scientific than it looks. It is run by (appropriately named) **African Extreme** (see chapter 13 for details). Booking is not necessary and, under the circumstances, they could not be easier to find.

The Victoria Falls have become famous for probably the most exciting but safe white-water rafting in the world and for many a visit would not be complete without doing the one-day run down the Batoka Gorge. A number of companies including **Safari Par Excellence, Bundu Adventures** and **Raft Quest** operate from the Zambian side and have the advantage over Zimbabwean operators of being able to begin right from the Boiling Pot. Experienced guides pilot inflatable rafts down a series of impressive rapids interspersed with pools whose tranquillity belies their inevitable slide into a further tumult of white water. The gorge itself is beautiful, the skies above filled with numerous birds – especially raptors – and the waters below with crocodiles and other exciting nasty creatures. Rafting doesn't require extraordinary fitness, only the capability of walking down the gorge and back out again at the end, but do not underestimate the latter, it is a serious hike.

As if bungee jumping were not enough, another fine imported New Zealand invention and newest craze on the river is **river boarding**. Don a helmet, wetsuit and flippers and dive into the foaming water with a boogie board. The gigantic 'stopper waves' you are supposed to surf will terrify all but the certifiable. Contact Safari Par Excellence and Serious Fun to sign up for this particular thrill.

The so-called 'float of the angels' is a non-white-water boat ride around the Boiling Pot.

Batoka Sky offers a 'flight of the angels' in two-seater microlights and perhaps the most spectacular aerial view of the Falls.

Tongabezi, Makora Quest and Chundukwa Safaris offer **canoe safaris** on the Zambezi above the Falls, which include camping or picnics and game viewing on islands in the river. Tongabezi also offer specialised birding and painting safaris.

For hikers the **Batoka Trail** is a four- or five-day guided trail arranged through Songwe Point Village. It is offered only from April through to September. The hike takes participants from the top of the gorge down to rapid 14, along the river to rapid 25 and then up again. It is self catering and participants need to bring all their own gear. Avid birders might be particularly interested as the hike is one of few opportunities afforded to see the gorge and its breeding raptors.

If you like your experiences a little more mellowed then a **Zambezi booze cruise** could interest you. Mapopoma Sunset

Cruises launch from the boat club. Zambian cruises are likely to be quieter than those operating on the heavily over-traded Zimbabwe side.

Many of the tour operators offer historical tours of Livingstone, but you could as well pick up some of the reference guides we mention, walk yourself around the town and absorb its gentle delapidation and decay, footnotes to the history of this remarkable frontier.

The **Mosi-oa-tunya Zoological Park** is a very small but scenically attractive game reserve with lovely riverine trees and a variety of animals that can be seen at reasonably close quarters. (Tourist brochures credit the park with all sorts of species but many of these have long since departed via Livingstone kitchens.) Some white rhino are kept in a special enclosure. Their establishment was vaunted as a major conservation exercise after rhino were poached to extinction in Zambia in the '70s and '80s. But since it is unlikely that white rhino ever occurred here, the claim rings a little hollow. They are, however, the only rhino in the whole region and perhaps interesting for that reason. There is not much other big game although elephants are beginning to cross over from Zimbabwe with increasing frequency, something of dubious advantage to the park as they are wreaking havoc upon the long undisturbed riverine trees.

Do stop at the **Old Drift cemetery**, which is a poignant remnant of the first European settlement. Before the construction of the rail bridge all people and goods crossed the river at this point and the first settler, one FJ Clarke, arrived in 1898 to trade and start a hotel. By 1903 the European population totalled 68. But the settlement was ill-sited in a flat and marshy area and lost many of its inhabitants to malaria. Here they remained buried when the town was moved to healthier ground at the coming of the railway in 1904. About 500 m downstream of the cemetery a monument marks the site of the old drift. Unfortunately visitors are required to have cars to see the park, or use the services of operators with a vehicle, but perhaps the increasing presence of elephants makes this a sensible precaution.

The **Livingstone Museum**, located just behind the tourist centre, is worth a visit. It is Zambia's national museum and has informative archaeological and ethnographic displays. Its premier feature is a collection of letters, notes and other paraphernalia that belonged to David Livingstone. There is a natural history section in which the most interesting exhibit shows the three different kinds of lechwe found in Zambia. The entry fee is US$5, children free of charge. There is also a craft shop.

The **Railway Museum** off Chishimba Falls Road has a large collection of old trains and is fairly interesting, particularly for its collection of old photographs which graphically illustrate the trials and tribulations of pioneer days. Adults must pay $5, children can enter free.

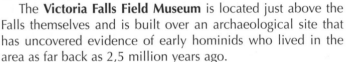

The **Victoria Falls Field Museum** is located just above the Falls themselves and is built over an archaeological site that has uncovered evidence of early hominids who lived in the area as far back as 2,5 million years ago.

Next door to the Field Museum is a curio shop in which a number of craft sellers tout their wares. Products are of reasonable quality but the competition for your patronage can be exhausting.

The **Maramba Cultural Village** between the Falls and Livingstone purports to give visitors a fascinating glimpse of Zambian culture, but on our last visit some Zimbabwean elephants on a cross border adventure had enthusiastically demolished it. Nationally, there is a renewed interest in cultural dancing and it is worth finding out if events or competitions coincide with your visit.

For a glimpse of contemporary traditional Zambian life try to visit the **Maramba Market** (not to be confused with the cultural village described above).

The Leya people of **Makuni Village** open their village and lives to visitors for a contribution of about US$5. They also have a small craft market. If you are there in July you might catch the Leya and their chief, Senior Chief Makuni, partake in the *Luwindi* ceremony which invokes the rains. To find the village, turn off the main road between Livingstone and the Falls down the road to the Lookout Tree. After the Lookout Tree the road forks and is signposted right to Songwe Point, left to Makuni. The road is not good and a four-wheel-drive is recommended. At Songwe Point Village, 20 or so kilometres down the road and right on the lip of the gorge an interactive village has been created that gives insight into the traditional life of the region, past and present.

Another traditional ceremony around Livingstone is the *Lukuni Luzwa Buuka* ceremony of the Toka. Held every August it celebrates the Toka conquest of other tribes. If lucky enough to see them, visitors should note that these ceremonies are not designed for tourists, they are wholly authentic and of great spiritual or cultural significance to their communities and should be accorded their due reverence.

The Livingstone Arts and Cultural Festival is held annually during the last week in April.

For crafts try the market behind the Falls described above, bearing in mind the stamina required for bargaining. Otherwise there is **Kubu Crafts** in the town centre which sells items of a more contemporary, and often domestically useful, nature or there is **African Visions Arts and Crafts** in the Faulty Towers centre below Nakatindi Road, which sells African crafts such as masks and jewellery from all over the continent.

Lake Kariba

Below the Victoria Falls and the Batoka Gorge the Zambezi has carved a wide, deep valley that for centuries was a major impediment to exploration and trade to the north. Then in 1955 the government of the then Federation of Rhodesia and Nyasaland decided to dam the Zambezi. The site chosen was the Kariba Gorge, where the mighty river was constricted through an arched gap of solid rock about 100 m wide. Shaped like a giant fish trap, Kariba is named after the *kariwa* (Shona) or *kariba* (Makorere), a small trap for catching birds and mice. Apparently in days gone by a great slab of rock overhung the gorge that resembled such a device on a giant scale.

The contract was awarded to an Italian company, Impresit, which began work in November 1956. The surrounding country was so rugged that the site could only be reached along centuries-old elephant trails. On 22 June 1959 the last skip of concrete was poured. The result was a wall 128 m high, 600 m wide, 26 m thick at its base and 13 m wide at the top that holds back the might of the Zambezi for 280 km. Thus was tamed at last, against all predictions, the legendary river god *Nyaminyami*.

The story of Nyaminyami's struggle against the forces of the 20th century is integral to the mythology of Kariba and one cannot look at the wall and the vast waters behind it without knowing a little of its legendary history. For centuries prior to the damming the Zambezi Valley was inhabited by the

BaTonga, an essentially hunter-gatherer people who lived in a symbiotic relationship with the teeming wildlife of the valley. According to their folklore this existence was presided over by a benevolent spirit and guardian of the river, who is depicted as a kind of giant snake and was called Nyaminyami. The Tonga elders protested against the building of the wall and refused to leave their ancestral grounds. The tribes even took up arms to prevent their removal, but their bows and arrows could hardly match firearms and after several tribesmen had been killed they reluctantly departed at gunpoint.

The elders prophesied, however, that Nyaminyami would destroy the dam. No one associated with the project has ever forgotten that this did in fact almost happen. In 1957 the river rose a colossal 100 feet as 3,5 million gallons of water surged through the gorge every second, flooding the coffer dam and setting back the works. The Zambezi has a double flood regimen from local and distant rains. This time, as usual, they followed one another but did not coincide. The following year, at odds of one in a thousand, the river flooded again as both local and distant catchment areas received unusually heavy rains. As had never happened before the runoff plunged into the Zambezi Valley all at the same time and the combined floodwaters smashed down on the emerging wall in the greatest tide the river dwellers had ever witnessed.

Nyaminyami threw all the power he could muster at the project, causing extensive damage and washing away a whole section of wall. In all, 17 men lost their lives building Kariba; some of those men are now entombed forever in the one million cubic metres of concrete into which they slipped and with which Nyaminyami was finally subdued.

The building of Kariba generated many other stories of heroism and endeavour. One that caught the imagination of the world was Operation Noah, in which thousands of animals were rescued from the rising waters.

The primary function of Kariba is to generate hydro-electric power. Ten turbine generators produce a combined output of 1 350 megawatts of electricity, supplying both Zimbabwe and Zambia. A second major industry was introduced in the form of a small sardine-like fish from Lake Tanganyika (see page 142).

These 'kapenta', as they are known, multiplied exceedingly rapidly in the early nutrient-rich years of the dam and today the lights of the commercial fishing boats used to lure big shoals into their nets can be seen spread right across the lake at night. But perhaps the most successful industry on the lake now is tourism. The Zimbabwean side, where the herds of game have been preserved, is a much more desirable tourist destination. On the Zambian side almost every living wild thing has long since been eaten, and the tourist industry focuses on water-sports and game fishing at Siavonga and to a lesser extent at Sinazongwe.

Siavonga

The road to Siavonga turns off the Lusaka-Chirundu road (see route 1, page 79) just 18 km from Chirundu. It comprises 65 km of reasonable tar road winding alternately through pretty hills and the rather overgrazed settlements of the Tonga people. You are likely to be offered great lumps of amethyst and other semi-precious rock along the way.

Siavonga is Zambia's premier 'seaside' town. Primarily a weekend destination from Lusaka and for the innumerable conferences to which the Zambian bureaucracy retire at the drop of a hat, Siavonga may with a certain stretch of the imagination be said to resemble a slightly sleazy Mediterranean resort. As most of the lakeshore trees have been cut down and the game long since killed, Siavonga cannot offer the immediate attractions of Kariba in Zimbabwe. Nevertheless there is the possibility of exciting fishing on the lake and a relaxed atmosphere with a magnificent view across the waters to the blue hills of Matusadona in Zimbabwe. Consider Siavonga as a first or last stop *en route* to Zimbabwe or as a stopover while exploring the remote and winding roads of Tongaland between Livingstone and Chirundu.

Although the main attractions are fishing and lazing in the sun, there is a crocodile farm just outside town where, for a very small fee, visitors can examine enclosures full of beady-eyed proto-handbags. And of course there is the Kariba Dam wall, which has been described above. The turnoff to the dam wall and border post is clearly marked.

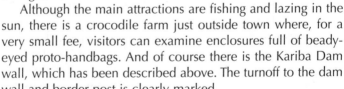

There is a wide choice of places to stay in Siavonga. The **Manchinchi Bay Lodge** is probably the most attractively positioned of the three main lodges, but otherwise is similar to the Zambezi Lodge and Lake Kariba Inn. For budget and self-catering travellers **Eagles Rest Chalets** are recommended. Accommodation is simple but comfortable and the setting is beautiful. To get there, take the left fork at the entrance to the Manchinchi Bay Lodge. Another budget facility, the **Leisure Bay Motel**, is currently being renovated.

Sinazongwe

This is the only other major development on the Zambian shores of Lake Kariba. It is primarily a harbour for the kapenta fishing industry and has little to offer tourists. **Gwembe Safaris** have a 45-ft houseboat moored here that is available for hire.

Chete Island Safari Camp use Sinazongwe as a port and base. Chete Island is perhaps really the only Zambian destination on Kariba that can offer a big game experience, sharing its game with the Chete Safari Area and Matusadona of Zimbabwe.

Lochinvar National Park

Lochinvar lies south of the Kafue River where it floods over the vast Kafue Flats, just a short distance to the north of the Lusaka-Livingstone road.

Proceed to Monze from Lusaka or Livingstone as described in route 3 in this chapter. From Monze the road is clearly signposted. It is 44 km long and rather rough so a four-wheel-drive is recommended, although not strictly necessary in the dry season.

The **Kafue Flats** are covered in places by vast stretches of water or lagoons which attract large flocks of birds, including many species not found in large numbers elsewhere. Otherwise rare birds such as the wattled crane appear in flocks of hundreds in the summer.

Although the park does not have big game other than buffalo and hippo, there is a large variety of antelope, in particular thousands and thousands of Kafue lechwe which occur only on these floodplains. To see these herds and the skeins of birds that seem to rise and fall continually over the water is enthralling.

The Kafue Flats have been designated a wetland of international importance under the Ramsar Convention by the IUCN and the World Wide Fund for Nature (WWF), who have sponsored a management project for the area that attempts to give local people an interest in conservation both through redistribution of tourist revenue and controlled harvesting of natural resources. Visitors will at first be surprised to see fishermen in the park, but they will soon realise that as they pole their mekoro across the swamp they are very much a part of a unique and fascinating ecosystem. The Zambia wetlands scheme is in many ways a pilot project for future wildlife conservation in Africa which recognises the interdependence of humans and wildlife. Enquire at the gate or at the lodge for the leaflets explaining the project as well as the bird checklist published by the WWF and ZOS, which lists the 428 bird species found at Lochinvar.

There are two national monument sites in the park that are worth seeing as much for their scenic value as their historical significance. The **Gwisho hot springs** are well signposted and lie about a kilometre west of the lodge.

Archaeological digging in the 1960s showed that the low mounds around the spring result from Late Stone Age habitation on the site between the second and third millennia BC. Several skeletons of these early inhabitants were discovered in the excavation, giving detailed evidence of their hunter-gatherer lifestyles. Nowadays game comes to lick tentatively at the salts deposited where the sulphurous waters seep and trickle into lush meadows at the edge of the Kafue Flats. On the top of **Sebanzi Hill**, which is clearly visible from the springs, is the site of an Iron Age village which has been shown to have been inhabited for most of the last 1 000 years. Little remains to be seen but the view over the surrounding flats is dramatic. The thick bush at the base of the hill is the most likely place to find Lochinvar's elusive herds of buffalo.

There is only one place of accommodation at the moment. The park runs a modest, pleasant campsite where a few chalets were built, although not completed at our last visit.

Better known is **Lochinvar Lodge** (see route 3, page 99), which is the original farmhouse. Run to date by the parastatal NHDC, it has unfortunately become sub-standard. The rooms are fairly clean with *en suite* facilities and the food is very basic. An astronomical sum is asked for this third-grade fare, but the staff are willing to acknowledge its shortcomings and it is possible to bargain down prices considerably. Lochinvar is being privatised at the time of writing, so you are advised to consult the Zambian National Tourist Board or Lusaka tour companies for new accommodation options in the park.

ROUTE 3
LUSAKA TO LIVINGSTONE

DISTANCE: 472 km **TIME:** 5,5 hours **ROAD CONDITIONS:** All roads are tarred **FUEL:** Kafue, Mazabuka, Monze and Choma **RECOMMENDED STOPS:** Tonga Craft Museum, Choma; or overnight at Lochinvar National Park or Wildlives Game Farm

The road out of Lusaka is in reasonable condition and provides a smooth drive. Just over 11 km from the bridge turn right at the clearly signposted junction. A reasonably good road winds pleasantly through undulating country until Mazabuka, when the great Kafue Flats suddenly open out before you. Beware of quarry blasting in the hills. **Mazabuka** is a pleasant farming town with a pre-war atmosphere. Between Mazabuka and Monze the road deteriorates and is currently undergoing reconstruction. In Monze large signboards proclaim the turnoff to Lochinvar Lodge. Note that the Lochinvar access road is poor and unsuitable for ordinary vehicles in the wet season. Of historical interest, at the south end of town a sign points right to the old **Fort Monze and cemetery**, one of the earliest police posts in the territory. Only a mound of earth, a commemorative plaque and nearby graves remain. The site is 16 km from town on a road traversable only in the dry season.

The distance from Monze to Choma is 97 km on a good tar road. **Wildlives Game Farm**, 15 km before Choma, offers basic camping facilities. **Gwembe Safaris** have a few chalets and a secure campsite in town (see chapter 12). As you enter Choma, directly opposite the BP petrol station on the Lusaka side of town is the **Tonga Craft Museum**. This is definitely the place to stop, stretch your legs, eat a snack and see the best craft display in the country. Permanent and temporary exhibitions are housed in a beautifully restored old school. A shop sells local and other African crafts of excellent quality. To get to Sinazongwe turn off either at Batoka or in Choma itself.

After Choma the road leaves the Kafue Flats and deteriorates, becoming potholed as it passes into gently undulating woodland country for about 70 km to Kalomo. Do keep a lookout just 3 km before Kalomo, where the road bisects a gentle mound. This is the **Kalundu Mound** and although apparently insignificant it is of considerable archaeological importance. It is an Iron Age site dating perhaps as far back as AD 300, and was formed by the accumulation of refuse and rubble for a thousand years thereafter.

Kalomo is a town of little note except for a delightful corrugated iron house on stilts and the local magistrate's house, which was the residence of the former Administrator of Northwestern Rhodesia between 1903 and 1907. Unfortunately it is not open to the public. It is about 115 km from here to Livingstone and the road leads eventually down into the Zambezi Valley and straight into Mosi-oa-tunya Road.

ROUTE 4
LIVINGSTONE TO KAFUE NATIONAL PARK VIA NDUMDUMWENZI GATE

DISTANCE: between 200 and 300 km depending on destination **TIME:** 3 hours to gate and then a further 2-3 hours to Ngoma **ROAD CONDITIONS:** Dry season only; four-wheel-drive recommended. **FUEL:** Kalomo, but not always available. **RECOMMENDED STOPS:** No specific stops but the route is scenic, especially in the hills around Ndumdumwenzi

Take the Lusaka road by following Mosi-oa-tunya Road northwards out of Livingstone. It is tarred for about 115 km to Kalomo, where a rusty sign to the Kafue National Park directs you left through the village past a government services depot. At the fork keep left and then bear left again at the next fork. It is 75 km to the national park. The road is a little bumpy and sandy but reasonable and proceeds through rural Tonga villages for an hour before climbing through a range of wooded hills and then descending to Ndumdumwenzi Gate. Sign in. It's approximately 100 km to Ngoma or 60 km to the recently rebuilt camp of **Nanzhila**. Permission to stay here must have been obtained from the NPWS at Chilanga or the regional HQ at Ngoma – it will not be given at the gate, if given at all.

The road proceeds into the most beautiful mopane and baobab woodland and is good in the dry season, but could be treacherous if wet. Then the **Nanzhila Plains** open up to the west. Keep right if proceeding to Ngoma. A left fork takes you to **Nanzhila Camp** across the plains, on which the dried and cracked mud makes for very uncomfortable travelling. It is necessary to go through Ngoma and the riverbed east of the camp to proceed up the main road to **Musungwa Lodge** and the **Itezhi-Tehzi Dam.**

Other options in the southern region for those inclined to explore are: the road from Monze to Namwala and Ngoma, which is a possible alternative route to the South Kafue from the Mumbwa road. The by-roads that wind through Tongaland between Siavonga and Sinazongwe pass through some breathtaking landscape where elephants are still said to roam. Sturdy vehicles are recommended for both options. Please be aware that as this book went to press a United Nations official was killed in the Gwembe region of Tsongaland, when his vehicle blew up a landmine left unexploded for 20 years after the Zimbabwe war. Heed warning signs.

8

THE WESTERN REGION

Between its source in the north-western tip of the country and the Victoria Falls (see chapter 7), the Zambezi River grows from a trickle to one of the mightiest rivers on the continent.

Although it has barely influenced the wider topography because it has not eroded the kind of deep valley that the Luangwa has in the east, it goes without saying that the Zambezi is the focus of all life in the region. It is the principal reason for tourists to visit the area, and even if it is not, it will certainly be a major influence on their travels there.

Western Zambia is predominantly Lozi-speaking, being the traditional kingdom of Bulozi or Barotseland. In north-western Zambia the people are Lunda or Luvale (see the section on Population in chapter 1).

This is probably the least developed region in the country and the most difficult to explore. Although Mongu, the administrative capital of North-western Province, and Senanga can be reached in ordinary cars along reasonable tar roads from Lusaka (see chapter 6), a four-wheel-drive vehicle is essential for wider exploration, particularly west of the river. Tourist destinations include three remote national parks, the Barotse floodplain and the course of the great river itself.

Travellers would be well advised to keep abreast of the political situation between Zambia and Angola, which is uncertain at the time of writing and may have implications for travel close to the border.

Barotseland

The ancient kingdom of Barotseland covered almost the entire region, but its traditional heart has always been the fertile plains annually flooded by the Zambezi. Such a large river would have cut a deep valley for itself aeons ago were it not for the presence of several hard basalt dykes that lie across the river's path. The Victoria Falls are the last and most dramatic of these, but several others upstream hold back both the waters and the deep Kalahari sands – with profound implications for navigation, transport and settlement in the area. Archaeological finds have shown that Bantu settlement on the upper Zambezi dates back at least three centuries before Christ and San (Bushman) habitation occurred tens of thousands of years before that. However, the forefathers of today's Lozi people are thought to have migrated down from the region of central Democratic Republic of Congo in about the 17th century, conquering or assimilating those who had preceded them.

Although early central African kingdoms such as the Lozi traded with other kingdoms and thence the outside world, it was only in 1798 that Europe began to take an active interest in the region when a Brazilian named Jose de Assumpcão e Mello penetrated as far as Luvale country in what is today north-western Zambia.

From the middle of the 19th century a succession of missionaries, traders and rogues began to explore the territory. The Portuguese were by then well established in Angola and began to make moves eastwards with the ultimate goal of uniting east and west Portuguese Africa.

In 1849 a Portuguese trader, Silva Antonio Francisco Porto, based himself in Barotseland. The next European to enter the territory was a Hungarian named Lazlo Maygar, who passed through the Mwinilunga district in 1851. It is a fascinating insight into David Livingstone's character that he had the opportunity to meet Maygar but deliberately chose not to, so that he would not have to mention him in his diaries and thus refer to any European penetration prior to his own. As for Silva Porto, his story is a fascinating one. He continued to live and trade in the area until 1890, when his village was attacked. He was so mortified by this sign of rejection from the people among whom he had settled that he wrapped himself up in the Portuguese flag, lay down on 13 barrels of gunpowder and blew himself through the roof of his house; dying (from shock) the following day.

On Livingstone's return journey from Loanda (Luanda) in 1855 he was shown and named the Victoria Falls (see page 82) and following its announcement to the world a succession of traders and missionaries began to move over the Zambezi. Primary among these was a hunter and trader named George Westbeech who came to Barotseland in 1871, apparently with a toothbrush in the band of his hat. Westbeech said that it represented the only bit of civilisation that he had and that he wanted. His influence at the Lozi court, then situated at Sesheke, saw to it that François Coillard and the Paris Evangelical Mission became established in Barotseland. It was a time of considerable politicking for the Lozi throne. The Kololo, Sotho migrants from southern Africa, had been established as overlords over the Lozi for half a century, but under the leadership of one Sepopa the Lozi throne was restored when in a single bloody night the Lozi rose up and slew every single Kololo, including women and children.

Interestingly however the original Lozi language has disappeared and it is the Sotho language of the Kololo that Lozis have retained as their own. When the missionary Fred Arnot stayed at Lealui, blood still flowed freely and he reported a veritable 'Golgotha of skulls'. He witnessed the sort of events that coloured the Victorian English perception of central Africa. Important occasions or objects were sanctified with human blood by chopping off a child victim's fingers and toes, then sprinkling the blood over the boat or object before ripping open the child's stomach and throwing the entrails into the river. Alternatively, victims were staked out at ant nests to be eaten alive. In 1885 a former claimant to the throne called Lubosi returned to drive out his usurper. To ensure that this time he stayed on the throne he purged the land of any other claimant's supporters. Westbeech witnessed it and described how every man and woman who surrendered was disembowelled or had their limbs smashed and were then left to die of starvation. Children were simply fed to the crocodiles.

Lubosi called himself Lewanika and it was he that the British South Africa Company deceived into giving away the mineral rights that eventually led Britain to formally take over Barotseland as a protectorate in 1900.

Today's king of the Lozi is Lewanika's grandson. He is known as His Royal Highness the Litunga Ilute Yeta IV. Although blood has long since ceased to be the currency of life in Barotseland, the Lozi are a proud nation who pledge allegiance to the king and insist that their protectorate status prior to Zambia's independence in 1964 entitles their kingdom to its own independence now. This is an ongoing political issue which visitors are likely to read a lot about in the Zambian press. The greatest display of Lozi tradition is marked in the annual *Kuomboka* ceremony (see the section on Festivals and Cultural Events in chapter 2, page 21).

From a visitor's point of view the centre of Barotseland is the great **Barotse floodplain**. At Sioma the **Ngonye Falls** (see route 5, page 115) mark the basalt dyke that is the lynchpin of the entire floodplain. The basalt has checked the erosive power of the Zambezi, and at the end of every rainy season causes the great tide of water that washes down from the Angolan highlands to flood the river's banks and turn the surrounding grasslands into an inland sea.

The Barotse floodplain stands in marked contrast to most of the rest of the country because the otherwise ubiquitous woodland gives way to wide open grasslands. Years ago Lozi custom prevented the killing of lechwe other than by royal consent and the plains were covered with enormous herds of game. Alas, as elsewhere, the country's independence saw the erosion of that kind of authority and today the only herds remaining are those of Nguni cattle. Through the middle of the plains runs the great river, here and there diverted into oxbow lagoons and creeks. Mango trees are sporadically dotted like dark green islands on the yellow plain and the beautiful reed huts of Lozi villages nestle into their deep shade. It is a pastoral landscape, but its timelessness is paradoxically bound fast to the caprices of the seasons. When the river floods the villagers must retreat to higher ground.

When the river again subsides they can return to plant the refertilised land and graze their cattle on regenerated pastures. The change is exceptionally striking. At the end of the dry season the river has shrunk to a single channel. In March it begins to rise steadily and within weeks what was a dusty yellow plain is transformed into an inland sea of green and azure. Where previously you could walk and drive, boats become the only transport. Even fairly large craft such as the Zambezi post boat steam up and down, connecting towns hundreds of kilometres apart.

With such water it is obvious that angling is another major reason to visit Barotseland. And conveniently the fishing here is at its best just when it is deteriorating elsewhere. In June and July the floodwaters begin to recede, bringing back both the fish that have spread over the floodplain to the more concentrated waters of the main channel and the nutrients they eat. For the deep-water predator fish such as tigerfish this signals a time of great feeding activity and consequently it is an excellent time to catch them. Fishing safaris to the region are becoming increasingly popular and there are an increasing number of companies offering such safaris. Between Katima and the Sioma falls there is a number of safari options for fishermen and travellers. The first is **Zambalozi Lodge** situated on an island in the river 20 km upstream on the Senanga road. The lodge is on the island, but camping is available on the bank. The manager is prepared to cook for campers if given sufficient notice. Further upstream the road deteriorates considerably. A few kilometres beyond Zambalozi is **Sakazima Lodge**, scheduled for completion in March 1999.

Fifty-seven kilometres from Katima towards Senanga is **Mutemwa Lodge**, owned by Gavin Johnson, the ex-South African rugby player. It is 127 km south of the Ngonye Falls (see chapter 12 for more details), has six twin-bedded tents and offers canoeing and scenic cruises as well as trips into the Sioma Ngwezi. The closest lodge to the Sioma falls is **Maziba Bay Lodge,** 7 km down stream. In addition to fishing the lodge offers white-water rafting between April and August, game drives, canoeing and apparently even microlighting.

Then above Mongu Tiger Fishing Tours operate **Tiger Camp** which has seven twin-bedded tents. In addition Tiger Tours run a camp in the Liuwa Plains.

However, for visitors who cannot afford all that and do not have their own boat, there are numerous fishermen who will be more than willing to take you out on their dugouts for a small fee. Whether for fishing or simply for a sunset cruise this always surpasses a ride in a powerboat and is a highly recommended experience.

Unlike fish, game resources have considerably diminished in the region in recent years and in spite of the fact that the whole country west of the Zambezi has been declared a game management area, visitors cannot expect to see much outside the two major national parks. Even hippos have all but disappeared. The apparent scarcity of crocodiles, however, should not be taken as an invitation to swim.

Birdlife is excellent, though, and its abundance can be attributed to Lozi traditional law which protected all birds and their eggs, especially egrets, marabou storks, white-bellied storks and vultures. Birdlife also responds to the flood regimen, moving away during the floods but returning in huge flocks to feed on the exposed banks and shallow pools when the waters begin to recede.

Mongu

This is both the regional capital and commercial hub of the province. It is close to Lealui and Limulunga, the *Litunga's* palaces, and therefore the seat of the provincial administration. Set on a hill that rises relatively high above the surroundings, Mongu commands a wide prospect out over the floodplains, but the Zambezi itself lies several kilometres to the west and the view of it is unspectacular. It might seem peculiar then that Mongu has a harbour, but this is connected to the Zambezi by an 8 km-long channel.

There is not a great deal to see but a worthwhile excursion is to go down to the **palace at Lealui** where there is a museum outlining the great Lozi heritage. The ramshackle fishermen's village at the harbour is perhaps the most photogenic part of the town although the tremendous poverty associated with it can be depressing.

There are three hotels, details of which are given in chapter 12. Fuel and vehicle repairs and some spare parts can be found. Be careful, however, of local mechanics abusing your dependency on them by charging exorbitant prices. Now blessed with a Shoprite Checkers, Mongu offers most necessary food supplies.

Senanga

Some 95 km south on the tar road from Mongu, this is a smaller and more attractive village also set on a small hill, but unlike Mongu the Zambezi flows by immediately beneath it. Consequently, Senanga offers a marvellous view of the floodplains.

Petrol and groceries are available, but motor spares and mechanical help are likely to be basic. Three alternatives for accommodation exist. There is the usual typical government rest house. The **Barotse Fishing Safari Lodge** is private and must be booked through Barotse Fishing Safaris in Lusaka. It is superbly sited on the water's edge. Next door is the best option for casual travellers, the **Senanga Safari Lodge**, which has a wonderful view and offers a range of accommodation to suit most budgets in clean, well serviced and private rondavels set in a pleasant garden. Alas, a satellite dish placed in the middle of the lawn with all the reverence a Catholic mission might accord a statue of the Madonna intrudes on the view almost as much as does the noise it produces from the set in the bar. Still, the terrace is the place to meet in Barotseland and there is a pleasant atmosphere. The lodge has boats for hire and some fishing tackle.

The Ngonye Falls

These falls at Sioma are second only to the Victoria Falls in magnitude and splendour. Although they are not particularly high, the sheer volume of water that thunders over the dyke is spectacular. Many visitors are misled into thinking that the view from the village of Sioma represents the sum total of the experience. In fact to see the falls properly it is necessary to cross the river by proceeding about 2 km downstream where a dugout canoe ferries people to and from the opposite bank. Precise directions are difficult, so ask around. A vehicle track leaves the road for a few hundred metres to finish above a small dune-sided gorge. It is advisable to ask a local or scout from the NPWS office at Sioma to guide you. But if you insist on going alone: having crossed the Zambezi by means of this canoe there is a path that ascends a sand dune and then forks. Take the left fork upstream and follow this footpath for about 2 km. It is reasonably clear. Eventually the roar of water will indicate that you are getting close. The footpath emerges from the woodland at a wide and shallow stream of water running over a small fall to your left. Other than in March or April this stream should be quite safe (there are no crocodiles here), so ford it. From here the way to the falls is fairly obvious. Another fall and the buildings of Sioma can be seen on the opposite bank behind, but keep right and after crossing another small stream and some rocks you will arrive at the main fall, which sweeps away from under your feet in a great arcing deluge of foaming water. June or July are the best seasons to see the falls. In the months before them the water is so high that it rushes right over and by the end of the dry season the falls lose a lot of their grandeur. **Maziba Bay Lodge**, downstream, offers boat excursions to see them and even white-water rafting through local rapids. See chapter 12.

Sioma National Park

This harsh wilderness without roads, landmarks or even much water is located in the south-western corner of Zambia between the Zambezi and the borders with Angola and Namibia (see route 5, page 114).

Only one safari company operates in this park at the moment, but there are no permanent facilities. The park is reached from the Sesheke/Katima Mulilo-Mongu road (see Route 5 in this chapter). Prospective visitors should be well equipped, preferably with two vehicles, and four-wheel-drive is essential. Fuel is only available at Sesheke or across the border at Katima Mulilo in Namibia and at Senanga. The park has no roads other than one around its fringes connecting the main road at Kalabolelwa (35 km north of Katima Mulilo) via Ngwezi Pools to the Quando River. Finding this road is an adventure in itself and you will save yourself much trouble by reporting to the NPWS office at Sioma opposite the Ngonye Falls and requesting the services of a guide. Even then you are dealing with a huge intractable wilderness in which you may need several days to find the harassed wildlife. A word of caution: the authors know from experience that it may be very hazardous indeed to attempt to depart from existing tracks without the services of an experienced scout.

This is Kalahari sandveld country with dry miombo or acacia and terminalia woodland. There are areas of Zambezi teak forest and a few open grassy dambos around pans or pools. The eastern side of the reserve around Ngwezi Pools is fairly well populated. Deep in the thickets and undisturbed dambos this reserve is said to continue to harbour considerable herds of game, including as many as 3 000 elephants. Alas, poaching remains rife and animals, particularly elephants, are shy although strife beyond the border and poaching is driving them to water on the Zambezi, leading to more frequent sightings on the road.

However, you are likely to see sable, roan and tsessebe, and this is the only place in Zambia outside South Luangwa (see page 152) where there are giraffe. It is also lion country.

There is no infrastructure in the park for accommodation or anything else. Try to reach Malombe, Kasaye or Kalau waterholes on the western side of the park for the greatest likelihood of finding game. For this a guide is essential.

An alternative to venturing too deep into the park itself might be to take the track from Kalabolelwa to Ngwezi Pools and then turn right and return on adequate track along the northern boundary of the park towards Sioma. If attempting this in the reverse direction, the road is fairly clear a few kilometres south of Sioma, but you are advised to seek more explicit directions from the wildlife officer in charge at the NPWS office in Sioma. This should still only be attempted by experienced bush travellers in reliable four-wheel-drive vehicles. Even though there are occasional villages, there's some chance of seeing game – perhaps even elephant – and it certainly gives you a taste of an Africa little changed by the passage of centuries. The journey can be accomplished easily in two days.

Mutemwa Lodge operates mobile safaris into Sioma and in time this park will be further developed. There are plans to make better roads into it. But until then it is a wild corner suitable only for hardy and experienced bush travellers.

Liuwa Plain National Park

Situated between the Zambezi and Angola, north of Kalabo, this is a very difficult park to access and it is recommended that use is made of **Robin Pope Safaris** – the only company currently operating in the park. However, permission for private parties can be obtained from the NPWS offices at Chilanga or the local NPWS headquarters at Kalabo. But be warned, although the terrain in the park itself makes for relatively easy driving, getting across the Zambezi and as far as Kalabo is another matter altogether. Four options exist. The post boat which can carry one vehicle runs between Mongu and Kalabo when the water is sufficiently high between April and June. When the water is low there are two ferry options, one directly out of Mongu at Sandaula and one at Libonda. The roads to and from these ferries are both difficult, even hazardous. When the water is too low for the post boat but still too high for these ferries, the remaining option is to cross the river below Senangu at Sitoti and proceed north to Kalabo. But treat this as a last resort as the road is terribly sandy. Big four-wheel-drives may do the trip in a day, but it took the authors two full days of low-range driving in a Land Rover to complete the 180 km journey (see route 5, page 115). And remember there is no fuel in Kalabo, so all fuel requirements must be carried on board and heavy sands will dramatically increase consumption. In Kalabo the NPWS officer in charge will supply a guide, who will be essential for navigation in the park.

It will then be necessary to commandeer the pontoon to cross the Luwinginga River. It is likely that the pontoon rope will have disappeared; enquire at the municipal offices. You will then have to row the rope across the river, before pulling your vehicle across on the pontoon. Once across the river it is a distance of some 30 km to the park, although there is no formal gate.

The park is unique in Zambia, consisting of a vast, flat, grassy plain fringed with low broad-leafed woodland. Crossing the middle of the plain and seeing nothing but a sea of waving grass stretching to the furthest horizon all round you is a spectacular experience. Large perennial herds of zebra and tsessebe and vast herds of migratory wildebeest are the main game. The most numerous predators are wild dogs and hyena but lions are also often seen. Other species include roan and a prolific number of oribi. Buffalo and red lechwe occur in the northernmost corner of the park near the Luambimba River.

Birdlife is excellent, particularly around waterholes and pans.

Besides the temporary and exclusive camps put up by the few safari companies who occasionally venture here there are no facilities whatsoever and there is no potable water other than a spring near Minde game scout village.

Remember all fuel and water will have to be carried on board. Other than the tracks to Minde and Luula camps there are no roads to speak of. Please take a guide; don't consider venturing off the track without a compass.

The park is still heavily poached both by Zambians and Angolans who may be heavily armed. Obtain advice on the security situation beforehand. Neighbouring Angola is close by with no recognisable border. If, in spite of all the above, you still want to see this barely travelled area, we vouch for its unique and delicate beauty and ask that special care be taken to preserve an environment so fragile that even vehicle tracks can cause irreparable damage.

West Lunga National Park

Located between the West Lunga and Kabompo rivers, this park is undeveloped and not easily accessible at the moment. However, the Kabompo River at the park boundary can be accessed at Jivundu some 40 km north of Kabompo on the

Kabompo-Solwezi road (see route 7, page 119). From Lusaka proceed either to Mumbwa and then on to Kasempa via the Lubungu ferry, a route that passes through wilderness in the Lunga-Luswishi Game Management Area or go round through the Copperbelt and Solwezi (see route 8, page 120, and route 9, page 132), turning off to Kabompo just after Mutanda. The latter is a better road but longer in distance.

The turnoff to Jivundu has a signpost clearly visible from the Solwezi side, but if coming from Kabompo watch carefully for it, the left turn doubles back sharply. At the time of writing the pontoon was broken and the river cannot be crossed to get into the park itself. Alternatively a scout from the Solwezi NPWS office may be persuaded to guide visitors in from the north, a dubious route untried by the authors. Whichever route is chosen, a four-wheel-drive vehicle will ultimately be essential.

Magnificently tall forests of several types are interspersed with grassy dambos and perennial papyrus swamps along the rivers. Poorly managed in recent years, the park has lost most of its once considerable wildlife to poaching. However it is said to still harbour a fair quantity of elephant and buffalo and scouts report hearing lions.

There are sable and certainly puku, sitatunga and Defassa waterbuck. Unusual animals to look out for are blue and yellow-backed duiker and a number of the lesser carnivores. The village of Jivundu is dreary but a scout will guide visitors to the river's edge a short distance away, where you can camp in beautiful solitude under big riverine trees and palms. Although there's little likelihood of seeing all the species listed above there are plenty of puku and bushbuck and great birdlife. A unique albino puku is the toast of the village. There are hippos but they are shy. Beware of crocodiles which, according to a local missionary, have acquired a taste for human beings.

An interesting adjunct to the history of the park is found in the legendary exploits of a former warden, one Mushala, who in the 1970s rebelled against the former regime, went to Angola for training in guerrilla warfare and returned to establish a Robin Hood-like camp in the West Lunga forests, apparently from which he sallied forth at intervals to rob banks and harass government agencies before retreating to distribute the spoils to local villagers. It says something of the West Lunga that it took the Zambian army 10 years to hunt down and finally shoot him. It is said by some that he was responsible for the radical decline of game, but by others that the blame for the destruction lies with the government forces who hunted him; and that Mushala should be thanked for the fact that game remains at all. If you want to see what this legendary brigand looked like, there is a picture of his corpse in the Lusaka Museum (see page 65).

At the time of writing there were no facilities whatever in the park, so visitors should ask at Jivundu for directions to a suitable campsite.

ROUTE 5

LIVINGSTONE TO MONGU VIA SESHEKE

DISTANCE: 525 km **TIME:** Approximately 10 hours
ROAD CONDITIONS: Potholed tar and sand; four-wheel-drive preferable **FUEL:** Sesheke/Katima Mulilo, Senanga
RECOMMENDED STOPS: Ngonye Falls; Senanga

From Livingstone (see page 82) the gateway to Western Province is Nakatindi Road, leading to Kazungula about 60 km away on a reasonable tar road. Although seldom visible, the Zambezi is ever present in its shallow valley to the left of the road. From Kazungula there are two options; either to proceed straight ahead on the main road or to cross the river and continue via Botswana and Namibia.

The first option through Mambova to Sesheke may seem the obvious choice, but it is an appalling road. The tar has collapsed and broken up to such an extent that it is no exaggeration to say there are more holes than surface. The tar has now mostly been removed, but the road is little improved. There is a campsite on the north bank at Sesheke called **Laughing Dove**. Camping is free and has been highly recommended to the authors.

The 100-odd km will take several bone-crushing hours to traverse. Then at Sesheke take the first major road to the left which leads down to the ferry on which it is necessary to cross the Zambezi at a cost of US$25. If you have a sturdy vehicle you may opt for this rather than the fatiguing series of six border procedures carried out on the other route. Sesheke itself was once the capital of the Lozi kingdom and near here the earliest traces of Bantu occupation in Zambia have been found, but of this illustrious history nothing remains to be seen and there is little to detain travellers on either bank of the river at this point.

The advantages of going through Botswana and Namibia are that Kasane and Katima Mulilo are well supplied, have reliable petrol and diesel and a choice of places to stay that vastly outclass anything on the other side of the river. The roads are gravel, but well maintained. At Kazungula after going through border procedures cross the river by ferry. Check that you have a multiple entry visa for Zambia otherwise you will have to pay for another one on re-entry. Alternatively negotiate with the border officials for a temporary exit permit. From Kasane proceed for 64 km through the Chobe National Park to Ngoma Bridge, the Namibian border. The stretch through Namibia to Katima Mulilo is 63 km long and consists of a good dirt road in the dry season, but is slippery in the wet. However, it was being tarred at time of writing. Katima Mulilo in Namibia is a slightly disorderly town but all basic supplies and fuel are available there. The village of Katima Mulilo in Zambia has nothing besides a government rest house of questionable respectability.

Whichever of the above options you have taken, the road north from here proceeds on the west bank of the Zambezi. It is 140 km to the village of Sioma at the Ngonye Falls along a reasonable gravel road that gets sandy in a few places. Off to the west lies the **Sioma National Park**, which is described on page 109. The river is almost always visible from the road and the area is continuously populated. The practice of *chitemene* agriculture has cleared much of the vegetation close to the road, but travellers will notice that certain trees have been exempted from this destruction. This is because they belong to species specially protected under Lozi traditional law for their medicinal and nutritional value or simply because they provide good shade.

At Kalabolelwa there is often an NPWS picket. The village of Sioma is small and only the brick walls and tin roofs of the National Parks and Wildlife Service offices a few hundred metres off to the right indicate that you have reached it. There is no petrol and there are no shops to speak of. But do stop to see the **Ngonye Falls** (see page 108). The NPWS have a basic campsite. The fishing lodges on the river are described above and in chapter 13.

The Ngonye Falls mark the first of the basalt dykes that hold back the sands and waters of the Barotse floodplains. As the road approaches Sitoti it leaves the bush behind. At Sitoti turn down to the river. The road straight ahead is the track to Kalabo. A short description of the journey further north on this side of the river is given at the end of this route.

The ferry at Sitoti will again cost foreign visitors the astronomical sum of US$25 or R60. Travellers dismayed by this expense need look no further than 100 m downstream for an explanation – here lies the mangled remains of the old ferry, which was bombed by the South Africans during the Namibian war. Normally the Sitoti ferry simply crosses the river directly but at the height of the annual flooding in April, when the road on the other side may be under water, it is forced to travel 17 km upstream to Senanga which is very time-consuming and will cause considerable delay.

Normally, however, the road to Senanga is dry but potholed. For the first time northbound travellers become aware of the floodplains which stretch away on all sides. There is fuel and accommodation in Senanga. From Senanga to Mongu there is a good tar road 116 km long.

Maps of Zambia indicate a direct road from Sitoti to Kalabo on the west bank of the river, but rather than attempting to negotiate it it is much simpler to go to Mongu and take a ferry back across the river from there.

However, occasionally when the water is too high for normal ferries yet too low for the post boat, it is necessary for traffic to Kalabo to use this route. The entire 180 km is deep Kalahari sand and in most seasons it will require a lot of low-range four-wheel-driving to plough through. The road proceeds through thick miombo woodland punctuated by villages.

Alternatively, a route that is more fun but no less arduous can be found along the very edge of the floodplain. This is no more than a sled track that winds through a continuous chain of villages. Skilled driving is called for so as not to run down dogs, chickens, children or the old and infirm. In the latter half of the dry season it is possible to find a track that traverses the middle of the floodplain itself, which will make for much easier driving. But it is difficult to find. To get onto the floodplain turn right at the first big tree after Sinungu. Note that many maps indicate a ferry across the Southern Lueti. In fact a dyke and bridge have been built. This side of the Zambezi is remote and little travelled, so visitors should be self-sufficient and well prepared. There is no fuel to be had anywhere, so carry enough for at least 500 km of low-range driving. There is no potable water until Kalabo.

However, for those willing to make the effort the floodplain is an inspiring experience. In the evenings when the cattle have been kraaled and the fish hung up to dry, the sound of cowhide drums and xylophones gently fills the vast, gathering darkness with a rhythm that seems to echo the timeless heartbeat of the continent itself.

ROUTE 6
LUSAKA TO MONGU

DISTANCE: 581 km **TIME:** 6 hours **ROAD CONDITIONS:** Tar with potholes, poor in places but will be upgraded **FUEL:** Mumbwa and Kaoma **RECOMMENDED STOP:** Kafue National Park

Leave Lusaka on the Mumbwa road to the Kafue National Park as described in route 2 (see page 80). Mumbwa itself lies a few kilometres north of the road 150 km from Lusaka. Petrol and basic supplies are available there. After Mumbwa the road deteriorates. After the first picket at Nalusanga the **Kafue National Park** (see page 71) lies on the north side of the road until you cross the magnificent Kafue River. Try to drive this section in the early morning when the possibility of seeing game *en route* is good.

This region has some magnificent deciduous forests. Sadly, outside the park they are being harvested at an alarming rate, especially for the much sought after 'Rhodesian teak', *Baikiaea plurijuga,* and mukwa tree, *Pterocarpus angolensis.* Kaoma is 78 km from the west gate of the national park. Again the town lies a little north of the road but there is a fuel station on the road itself. Travellers wishing to turn towards Lukulu and North-western Province note that the turnoff is a distinct gravel road heading north-west immediately beyond the second

river crossing after the fuel station. Some 15 minutes down that
road it forks and you should bear right.

Those proceeding to Mongu just carry on straight down the
tar road for 186 km.

ROUTE 7

FROM MONGU NORTH TO THE SOURCE OF THE ZAMBEZI VIA LUKULU, CHAVUMA, ZAMBEZI, KABOMPO AND MWINILUNGA

DISTANCE: 2 or 3 days **ROAD CONDITIONS:** Sandy tracks
for which four-wheel-drive is advisable **FUEL:** Scarce; the
only fuel station is in Mwinilunga, but fuel can sometimes be
bought from IRDP depots or missions in other towns
RECOMMENDED STOPS: Sancta Maria Mission, Lukulu,
Zambezi Motel in Zambezi for the view but nothing else,
Chinyingi Mission and suspension bridge

The best road to Lukulu is the one from Kaoma mentioned in
route 6, page 116. In the dry season it is possible to proceed
north from Mongu by taking the road across the floodplain to
Lealui and then heading north past the Libonda ferry. This way
is extremely sandy and although more picturesque it will be
slow going. Between Libonda and Lukulu is the camp of
Barotse Fishing Safaris, accommodation at which is best
booked in advance. Lukulu itself is not particularly interesting
although the view from the **Sancta Maria Mission** over the
Zambezi toward the Liuwa Plains is quite magnificent.

From Lukulu the road turns eastwards and improves a little
for the 72 km to the Watopa ferry. Be sure to turn down to the
ferry rather than proceeding straight on through the village,
where the road becomes a narrow track back to Kaoma. The
Watopa ferry is manually operated and like all pontoons of this
size gives free passage across the river – in this case the
Kabompo, which is a major tributary of the Zambezi.

It is possible to skip Lukulu and proceed directly to the
Watopa ferry from Kaoma by turning right about 102 km along
the Lukulu road. The road is boldly signposted as the M8, but

don't be deceived; it is a tiny, sandy track that winds its way for kilometres through uninhabited bush and dense forest. If you have time and preferably a four-wheel-drive, it is a delightful track to take. Eventually it becomes even narrower as it reaches a more populated region and then a right turn marks the pontoon. To proceed straight, as described above, would take you 72 km to reach Lukulu.

From the Watopa ferry it is 21 km to the main Kabompo-Zambezi road, the much touted M8. Turn left if heading for Zambezi and Chavuma. The road has recently been upgraded and is one of the best gravel constructions in the country. It is a beautiful drive, passing through kilometre after kilometre of seemingly untouched forests. The town of **Zambezi**, 75 km away, has a central African feel about it with its mission church, muddy streets and low-slung buildings under a green canopy of trees. The only place to stay is the squalid **Zambezi Motel** which won't win any prizes – architectural or otherwise – but does have an excellent view of the Zambezi River.

Don't stop. Head north out of town for 82 km to Chavuma. Worth seeing *en route* is the **suspension bridge** over the Zambezi to the Capuchin Mission at Chinyingi. Look out for an un-signposted but fairly obvious track branching to the west about 1,5 km after the bridge over the Mkondo River. If you miss this turn there is another, signposted to the Chinyingi Mission a few kilometres further on. The reason to see this remarkable structure, built by the missionaries after the old ferry capsized and several of their colleagues were drowned, is that it is the first of only four bridges across the entire length of the river. Victoria Falls, Chirundu and Tete are the other three. Walking over it is a thrilling experience and you can take spectacular photographs at sunset.

The only reasons to see **Chavuma** are that it is very close to where the Zambezi comes out of Angola, the river runs over the **Chavuma Falls** (which are greatly disappointing at all times other than in the flood season) and it is the site of one of the oldest missions in the region. The **Brethren Mission** is located on a hill and has a citadel-like command over the entire area.

If planning to spend a night here enquire at the mission about their campsite. It is reached by taking the road to the erstwhile pontoon immediately below the falls and then proceeding along a right fork past the school. Follow this sandy track for about 3 km. The campsite is used as a place of seclusion by the mission and has a few ramshackle buildings with some rooms of monastic appearance. The site above a broad sandbank is pleasant. Plans are afoot to provide another campsite downstream for campers only. A pleasant walk can be taken from the west bank of the river upstream to another waterfall on the Kashiji River. Take the *mokoro* ferry across the river directly west of the mission. There is a fairly obvious path, but ask locals for directions. At the falls there is a beautiful clear pool, but beware of crocodiles. Because Chavuma is close to the Angolan border, local police and military are strict about security and if planning any such local excursions it is advisable to inform them of your intentions beforehand.

To proceed north from here it is necessary to go back through Zambezi to Kabompo, a distance of 153 km. The gravel road is excellent most of the way. Spread out as it is under the trees on the south-east side of the road, Kabompo slips by almost unnoticed. While driving on these north-western roads travellers may notice curious structures made of bark high up in some of the trees. They are beehives and the best reason to stop in Kabompo is to visit the honey factory and buy some of this absolutely delicious forest honey. (It is also available in some Lusaka shops.) Anyone will be able to direct you there. If not, ask for the IRDP depot. It is just next door. Fuel can also be bought from the **honey factory** but note that it is closed at weekends. In addition to the above Kabompo has a Catholic and a CMML mission. There is a government rest house that is pleasantly located but rather disreputable.

If looking for somewhere in the region to spend the night, rather ask directions to where you can camp on the Kabompo River or proceed up to Jivundu about 70 km away, where the river marks the border of the **West Lunga National Park** (see page 112). A local politician and businessman is planning a campsite near the town.

From Kabompo there are two options for proceeding north. Either continue along the main road for 327 km to the Solwezi-Mwinilunga road, from where it is 242 km to Mwinilunga. It is a good road through woodland country and you may even be lucky enough to see elephants crossing it. Or take the back road to Mwinilunga which turns north at Loloma. This road is suitable for four-wheel-drive vehicles only. Moving north from Kabompo you cross a small, clear stream after about 25 km.

Shortly afterwards turn left and double back to **Muzama Woodcrafts** (where incidentally some excellent furniture is made from local timber). Proceed past the workshop and bear right past Loloma Primary School. There are some thatch cottages on the left; bear right and keep right where the road forks along the most used track until it joins what was obviously the original route from Manyinga. From there the track proceeds for 218 km more or less straight north through sporadic villages and large tracts of truly magnificent forest. The road is rather sandy in places and sometimes, especially through Lusongwa village, it is rutted and bumpy. Set aside at least seven hours for this trip. The track eventually comes out just west of the bridge over the West Lunga River, immediately before Mwinilunga.

In Mwinilunga there is both a council and government rest house. The latter is quieter and more hygienic than the former. Petrol and diesel are usually available. If you encounter mechanical problems ask for the mechanic at the ZESCO depot.

The main road heads straight west out of town where, after a few kilometres, it reverts to a dirt track. The turnoff to the source of the Zambezi is about 50 km away and marked by a faded blue sign (see route 8, page 121). The road to Kalene Hill and Sakeji is 67 km from Mwinilunga.

ROUTE 8
COPPERBELT TO MWINILUNGA

DISTANCE: 450 km **TIME:** 5 hours **ROAD CONDITIONS:** Reasonably good tar road **FUEL:** Solwezi **RECOMMENDED STOPS:** Chimfunshi Wildlife Orphanage, Kalene Hill

Visitors wishing to see the north-western corner of Zambia and the source of the Zambezi, but not able to take the four-wheel-drive route described earlier, can reach this destination in a normal car by proceeding through the Copperbelt. From Chingola it is 173 km to Solwezi. The road is straightforward and the only warning that need be given is that this is the one road in Zambia where it is inadvisable to pick up passengers or leave your vehicle unattended. The area is plagued by bandits from the Democratic Republic of Congo who hijack vehicles and take them back over the nearby border.

About 60 km from Chingola is the turnoff on the right-hand side to **Chimfunshi Farms and Wildlife Orphanage**, which has become famous as a refuge for chimpanzees. Dave and Sheila Siddle welcome visitors, but have their hands full implementing an ambitious programme to re-introduce these abused primates to the wild.

Solwezi is a bustling town. There is fuel, there are banks and shops for basic supplies and the **Changa Changa Hotel** is a reasonable establishment with decent *en suite* facilities.

From Solwezi the road turns south for about 35 km to meet the Kabompo road at Mwelemu. Here there is usually a NPWS picket with a boom across the road. Then it swings west again and it is 240 km to Mwinilunga.

For the most part the area is densely populated with a string of villages flanking the road. There is little to stop for, but about 72 km before Mwinilunga a road heads south and by following it for 13 km and then turning right onto a very poor track for another 2 km you can reach the **Nyambwezu Falls**. They are not spectacular, but there is a rock shelter just the other side of the lip of the falls which has prehistoric engravings of curious lines and dots.

You would imagine that finding the **source of the Zambezi** requires a Rider Haggard-like expedition through mysterious 'jungly' mountains. Actually there are no mountains to speak of and it couldn't be easier to find. You can reach it by driving straight out of Mwinilunga in a westward direction for about 50 km. Shortly after leaving town the tar ends and the road narrows into a lane running for kilometres through the trees. A faded blue sign on the right-hand side of the road marks the entry to the heritage site. Having turned and signed in, proceed for about 4 km down the access road until it comes to an independence monument.

There is a clear footpath down the hill into a patch of 'rainforest'. Do apply mosquito repellent liberally beforehand as the valley is full of the little pests. The path ends at a delightful, clear rivulet of water that appears to emanate from the bowl of a fallen tree. In fact the real source is higher up and can be found by taking a small track upstream some 10 m back from where the main path ends.

This small path winds between the trees and occasionally you can see the tiny stream burrowing through the mossy roots underfoot. Eventually you come upon a clear pool of water and it is incredibly moving to watch it drain over the leaf-strewn ground on its first passage to becoming that mighty, mighty river. Incidentally, it is amazing to think that the source of that other huge African waterway, the Congo River, is only a few kilometres away. There is a campsite at the monument with a pit latrine.

For those interested in the history of the territory it is worth visiting **Kalene Hill** and **Sakeji** where the descendants of the pioneer missionary, Dr Walter Fisher, live at Hillwood Farm. A part of the farm has been set aside for game and there are plans to establish a small self-catering lodge and camping facility. This is an ideal stepping-stone for Kalene Hill. However, it is a private farm and visitors should enquire at the farm office before proceeding.

Kalene Hill is best visited in the company of Joan Hoyt, who can extract from the otherwise dull ruins a fascinating and lively story of the early days at the mission. A pamphlet is available for unaccompanied visitors. To get to the hill turn left at the T-junction if coming from Mwinilunga. (The road on the right goes to the farm and Sakeji School, so if coming from there simply go past the Mwinilunga road.) After crossing a bridge *en route* to Mwininyilamba keep right past the road camp and through a village and then bear left at the next fork (the right fork goes to the present mission and is the way to see the Zambezi before it runs into Angola). About 2 km further on the road bisects a large anthill at the end of a mud-brick village. Look for a track bearing right. It is about 1,5 km from there to the hill, the last part of which is very stony and probably requires a four-wheel-drive. The ruins of the old mission have all but disappeared and it is hard to imagine the once thriving community from the rocky outcrop, but the view out over Angola and the Democratic Republic of Congo is terrific.

The mission on Kalene Hill was founded in 1905 by Walter Fisher, a 'brethren' doctor who had followed Fred Arnot to Africa in 1889 and practised and preached from missions in the Angolan hinterland. Arnot was married to Fisher's elder sister. The name Kalene Hill is derived from that of Ikalenje, a Lunda chieftain in the region. It was wild and primitive country and the story of these early missionaries is one of striking faith and endurance in the face of persistent hardship. It is told in two books: *Ndotulu – The life stories of Walter and Anna Fisher* by W Singleton Fisher and Julyan Hoyt, and *Nswana – The Heir* by Monica Fisher. The former is out of print but the latter was published fairly recently and can be found in bookshops in Lusaka.

A little way down the north-western side of the hill on the path from the new mission are the graves of Walter and Anna Fisher. Their graves look out over a vast intractable wilderness still lost in a hazy tropical ether where so much and yet so little has changed since their arrival a century ago.

THE COPPERBELT

Between 600 and 1 000 million years ago the landmass of what is now central Africa underwent an oceanic invasion from the west. Over aeons water erosion leached gravel and clay, and dissolved mineral salts from the highlands. And in the shallow lagoons and estuaries of that primordial soup primitive plant and animal matter produced sulphurated oxygen which in turn precipitated sulphides of copper as well as cobalt, nickel and iron. Then the oceans advanced; huge sediments were laid down. The globe cooled and glaciers pushed enormous boulders down from the north. In the chilly seas primitive life flourished.

When the climate warmed more sediments were deposited and the landmass was then subjected to terrific tectonic uplift and folding. Two hundred and fifty million years ago a second ice age occurred, after which the land became a dry and waterless desert. Another massive tectonic shift lifted this part of the continent a thousand metres. When streams broke through they stained the rocks green. From about the 4th century Bantu populations long settled in the area began to exploit the traces of copper that this revealed.

Then in 1902 a prospector named William Collier was hunting (or so it is said) along the Luanshya River, when he shot a roan antelope bull in an open dambo and it fell on a green-stained rock. And so was unleashed a process that disembowelled in a century a geomorphology wrought over a billion years. The Copperbelt, in an area 50 km wide and just twice as long, became one of the greatest copper-producing areas of the world; at one time churning out as much as 800 000 tons of copper a year. The decline of world copper prices and depletion of resources have somewhat jaded the once-thriving industry.

In truth the Copperbelt is of limited interest to anyone little fascinated by mining. It is densely populated and environmentally ravaged but it has for a long time been the commercial and industrial centre of the country. Kitwe considers itself the hub of the Copperbelt, but Ndola is the largest and most important city.

Ndola

Ndola is really more of a sprawling town than a city, but it is the second biggest city after the capital. Its origins were as a railhead and distribution centre. The Ndola boma was established in 1904. With the growth of secondary industries around the copper mines, rapid and extensive development has turned it into the commercial and industrial hub of the country. But a typical industrial city it is not, being a rather pleasant town with bustling, colourful President Avenue contrasting with the broad and leafy expanses of Independence Avenue and Broadway Road.

Access

By air: There are four Aero Zambia flights a week from Lusaka and Interair fly from Johannesburg to Ndola twice a week (see page 46).

By bus: The bus terminus is in Chimwemwe Avenue, just a short walk from the city centre. Some buses seem to arrive and depart behind the Savoy Hotel off Main Soko Road.

By rail: Two passenger trains operate between Livingstone and the Copperbelt via Lusaka. The railway station is at the extreme north end of President Avenue. To reach the city centre proceed down President Avenue until it intersects with Broadway Road then turn up Broadway for two blocks and turn right into Moffat. Or go straight down President as far as Main Soko Road.

By car: Ndola is 320 km north of Lusaka on the main road, passing straight through Kabwe and Kapiri Mposhi. You can enter Ndola in one of two ways, from Lusaka straight down Main Soko Road or from Kitwe and Luanshya down Luanshya Road (which becomes Broadway Road).

Tourist information

Most banks and travel agencies are located in Buteko Avenue near the Savoy Hotel. President Avenue is the main commercial street. The Central Hospital is on the corner of Nkana and Broadway roads. Vehicle repairs and spare parts are best sought in Chisokone Avenue, one road down from and parallel to President Avenue.

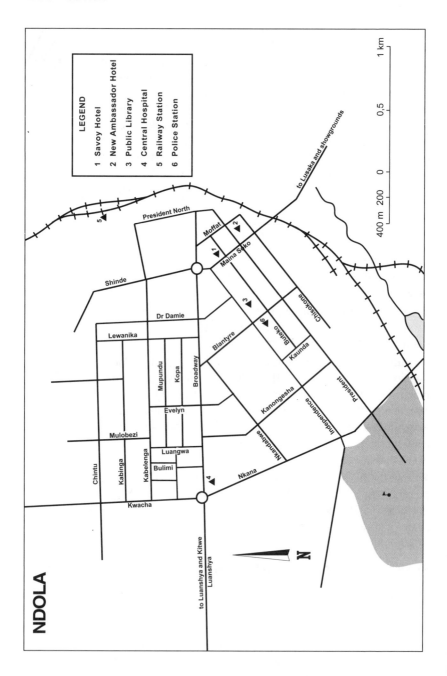

Accommodation

There are really only three alternatives in Ndola. The **Savoy** in Buteko Avenue is the most exclusive and centrally located with a quietly cosmopolitan atmosphere. The **New Ambassador** in President Avenue is at the other end of the market but is also central, and then there is the **Mukuba Hotel** in the Trade Fairgrounds and so a little out of town but nevertheless very pleasant. Take Main Soko Road out under the railway line and round to the industrial area, look for a signposted turn to the right and then follow the signs.

Kitwe

With the start of mining in the 1920s and further prospecting, extremely rich ore deposits were found close to the Kafue River and what became the Nkana Mine was first sunk in 1928. In 1935 a township was laid out along the Kitwe stream for the benefit of traders attracted to the mining operations. By a curious proclamation the colonial government decreed that no other township could be established within a ten-mile radius and so Kitwe became, as it still asserts itself today, the hub of the Copperbelt. Rivalling Ndola in size, it is not an unpleasant town although it has little to offer tourists besides essential services.

Access

By air: Kitwe has a reasonable airport at South Downs, 10 km west of the city, but flights from Lusaka land at Ndola Airport, 60 km away.

By rail: The Zambian railways passenger service from Livingstone and Lusaka operates as far as Kitwe. The railway station is very close to the city centre, off Oxford Road.

By bus: The inter-city bus station is in what is known as the second-class trading area.

By car: Kitwe is 58 km from Ndola. Those arriving from Ndola and the south will enter Kitwe on a dual carriageway, which becomes President Avenue. One block west is Independence Avenue, which from Oxford Road is the main thoroughfare through Kitwe and continues northwards to connect Kitwe with Chingola.

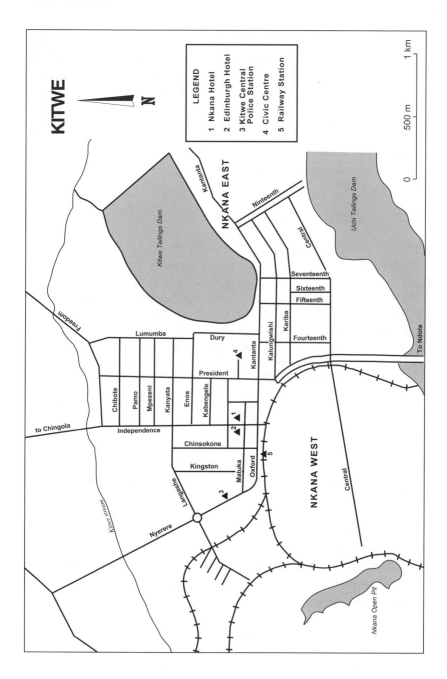

Tourist information

The city centre lies astride Independence and President avenues and most shopping and banking will be found here. The Civic Centre is on the west side of President Avenue and Kitwe Central Hospital lies just 2 km down Independence Avenue, immediately behind the fire station. Vehicle repairs are best sought along and west of Independence Avenue.

Accommodation

There are a few choices, two of which are preferable: the **Nkana** and **Edinburgh** hotels, which stand directly opposite each other on Independence Avenue two blocks north of Oxford Road. Both have assumed the status if, unfortunately, not the standards of international hotels and have corresponding prices. The **Buchi Hotel** is cheaper but about 6 km out of town. For backpackers there is a **YMCA** about 2 km further down on the left-hand side of Independence Avenue.

The other towns on the Copperbelt are Luanshya, southwest of Ndola, and then to the north-west of Kitwe: Mufulira, Chingola and Chililabombwe. Unless proceeding to the Democratic Republic of Congo, the only one of these that visitors are likely to pass through is Chingola, which is a not unattractive town with trees and broad avenues but with nowhere pleasant to stay and nothing to interest travellers.

What to see and do

For all its limited tourist potential the Copperbelt does have some places of interest which may be worth an excursion or detour on your way through.

The **Copperbelt Museum** on Buteko Avenue in Ndola has a display outlining the history of the Copperbelt, and provides examples of various ores as well as a small collection of stuffed animals so decrepit you might be forgiven for assuming they were representatives of extinct species. For better taxidermy see the bird collection in the foyer of the Mukuba Hotel.

Also in Ndola, in Makoli Avenue off Nkana Road 500 m south of President Avenue, stands an ancient *Afzelia quanzensis* or Mupapa tree. This is the **Slave Tree** and under its shade Swahili slave traders met and sold their captives. It is hard to imagine now, but the slave trade was finally abolished in this part of the world only with the establishment of the British colonial administration in the first decade of this century.

Another magnificent tree is the **Chichele Mofu Tree** — which you can't miss as it stands right in the middle of the dual carriageway between Ndola and Kitwe. According to local tradition it is an Ngulu, that is to say a house of spirits in which that of a long-dead chief lives. The tree was declared a national monument in 1976 to commemorate World Forestry Day and at its foot stands a plaque inscribed with this well-known anonymous poem:

> Ye who would pass by and raise your hand against me,
> harken ere you harm me.
>
> I am the heat of your hearth on cold winter nights,
> the friendly shade screening you from the summer sun;
> and my fruits are refreshing draughts
> quenching your thirst as you journey on.
>
> I am the beam that holds your house,
> the board of your table,
> the bed on which you lie
> and the timber that builds your boat.
>
> I am the handle of your hoe
> and the door of your homestead,
> the wood of your cradle
> and the shell of your coffin.
>
> I am the gift of God and the friend of man.
>
> Ye who passes by, listen to my prayer ...
>
> HARM ME NOT.

The spirit of that ancient chief must rest uneasily in those boughs as he surveys from the vantage of history the deforestation occurring around him.

Also on the Ndola-Kitwe road is a signposted turnoff to the **Dag Hammarskjöld Memorial**, a monument erected on the site where the former UN chief was killed in a mysterious air crash while on his way to intervene in the Katanga crisis in

Zaïre in 1961. The memorial can also be reached by driving from Ndola on the Mufulira Road and then turning south-west about 10 km from Ndola. It is of limited tourist interest.

Where the Chingola-Chililabombwe road crosses the Kafue River is a recreational area known as the **Hippo Pool**. There are no longer hippos in this stretch of the river, but the area is scenic and a good birding spot. Some misgivings are expressed about its safety from petty crime.

The **Collier Monument** in Luanshya is a 6-m copper obelisk marking the approximate spot where the prospector William Collier made the discovery related above that put the region on the map.

There are two interesting sunken lakes in the Copperbelt. **Lake Kashiba** is situated not far from St Anthony's Mission, about 70 km south-west of Mpongwe. It can also be reached by turning west down a secondary road some 32 km north of Kapiri Mposhi on the way to Ndola. There are basic camping facilities at the lake and it is a beautiful spot, well worth considering as a stopover for campers coming up from Lusaka *en route* to the north-west. There are no crocodiles so swimming is possible and there is said to be good birdwatching in the nearby forest. The lakes are apparently formed when schistose rock that makes up the surface collapses into sinkholes in the underlying limestone. Lake Kashiba is over 100 m deep.

The *National Monuments of Zambia* booklet relates a legend surrounding a clan who lived in the area known as the Bena mbushi. Insulted in some inter-clan argument, the Bena mbushi all tied themselves to a very long rope. And thus strung together they danced around their village before proceeding to the lake where link by link the great human chain threw themselves in and drowned. The very last person on the rope was a pregnant woman who was saved at the last minute and became the ancestor of the people today.

Another lake held in traditional reverence by the local people is **Lake Chilengwa**, which is smaller than Lake Kashiba and one of apparently several similar sunken lakes in the Ndola region. It is about 500 m across. It lies about 16 km south-east of Ndola, quite near the Democratic Republic of Congo border. To get there take the Ndola-Bwana Mkubwa road. Five kilometres south of Ndola turn east and then take a left turn north just before Chiwala Secondary School.

ROUTE 9
LUSAKA TO NDOLA AND KITWE

DISTANCE: 358 km **TIME:** 4,5 hours **ROAD CONDITIONS:** All tar **FUEL:** Kabwe, availability at Kapiri is unreliable **RECOMMENDED STOPS:** Possibly divert via Lake Kashiba

In Lusaka head straight north on Cairo Road, which beyond its north-end circle becomes the Great North Road (see route 10 in chapter 10). The road is being rebuilt and you can expect good tar at first and then roadworks *en route*, with long and uncomfortable detours for the foreseeable future. Where road-works have not yet commenced expect potholes. The distance is 68 km through the Chisamba farming block to **Landless Corner**, a large roadside store where you can buy fresh produce. Some kilometres before Landless Corner you cannot miss the sign to **Fringilla Farm** which aside from having an excellent butchery, dairy and restaurant, offers accommodation in luxury chalets and camping facilities with hot running water. Fringilla is owned by the Woodley family, and more welcoming and hospitable people you could not hope to meet. In addition there is a workshop where vehicle repairs can be carried out at far more reasonable prices than can be found in town.

There is usually a roadblock at Landless Corner, then it's 70 km to Kabwe, which is a pleasant, leafy town. From Kabwe it is 68 km to Kapiri Mposhi, railway junction for the famous Tazara line to Dar-es-Salaam and the place where the Great North Road splits to the Copperbelt and east Africa. It is a truckers' stop with a string of brightly painted bars and 'nightspots'. Colourful and fun to pass by, its highly questionable whether you would wish to spend the night.

The road through Kapiri is absolutely awful at the moment, with huge crater-like potholes. It is best to drive slowly and give way to other vehicles. About 30 km beyond Kapiri there's a turnoff left to Mpongwe and St Anthony's Mission which is the way to Lake Kashiba. Straight on it's about 67 km to where the road splits left for Kitwe. From Kapiri it is 115 km straight to Ndola. Between Ndola and Kitwe note the Chichele Mofu Tree mentioned on page 130 and the turnoff to the Dag Hammarskjöld Memorial (see page 130).

10

THE NORTHERN REGION

The rivers of this region are almost the only ones in the whole country that do not ultimately run into the Zambezi. Instead they drain from the watershed along the Great North Road first into the Bangweulu Basin and then the Luapula River, which runs into Lake Mweru and eventually meets the great Congo River itself. The Great North Road and the Tanzania-Zambia (Tazara) Railway are the region's lifeline to the rest of the country and for the most part follow the watershed between the Zambezi and Congo rivers. Today there is something awe-inspiring about driving up the Great North Road from Kapiri Mposhi, along the highway to east Africa, and seeing the hills roll away on either side of this continental divide between two of the greatest rivers on the planet.

It is a large region with a relatively undeveloped tourist infrastructure, but in addition to several national parks and wilderness areas, northern Zambia has many scenic diversions from its principal highways. It is an area of high rainfall and large rivers with many beautiful waterfalls and, of course, great lakes that have found their way into the pages of history as the quests and sometimes the nemesis of European explorers. The region had a somewhat colourful colonial history. If the first naval battle of the First World War was fought on Lake Malawi, this region can claim the last surrender of that war, when General von Lettow Vorbeck gave himself up near Kasama. The Bemba are the predominant tribe in the region. The Lunda, who trace common origins with the Bemba, live in Luapula Province.

Kasanka National Park

This marvellous little park, centred on the Kapabi Swamp, is privately managed and a must-see for visitors to the area. It is located in northern Zambia, south of the Bangweulu Basin.

Kasanka is easily accessed by turning off the Great North Road (see route 10, on page 148) 39 km from Serenje onto the Mansa road. About 54,5 km from the turnoff the entrance to Kasanka is clearly marked on the left. Four-wheel-drive vehicles are not necessary, only advised for further excursions. Kasanka also has its own airstrip.

This small park, only 420 km² in extent, is a gem. Once badly poached, it has been saved through the formation of the Kasanka Trust. It is the first privately managed national park in Zambia and tells a striking success story. The Trust represents the NPWS, private enterprise and the local population to ensure benefit to all from Kasanka's conservation. Although the park was almost devoid of wildlife in 1985, numbers of game have returned to its sanctuary – including elephant. But the park is famous for being probably the world's best place to view sitatunga. These normally rare and very shy antelope can be seen by the dozen from a hide built high in a magnificent *Khaya nyasica*, or mululu, tree.

Kasanka has a variety of vegetation from dry evergreen forest to swamps and magnificent riverine trees. There is prolific birdlife with over 350 species recorded to date, including shoebills which are sometimes found in summer in the papyrus swamps at the southern end of the park. Mammal species seen include puku, bushbuck, Defassa waterbuck and reedbuck. There are Lichtenstein's hartebeest and sable, common duiker and Sharpe's grysbok, warthog and bushpig. Occasionally yellow-backed duiker are seen. There are hippos and crocodiles, including some very large specimens of the latter.

Perhaps uniquely in Zambia the slender-snouted crocodile *(Crocodylus cataphractus)*, which is a denizen of equatorial forests, has been recorded in Kasanka. Lions pass through but are not resident. Leopard and smaller carnivores are plentiful. In November and December Kasanka witnesses a quite extraordinary event: a million straw-coloured fruit bats emerge after sundown, filling the sky like a black cloud.

The park also offers good angling for tigerfish, bream and barbel.

Relatively close by are the **memorial** marking the spot where Livingstone died (see page 147), the **Kundalila Falls** (see page 146) and the **Nsalu Cave** (see page 149). Kasanka makes a good springboard for an expedition into the Bangweulu Swamp.

Kasanka is open throughout the year. Game viewing will be better in the dry season, birdwatching in the summer. November and December is the time to see the remarkable bat colony.

Kasanka has three lodges: **Wasa Lodge**, which is the main camp, consists of small, charming rondavels with shared facilities set above a small lake, whereas the **Luwombwa Fishing Lodge** and **Musande Tented Camp** are both situated on the Luwombwa River. All are reasonably priced and available on a self-catering basis or with full board if booked in advance. Campers can also use a fourth camp at Kankonto which has its own access at the 91-km mark on the Mansa road. Here basic cooking and washing facilities are provided, although visitors are expected to provide their own tents and bedding.

Kasanka will also organise trips to **Shoebill Camp** in the Bangweulu Swamp (see page 137).

Lavushi Manda National Park

Directly east of Kasanka, between the Mansa Road and the Great North Road, you will find this little park. It is relatively easily accessed from the Great North Road. Turn west 46 km south of Mpika, or take the road to Chiundaponde from the Mansa road, 10 km from the Kasanka turnoff. This is also the road to the **Livingstone Memorial** (see page 147) and is signposted as such. After some 8 km the road forks left to the memorial. Keep right and then turn left about 12 km further on. From Chiundaponde the road goes directly to the park, with the entrance marked by a picket. This road eventually comes out on the Great North Road south of Mpika. In the dry season the road is relatively good most of the way, but is washed out with big gullies in the region of the park.

The park runs from the Lavushi Hills on the Zambezi Congo watershed down toward the Bangweulu Basin. Mixed broadleafed woodland and open, grassy dambos make for pretty terrain, but sadly the area has been poached of almost every living creature.

If you are lucky you may see a reedbuck or a grysbok. So the park is at most recommended as a scenic diversion *en route* northwards.

There are no formal facilities but with relatively easy access (although a four-wheel-drive or high clearance pick-up is recommended) there's many a scenic spot to choose in which to camp. The road that traverses the park is the only one.

Isangano National Park

This is situated north-east of the Bangweulu swamp. Take the Great North Road to Mpika and then proceed towards Kasama for about 86 km. Turn left onto a secondary road which proceeds 43 km south-west to the village of Mbati which is on the Chambeshi River, the park boundary. The park has no internal road network. It is doubtful whether visitors can proceed across the river by vehicle at all.

The park comprises mostly well-watered floodplain, being part of the Bangweulu Basin. Once prolific game has, according to latest reports, virtually been poached out. Visitors are in fact better advised to go into the Bangweulu Game Management Area where the local game populations, including the unique black lechwe, are still plentiful (see below).

There are no facilities in this park whatsoever.

Bangweulu Game Management Area

Bangweulu means 'where the water meets the sky'. This vast wetland is notorious as the morass in which Livingstone died under the delirious misconception that he had found the source of the Nile. The real lake is best seen from Samfya, but currently that offers little beyond a beach holiday in slightly seedy surroundings (see page 140). Much more interesting is the Bangweulu Game Management Area, which is probably the most exciting wildlife destination in northern Zambia and, like Lochinvar (see the Lochinvar National Park in chapter 7, page 97), a wetland listed as having international conservation importance under the RAMSAR Convention.

The Bangweulu Basin in its greatest extent lies between the Mansa road and the Great North Road, to the north of Kasanka and Lavushi Manda national parks.

There is an airstrip at the WWF Wetlands Camp at Chimbwi. By vehicle from the Great North Road turn to Mansa and then, just after the Kasanka turnoff or about 64 km from the GNR, a sign marks the way to the Livingstone Memorial. Turn right. At the next fork, where a sign points left to the memorial, proceed right then turn left at the next fork, to Chiundaponde. At Chiundaponde, instead of forking right to Lavushi Manda proceed straight to Ngungwa. The journey from the tar road is about 140 km and lasts about six hours.

The Bangweulu is a magnificent wilderness but quite unlike any other in Zambia. It consists mainly of vast grassy flatlands and papyrus swamps interspersed with river channels and lakes. Because it is a game management area rather than a national park, the local population continues to support itself by fishing. Wildlife is prolific. The black lechwe is endemic to these floodplains and can sometimes be seen in herds of up to 10 000 animals. In addition elephant, buffalo and tsessebe have adapted to life in the wetland and smaller antelope such as reedbuck, oribi and sitatunga are common.

Bangweulu has stunning birdlife with prolific numbers of waterfowl as well as Denham's bustard and that great central African 'dodo', for which these swamps are famous, the shoebill stork.

The Bangweulu is accessible by vehicle only between May and December. However in the wet season boat transfers to Shoebill Island can be arranged.

Kasanka Wildlife Conservation Ltd run **Shoebill Island Camp** for full catering or self-catering guests. It is best to book in advance through Kasanka. Some of the safari companies based in the Luangwa Valley also run safaris to Bangweulu (see chapter 13).

Lusenga Plain National Park

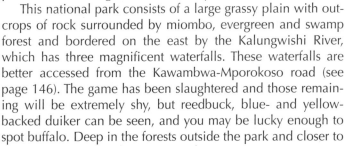

To reach this park in the far northern part of Zambia, near Lake Mweru, proceed to Kawambwa, either via Mporokoso or, preferably, by turning off the Great North Road (see route 10, page 148) to Mansa along a good tar road. At Mansa turn right and travel northwards for 168 km to Kawambwa. Enquire at the National Parks and Wildlife office in Kawambwa for a scout who can guide you into the park. Attempts to reach the park without such guidance are likely to fail.

This national park consists of a large grassy plain with outcrops of rock surrounded by miombo, evergreen and swamp forest and bordered on the east by the Kalungwishi River, which has three magnificent waterfalls. These waterfalls are better accessed from the Kawambwa-Mporokoso road (see page 146). The game has been slaughtered and those remaining will be extremely shy, but reedbuck, blue- and yellow-backed duiker can be seen, and you may be lucky enough to spot buffalo. Deep in the forests outside the park and closer to

Nchelenge a small herd of elephants apparently survives.
It is best to go between May and December.
There are no facilities whatsoever in the park and no roads.
A guide will direct you to the best place to camp.

Mweru Wantipa National Park

This is located in far northern Zambia between Lake Mweru
and Lake Tanganyika.

Take the Great North Road (see route 10, page 148) to
Mpika and Kasama. From Kasama proceed to Mporokoso.
Here the main road proceeds to Lake Tanganyika, but continue through the town westwards toward Chiengi where the
main road from Mununga on Lake Mweru swings north. Turn
right along this road which proceeds straight through the park
with Lake Mweru Wantipa on your right. There are no other
roads in the park.

This park used to be home to vast herds of elephant. Alas,
poaching has wiped them out. There are still some buffalo
herds and there are said to be a few herds of hartebeest, roan
and sable, although evidence of these is slim. There may still
be lions. Birdlife is excellent, especially along the shoreline.

The best time to visit is from May through to November or
December.

There are no facilities, but during the dry season some of
the large trees on the lakeshore and floodplain may be accessible for camping. The park is inaccessible during the rainy
season.

Sumbu National Park

This park is in far northern Zambia, on the shores of Lake
Tanganyika.

There is a tar airstrip at Kasaba Bay to which there are
weekly charters by Roan Air. By road you proceed up the Great
North Road past Mpika to Kasama. From there take the
Luwingu road and then 18,5 km from town turn right to
Mporokoso, where you turn right in a northerly direction
towards Sumbu. At Sumbu there is a boom across the road and
you will be directed right into the park. The road network in
the park is limited to one bumpy and stony track to Nkamba
Bay and Kasaba Bay. For this last section it is necessary to have

a four-wheel-drive or certainly a rugged vehicle. On some maps Sumbu National Park appears to be accessible from Mbala; note that this is impossible as there is no way across the Lufubu River.

Despite the efforts of insensitive development and poor management, this remarkable national park has not lost its appeal. The hillsides consist of dense, near-impenetrable thicket which is not particularly attractive in the dry season, but the lakeshore and floodplains are more open for game viewing. Poaching has not yet entirely wiped out the elephants, some of which frequent the **Kasaba Bay Lodge**, and can be seen at quarters closer than anywhere else in the country. There is also buffalo, lion, leopard and a reasonable number of antelope including roan, sable and waterbuck and a healthy population of puku. Hippos can be seen in the unusual setting of the lake which also harbours some of the largest crocodiles south of the equator. One look at 'the poacher' hauling all 6 m of his vast reptilian bulk out of the lake at Kasaba Bay will convince visitors of the danger of swimming.

The primary reason people come to Kasaba Bay is to fish for Goliath tigerfish and Nile perch. Boats can be hired from the lodges.

The park is open all year round. There are unfortunately no camping facilities in the national park and visitors will have to stay at either Kasaba Bay Lodge or Nkamba Bay Lodge, which despite proclaiming all the conveniences of modern hotels (unless they have run out of diesel or supplies, which is a not-infrequent occurrence) are overpriced.

The design and management of the lodges implies much about Zambia's former seclusion from modern eco-tourism (for details see chapter 12). Game drives are probably better from Nkamba Bay although you can be guaranteed elephants, puku, hippos and crocodiles at Kasaba Bay.

Camping and slightly cheaper accommodation is available at **Ndole Bay Lodge**, which lies about 8 km west of Sumbu and hence well outside the boundaries of the national park.

Shiwa Ngandu and Kapishya Hot Springs

Shortly before the First World War, a young British officer who had served on an Anglo-Belgian boundary commission to determine the border of the Congo decided to make his way back from Ndola to Dar-es-Salaam on foot. After crossing the Luapula River and the Bangweulu Swamp he found his way into a temperate region where he came upon a small but beautiful lake called Ishiba Ngandu, the Lake of the Royal Crocodiles. According to legend, at the beginning of this century the lake teemed with hippos and crocodiles, which terrorised the local inhabitants. An army of 200 warriors was sent to destroy these marauding denizens. At the end of a day of great carnage the hippos and crocodiles had been slaughtered but of the brave 200 who had set forth in the morning, only a handful of warriors returned alive.

Whatever unquiet bones lay beneath its surface, young Stewart Gore Brown saw paradise reflected in the still waters and decided to make his home here. The war intervened and it was only in 1920, having survived the Battle of the Somme, that he could return. But return he did, with a building manual from his battle days and an extraordinary dream. In a wilderness barely explored and still teeming with game he imagined an English shire where the inhabitants would be drawn into working for his great estate and in return would be provided with houses, schools, clinics and a post office; in fact a utopian community over which he would preside from a seat befitting the grandeur of his ambitions.

Today, visitors who arrive at the gatehouse without being forewarned are likely to be bowled over, for they'll see just how much of a reality he managed to make his dream into. With bricks and timbers and roof tiles made on site and equipment and furniture (including a four-poster bed) brought from England to the railhead at Ndola and then carried 600 km across the Bangweulu Swamp (the Great North Road did not yet exist), he built the farm with all the amenities he had planned. And on the hillside overlooking it all he built a magnificent Tuscan manor house. He distilled essential oils from citrus and shipped out the high-value, low-bulk product on porters' heads to Ndola.

A thriving industry developed and ran until after the Second World War when imported trees brought a virus that killed off all the citrus groves. He became a figurehead in Northern Rhodesian politics, was knighted by the Queen and further honoured by President Kaunda, of whom he became a great friend. When eventually he died, an octogenarian, in 1967, he had acquired the venerable and aristocratic status of Zambia's grand old man.

After three-quarters of a century the rain and sun have so beaten down upon the walls and roofs and ramparts of his vast estate that they look as if they are centuries old. At the bottom of the gardens where cypresses and deodars, eucalyptus and pine become entwined with a jungle of creepers and collapse into rampant forest, there is a sense of Africa and colonialism peacefully reconciled. Of all the extraordinary and sometimes bizarre legacies the colonial period bequeathed to the continent, this house is one of the most moving. To see Shiwa Ngandu and then turn one's gaze from the mouldering terraces to the distant shimmer of the lake is to stand in awe of the vision, the self-assuredness, the paternalism, the compassion and the sheer bloody-mindedness that underscored the British colonial hand in Africa.

Today Stewart Gore Brown's grandchildren, the Harveys, have inherited the estate. It is still their family home. For many years they have run safaris from here down into the North Luangwa National Park (see page 157). At the same time they have run a small lodge at the Kapishya Hot Springs. Now they have decided to incorporate their home into the safari package and clients are invited to stay in the manor house and experience for themselves the lifestyle of a bygone era (see Shiwa Safaris, chapter 13).

Kapishya Hot Springs lies just 20 km from Shiwa Ngandu (see route 10, page 149). Part of the great estate, it falls under the umbrella of Shiwa Safaris, but casual visitors are welcome to book into the lodge (it is best to do this in advance) or camp close by. Zambia has many hot springs, but none to rival these. To bathe in the hot clear soda water of an unspoiled, sandy-bottomed pool overhung with palm trees is wonderful; to do so at night with only the light of the moon or a storm lantern is a sensation that has to be experienced to be believed.

The Great Lakes
Lake Bangweulu

This has been partly dealt with above. The open waters of the lake can be reached at Samfya, which is directly off the tar road between Serenje and Mansa. Plans have been made to establish a tourist resort here, but unless visitors have their own boats which are launched here for fishing, there is little to attract anyone to Samfya.

Lake Mweru

Lake Mweru is to be found up in the north-western corner of the region and, together with the Luapula River which drains into it, forms part of the border with the Democratic Republic of Congo. There is no established tourist infrastructure on Lake Mweru at all, and because its shores are densely populated there is no particular destination for travellers to try to reach. As part of a comprehensive tour of the great lakes it is worth seeing, however, just for its great expanse.

Fishermen are likely to find it particularly good for large bream, but it does not otherwise have the variety of fish existing in Lake Tanganyika itself.

The best place to stay is the **Lake Mweru Water Transport Guest House** in Nchelenge. It is a grey and white building down on the waterfront close to the municipal rest house. It is very reasonable indeed with spotlessly clean, if somewhat bizarrely furnished, rooms with *en suite* bathrooms. The complex is generally self-catering, but simple meals of nshima and fresh bream can be arranged.

The beach on which the local fishermen land their catches early each morning is a short walk from here and the ensuing gathering that comes to buy kapenta and bream is a colourful spectacle.

Lake Mweru Wantipa

Lake Mweru Wantipa lies directly between lakes Mweru and Tanganyika. Falling mostly within a national park, this is covered on page 138. It is worth noting that some maps, such as the green Republic of Zambia Tourist Map, have overprinted the lake so that it appears to be some kind of marsh. It is in fact an open lake, although subject to unusual changes in level in drought cycles.

Lake Tanganyika

Lake Tanganyika is perhaps the best known of Zambia's lakes, being by far the largest and most interesting. Although Zambia can lay claim only to about 7 per cent of the lake, it revels in sharing its statistics. Lake Tanganyika is the longest and seventh largest in the world. It is the second biggest lake in Africa after Lake Victoria and the second deepest lake in the world after Lake Baikal in Russia. It has a surface area of 32 914 km^2 and is 1 395 m deep, which is 642 m below sea level!

Lake Tanganyika is of course part of the Great Rift Valley, which explains its immense depth and the steep topography of its shoreline, so different from other lakes in the country. Consequently the Zambian shore is far less populated than Lake Mweru. In addition a considerable length of the shore falls within **Sumbu National Park** (see page 138) and so remains relatively wild and unspoiled.

Only the first 200 m or so of the lake contains oxygen. The relationship between those vast somnolent depths and the richly animated surface is still being studied, but it seems that chemical interaction between them is responsible for the incredible richness and variety of life forms in the lake. Scientists studying the lake say they have not yet documented all the species of fish to be found there. The majority are small cichlids and the like. Some are brilliantly hued and are caught for the pet trade, but what makes anglers' eyes gleam is presence in number of sporting fish. These are the southernmost waters in which Goliath tigerfish and Nile perch are found.

There are three lodges on the Sumbu side of the lake. The two inside the national park have been described above. The only camping facility here is to be found at **Ndole Bay Lodge**, which is reached by turning left 5 km before the gate at Sumbu. The 8 km access road is frightful but the lodge itself is pleasant and beautifully situated above a small beach where the absence of crocodiles makes swimming and other water sports possible.

The lodges hire boats and guides to prospective fishermen. For those with their own boats the only proper launching ramp is at Kasaba Bay, but getting the boat there on the road in its present state is likely to be an ordeal.

Note that there is no direct vehicular route between Sumbu and Mpulungu. By boat it is about 80 km. By car it is necessary to drive all the way back to Mporokoso and then proceed towards Kasama for another 81,6 km, where just as you pass a stand of tall eucalyptus trees a road veers off to the left. This is a shortcut obviating the need to go all the way to Kasama and it joins the Kasama-Mbala road after 71 km, 75 km from Mbala. The total distance is 320 km.

Before independence Mbala was called Abercorn. There are two hotels: the **Grasshopper Inn** and the **Arms Hotel** (formerly the Abercorn Arms). Nearby is **Lake Chilwa**, which is picturesque and said to be safe for swimming. While in Mbala it is worthwhile to visit the **Moto-moto Museum** for its interesting archaeological and indigenous cultural artefacts as well as colonial memorabilia.

A few kilometres south of Mbala there is a turning to Mpulungu some 40 km down the escarpment on the shore of Lake Tanganyika. Mpulungu is landlocked Zambia's 'port'. Here the big lake ferries from Bujumbura in Burundi and Kigoma in Tanzania dock (see the section By Boat on page 48).

There is also a thriving fishing industry, but the town owes its existence to the passage of trucks on and off the ferries. There is only one place to stay – **Nkupe Lodge**. This is a self-catering facility aimed at backpackers and is pleasantly low-key and inexpensive.

The primary reason for travellers to come to Mpulungu is to embark on one of the northbound ferries. Recently, however, a couple has opened a small camp a few kilometres west of Mpulungu offering snorkelling safaris. If you are spending a day in Mpulungu follow the track past Nkupe Lodge for about 150 m to the ruins of the **Niamkolo Church**. It is the oldest 'surviving' stone church in Zambia. In 1880 (only seven years after Livingstone's death, when the territory had barely been explored by Europeans) the London Missionary Society established a mission at Niamkolo, while looking for a site on the southern end of the lake on and from which to assemble and launch a steamboat, the *SS Good News*. In the face of aggression from Arab slave traders they had to abandon the site.

The British in Nyasaland to the south-east meanwhile were putting paid to the nefarious trade and in 1887 the missionaries returned to Niamkolo. In 1893 Alfred J Swann bought a piece of land and in 1895 work was begun on the church. One Adam Purves, a helper at the mission, is said to have been the architect. The walls were built by constructing two rows of rough-hewn stone almost a metre apart and then filling the gap in between with rubble. Both nave and tower were roofed with thatch. The high incidence of sleeping sickness however led to the mission being moved in 1908, and shortly afterwards it burned to the ground. There is something poignant in the thought that after so much work the church was probably in use for barely two years. In 1962 the walls were rebuilt and the cement grouting dates from this time.

If you have a boat or are able to organise one it is possible to go out to **Kituta Bay**, east of Mpulungu, where lies the hull of the other missionary enterprise, the *SS Good News*. The 54-foot ship was originally built in England and delivered to the mouth of the Zambezi from where it sailed up to the Shire River, where in places it had to be carried, then sailed the length of Lake Nyasa (Malawi) to Karonga. Here it was dismantled and then carried 400 km overland to Lake Tanganyika. Because Niamkolo was being threatened by Arabs the boat was carried to the Lufubu River, where after a year of reassembly it was launched in 1895. There is a monument on the site to commemorate the event. The *Good News* remained in service for many years. Her propeller and flag can be seen in the Moto-moto Museum in Mbala.

By far the most impressive spectacle in the vicinity and definitely worth the excursion is the **Kalambo Falls**. Here the Kalambo River – which at this point marks the boundary between Zambia and Tanzania – plunges 221 m in the second highest single-drop waterfall on the continent. That is more than twice the height of the Victoria Falls (see page 82). To see this when the river is in flood in February must be an awe-inspiring sight. In the dry season it is impressive enough. The gorge itself is almost 300 m deep and sheer-sided at the fall. These cliffs are a nesting site for marabou storks, who add a sense of the primeval to the spectacle as they soar like pterodactyls above the plunging waters.

The falls are accessible by car. Take the road north out of Mbala and then turn left as signposted. The falls are 33 km from Mbala and the road is poor, becoming terrible towards the end. For this reason you may have to walk the last couple of hundred metres. If you do so, be sure to lock your car and preferably leave someone to watch it. Apparently there are bandits from Tanzania who may otherwise help themselves to your belongings.

Another way to see the falls that is more fun but requires some effort is to hire a boat at Mpulungu which will take you round to the river and a little way upstream. Then it is a walk of a few kilometres to the foot of the falls and a good hike up to the top. For backpackers the cheapest and perhaps most exciting way to see the falls is to take one of the water taxis that run between Tanzania and Mpulungu. They will drop you at the river mouth on one day and collect you the next. Take basic camping gear and sleep next to the river.

Other Places to See

There are several other waterfalls in the northern region of Zambia that are worth making the effort to see. Many make ideal places to camp *en route* and some even have camping sites nearby that are clean and little used.

The **Kundalila Falls** are easily accessible to most travellers driving up into northern Zambia, as they are just off the Great North Road (see route 10, page 149) at Kanona about 20 km north of the Mansa road junction. A signposted track goes east from the road for 13 km. Just before the falls picnic site there is a boom across the road where you are required to sign in. The Kaombe River is a clear stream which gurgles out of a pretty meadow and then suddenly shoots over a 65-m drop to fall into a clear pool that invites an invigorating swim. There is a path to the bottom of the fall. The view from the top out over the distant **Luangwa Valley** (see page 151) is one of the loveliest in Zambia.

There are contradictory notices about whether camping is allowed here. Military installations in the vicinity have made it a sensitive area and the former government disallowed camping. In the authors' experience camping is now allowed but visitors are warned that the caretaker may use the ambiguous situation to extort money from prospective campers. A small payment for the upkeep of the site is advised, but no more.

The **Chishimba Falls** near Kasama (see route 10, page 150) are an ideal place to camp. About 18,5 km out on the road from Kasama to Luwingu there is a right turn to Mporokoso and about 5 km up that road, as it reaches the top of a small hill, a sign marking the Chishimba Falls power station points left down a small road leading directly into the campsite. The waterway actually consist of three falls. Above two of them weirs have been placed to channel water to a hydro-electric plant. All this engineering has been done discreetly and spoils the scenery very little. First the Mutumuna Falls crash down onto pitch-black rocks before flowing into a small clear lake made by the weir above the Kevala Falls. The Kevala Falls tumble over a series of rocks and then slide magnificently over a huge slab of rock as the Chishimba Falls. Then the river tumbles through a pretty gorge covered in evergreen forest. The campsite has a roofed cooking area and a pit latrine.

The **Chipoma Falls** near Chinsali are actually a series of large rapids which may be worth stopping to see *en route* between Mpika and Tunduma. To get there turn west off the Great North Road about 57 km after the Shiwa Ngandu turnoff or 24 km south of the Chinsali turnoff. Drive about 6 km, keeping left at forks and junctions.

To reach the spectacular **Kundabwika Falls** you need to take the road from Mporokoso to Kawambwa, and 64 km onwards a road turns north to Mununga on Lake Mweru. Some 40 km up this road a left turn leads directly to the falls on the Kalungwishi River, which at this point marks the northern boundary of the Lusenga Plain National Park.

From here the Kalungwishi River flows down the eastern boundary of the national park until it plunges over the most magnificent falls in the region, the **Lumangwe Falls**. To see these take the road west from Mporokoso for 84 km toward Kawambwa where, just 2 km east of the Chimpembe pontoon, a road turns to the right or north-west. There is a picket where you must sign in and then it is 13 km to the falls. There is an abandoned rest house near the water where visitors are welcome to camp. There is an even better spot to camp literally metres from the lip of the falls. It would be well worth spending a night here. Thirty metres high and easily 120 m wide, these falls are in every way simply a small-scale version of the Victoria Falls. The surrounding forest is beautiful.

The **Ntumbachushi Falls** on the Ng'ona River are about 15 km west of Kawambwa towards Kazembe where the access road turns back south-east for about a kilometre. The falls are lovely; indeed the whole area is particularly scenic. For a small charge visitors can camp at the falls. There are latrines and the caretaker will provide firewood.

The **Livingstone Memorial** is worth a visit only if you are in the immediate area, either at Kasanka or going into the Bangweulu. The memorial is rather uninspiring, although it is moving to stand at the spot where the great explorer finally met his end. David Livingstone started out on his last African journey in 1866. He travelled up Lake Malawi then explored westwards to lakes Tanganyika, Mweru and Bangweulu. For six years no news of him reached the outside world until the journalist-turned-explorer, Henry Morton Stanley, met him at the town of Ujiji on the eastern shores of Lake Tanganyika with the now famous words: 'Dr Livingstone, I presume?' Thereafter Livingstone headed west and south in search of the elusive source of the Nile. He could not have known that it lay in precisely the opposite direction.

At Lake Bangweulu Livingstone was delayed by floods and, unable to progress, suffered increasingly from dysentery. Eventually he was carried through the swamps to the village of Chief Chitambo, where he died kneeling beside his bed. His bearers and servants then buried his entrails beneath a tree that stood just where the memorial stands today. His body was salted and dried in the sun for a fortnight before his servants, in the most extraordinary gesture of devotion, carried it 1 500 km to the coast at Bagamoyo. From there it was shipped back to England to be buried in Westminster Abbey.

ROUTE 10
THE GREAT NORTH ROAD – KAPIRI MPOSHI VIA MPIKA, KASAMA TO MBALA AND MPULUNGU

DISTANCE: 812 km **TIME:** 15 hours **ROAD CONDITIONS:** Potholed tar **FUEL:** Petrol is not always available at Kapiri but is usually available at Serenje, Mpika and Kasama **RECOMMENDED STOPS:** Kapishya Springs or Kasanka, Kundalila Falls, Chishimba Falls.

At Kapiri Mposhi the road and the railway line from Livingstone and Lusaka fork and the Great North Road proceeds towards east Africa. As you might expect from such a major junction, Kapiri is a rough truckers' town of 'dosshouses' and nightspots. These vie with colourful murals for the attentions of the passing traffic. You might stop for a mosi and nshima with 'road-kill' chicken, but it is unlikely you would care to spend the night. Just 5 km from town turn east past the Chimulangi Nightspot. It is then 192 km to Serenje, bypassing Mkushi and coming close to the Democratic Republic of Congo border, after which the road begins a gentle ascent up onto the Zambezi-Congo watershed. This section of the road, particularly in the region of Mkushi, is potholed in places. The trucks coming in the opposite direction veer round the potholes like great lurching juggernauts with scant regard for any smaller oncoming traffic.

There are two motels in Serenje, but both are noisy. A better option if you need somewhere to spend the night would be to camp at the **Kundalila Falls** 60 km further on (see page 146). Forty kilometres from Serenje is the turnoff to the left of the Chinese-built road to Mansa which is the way to Kasanka and Bangweulu. At Kanona the track that turns down to Kundalila Falls is signposted, but not clearly so ask the locals if you are unsure. The falls are 13 km down the track. Note that under the previous regime camping was not allowed, but for a small fee the caretaker will allow you to do so.

The other place worth stopping to see is the **Nsalu Cave** with its remarkable rock paintings. To reach it turn west off the Great North Road 30 km north of Kanona then proceed 7 km to where the caretaker, Mr Thomas Mambwe, lives. After a further 7 km a road turns south to the cave. The cave is fenced off but the paintings can be seen clearly. Visitors wishing to go into the cave to examine the paintings must be accompanied by the caretaker.

Mpika is 236 km from Serenje. Just before Mpika the road forks. The Great North Road proceeds through Mpika to Isoka, 260 km away, and Tunduma on the Tanzanian border 109 km beyond that.

Note that you cannot rely on buying fuel at Isoka and for those travelling through, it will probably be available only at Mbeya in Tanzania.

The turnoff to Shiwa Ngandu which proceeds through to **Kapishya Hot Springs** (see page 141) is 89 km up the Great North Road from the Mpika road junction. This road eventually joins the Mpika-Kasama road some 86 km north of the place itself. The road to Kasama crosses the Chambeshi River about 35 km beyond this point. At the north end of the old bridge there is a monument marking the spot where the hostilities of the First World War were brought to an end when the legendary commander of the German Forces in east Africa, General von Lettow Vorbeck, surrendered to Mr Hector Croad, British District Commissioner, at Mpika on 14 November 1918, three days after armistice of which the Germans were unaware. The piece of artillery in the memorial is a breech-loading field gun of the kind used by German forces in that campaign. The war in east Africa that this concluded was perhaps the last 'gentlemen's war' in history and well worth reading up on.

Ninety kilometres beyond the bridge lies the town of **Kasama**, administrative capital of the region. Kasama has banks, petrol and a hotel. Travellers wishing to camp near here should proceed to the **Chishimba Falls** (see page 146).

From Kasama you can turn east to Isoka 175 km away, west to Luwingu 150 km away and Mporokoso 160 km away or proceed north on the main road to Mbala, which is 167 km from Kasama. Only the Mbala road is tarred.

Just a few kilometres before Mbala a left turn marks the 40 km road down the escarpment to Mpulungu.

THE EASTERN REGION

The eastern region of Zambia consists almost entirely of the Luangwa Valley drainage system between the Muchinga Escarpment and the hills of Malawi and Mozambique. And the primary reason for visitors to go there is to see the magnificent Luangwa Valley and the game reserves that have made the valley such a famous wildlife sanctuary and tourist destination. It covers a large region of the country yet it is serviced by only one major road – the Great East Road (GER), which runs from Lusaka to Lilongwe in Malawi via Petauke and Chipata. Only minor roads connect towns further north, such as Lundazi, to the GER. The Great East Road is tarred and both Lilongwe and the main gate of the South Luangwa National Park are easily accessible in normal cars, but for any diversions from that route four-wheel-drive is recommended.

The Luangwa Valley

Game protection in the Luangwa Valley has a long history. In the late 19th century elephant and hippo were heavily exploited by the Chikunda tribe from Mozambique as well as Arabs based on Lake Malawi. Hippo were at one stage so rare that the British South Africa Company which administered the territory imposed a total ban on hunting them until their numbers recovered. Nowadays the area positively teems with that large mammal.

With the establishment of the British South Africa Company administration in 1898 and control over elephant hunting, elephant numbers started to recover. The BSAC established the first game reserve in the valley in the Luamfwa region in 1904 to protect the last remaining population of Thornicroft's giraffe. Although this reserve was subsequently deproclaimed in 1911, elephant populations continued to develop, and did so well that by 1930 they began to pose a serious problem for local subsistence farmers. Contracts were issued to men who were to become legendary 'white hunters', such as Charlie Ross, Bill

Langham and Freddy Hall, to shoot marauding elephants. Hall was mauled by a lion while trying to capture giraffe and died of his injuries. Charlie Ross was killed by an elephant in 1938. In 1939 Ross was replaced by a young man, Norman Carr, who perhaps more than any other figure can be said to be the father of conservation in Zambia and particularly of the Luangwa Valley, where he lived at his camp Kapani until he died in 1997. At the same time the three major game reserves, North and South Luangwa and Lukusuzi, were proclaimed.

In 1950 Norman Carr proposed a scheme whereby the local population could become involved in conservation and benefit from it. He persuaded Chief Nsefu to turn some of his tribal land into a private game reserve. Revenue from the reserve was returned to the chief's administration. The project was so successful that the Chewa asked that a camp be established at Luambe, which was carried out in 1954. In the late 1950s tourist camps were established and after retiring from government service in 1961 Carr and a partner, Peter Hankin, established the first safari company in the country.

The tourist infrastructure was extended by the building of all-weather roads in the 1970s. Bridges over the Luangwa were constructed, as was the present airstrip. In 1972 all game reserves were abolished and designated national parks. A census in the early 1970s revealed an elephant population of over 100 000, but from about 1975 onwards poaching began to escalate dramatically. In 1980 the Save the Rhino Trust was established to combat poaching. In 1987 the Luangwa Independent Rural Development Project (LIRDP) was established to implement an overall management policy for the Luangwa Valley and direct revenues accrued through tourism to the benefit of the local population.

South Luangwa National Park

The most famous game reserve in the country, this is a magnificent park with abundant wildlife and a range of lodges and safari operations to cater for most budgets and travel tastes.

The Luangwa River runs right through the eastern part of Zambia and almost the whole valley is given over to wildlife management. South Luangwa National Park covers 9 050 square kilometres between the west bank of the river and the Muchinga Escarpment. Safaris and lodges are concentrated on

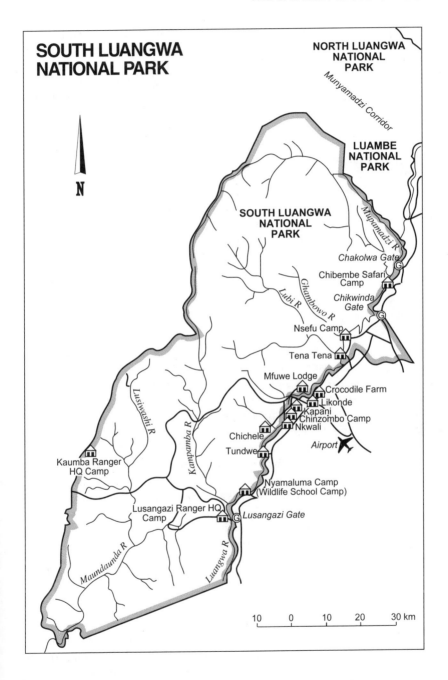

SOUTH LUANGWA
NATIONAL PARK

NORTH LUANGWA
NATIONAL
PARK

Munyamadzi Corridor

LUAMBE
NATIONAL
PARK

SOUTH LUANGWA
NATIONAL
PARK

Mupamadzi R

Chakolwa Gate

Chibembe Safari
Camp

*Chikwinda
Gate*

Luabi R

Ghambowo R

Nsefu Camp

Tena Tena

Mfuwe Lodge

Crocodile Farm

Likonde

Kapani
Chinzombo Camp
Nkwali

Chichele

Tundwe

Airport

Lusiwashi R

Kampamba R

Kaumba Ranger
HQ Camp

Nyamaluma Camp
(Wildlife School Camp)

Lusangazi Ranger HQ
Camp

Lusangazi Gate

Maundaunda R

Luangwa R

10   0   10   20   30 km

the river, the majority based on the east bank and conducting daily walks and drives across the river in the park.

Safari operators can meet clients in Lusaka (see page 57). There is an airstrip just outside Mfuwe, the main gate, and national and charter airlines make regular flights. A weekly flight from Lilongwe in Malawi has been considered but has not materialised as yet.

By road Mfuwe is about 698 km from Lusaka. Follow the Great East Road to Petauke, from which four-wheel-drivers can traverse a slow but scenically beautiful road straight to the park. Those without four-wheel-drive vehicles should proceed to Chipata and turn left just before the Independence Archway (see route 11 on page 162). The park itself has some all-weather roads and is suitable for normal cars although, particularly in the wet season, a four-wheel-drive may be more comfortable.

Hitchhikers will find the going slow but there is enough traffic to and from Chipata to get you through. At the moment it is the only national park that is reasonably accessible to hitchhikers at all.

The Luangwa Valley is part of the famous Rift Valley. To most visitors the Muchinga Escarpment will remain just a blue haze in the west. But between the Luangwa River and the escarpment lies a vast savanna sanctuary. Despite the endemic poaching of the 1980s there remains a fantastic amount of game. Of the 'big five', four are readily seen with rhino being the exception. There is considerable doubt whether any rhino at all remain alive in Zambia and if they do their whereabouts are either unknown or kept highly secret. Predators are common and South Luangwa is known particularly for leopard sightings. The elephant population is but a fragment of the 100 000-strong population of the 1970s, but small family groups are frequently seen and if the devastation still visible in some areas is anything to go by, the drastic reduction in population may have a beneficial affect on the environment in the long term.

Antelope include impala, puku, eland, Lichtenstein's hartebeest, kudu and common waterbuck. It is interesting that this, the species of waterbuck found elsewhere in southern Africa, is quite different from the Defassa waterbuck found in the Kafue region. Of particular note is that the park is one of only two in the country where giraffe occur naturally, and those found here are a unique subspecies, the Thornicroft's giraffe, which has different markings from giraffe elsewhere. Cookson's wildebeest is also a subspecies of blue wildebeest and unique to the valley.

Botanical variation between broad-leafed woodland, acacia, mopane, grassy plains and huge riverine trees along the sandy river make the valley a paradise for birds, and almost 400 species have been recorded. Specialities are the Pel's fishing owl, large numbers of African skimmers, the African broadbill and as many as 40 different birds of prey.

It is a pity that on a continent where wildlife and people have interacted since time immemorial, the latter seldom form part of contemporary tourist experience. But recently **Mwizala village** in Kawaza, 8 km from Mfuwe on the Tena-Tena road, have opened their village to guests. A hut costs US$15 for which you will be treated to Kunda cuisine, hospitality and possibly a visit to a traditional healer.

Kaingo Crafts, a shop close to Mfuwe and the airport, has a range of crafts produced locally and from elsewhere in Africa.

The park is open all year, although many of the private lodges are closed during the rainy season. It is best to visit between April and October, although October can be extremely hot.

There are two lodges inside the park, **Mfuwe** and **Chichele**, which were nationalised years ago and are run by the NHDC. Mfuwe has been privatised and totally renovated. Chichele still operates after a fashion but its current status is uncertain. Note that some lodges listed in tourist leaflets and maps are no longer operational or are currently being renovated.

Then there is a number of excellent upmarket lodges sporadically located along the east bank of the Luangwa River where they overlook the park. Most of these are best booked in advance. Many of these lodges or camps are owned and run by experts on conservation in Zambia, whose vast experience of the bush makes their guidance into the ways of the wild an experience worth every penny. Game drives are conducted in the park by experienced and knowledgeable guides and walks are additionally accompanied by armed scouts. Also, several lodges run bush camps in more remote corners of the park from which walking safaris are conducted. Walking safaris from bush camps are restricted to the dry season and some lodges close for the rains. The map shows the positions of the various lodges.

Not far south of Mfuwe is **Kapani**, run by Norman Carr Safaris and open all year. Kapani has a luxurious, old-fashioned atmosphere and there is a swimming pool. In the dry season Kapani runs three bush camps inside the park: Luwi and Nsolo, which are built of reeds in the tradition of old hunting camps, and Kakuli which is tented under thatch. In all the emphasis is on game walks although some drives are also undertaken.

Chinzombo, close to Kapani, is owned by the Save the Rhino Trust and is a medium-sized thatched lodge in a scenic location. Chinzombo runs two bush camps, Chamilandu and Kuyenda, which sleep only six people in rustic but comfortable huts. The bush camps are used only in the dry season but Chinzombo is closed just between January and April.

Robin Pope Safaris have two small and exclusive main camps on the east side of the river. **Tena Tena** is a tented camp situated inside the park where it encloses what was once called the Nsefu Game Reserve. Six large tents each have *en suite* flush toilets and showers. It is open in the dry season only. **Nkwali** is south of Kapani and Chinzombo on private land overlooking the Luangwa River. This is a beautiful camp with six chalets which superbly combine modern comforts with a sense of being open to the wild. Nkwali has a longer season, only closing for the very wet months of December through to March. Robin Pope Safaris also operate **Nsefu Bush Camp** inside the park which, started many years ago by Norman Carr, claims to be the oldest tourist camp in Zambia. It has six twin-bedded thatched rondavels with *en suite* facilities close to a waterhole, so there is plenty of game in and around the camp. Robin Pope Safaris also run walking safaris over five-day stretches in the remote and inaccessible Munyamadzi River region of the park.

Chibembe Camp, run by Chilongozi Safaris is 54 km north of the Mfuwe road. It has 40 beds in single, double and family-sized wooden chalets with *en suite* facilities. The camp is located overlooking a large hippo pool in the river and there is always game to see from the terrace and a swimming pool in which to wallow during the heat of the day.

Derek Shenton runs **Kaingo Camp** consisting of four *en suite* bungalows and family style hospitality.

Mchenja Camp comprises a small group of A-framed chalets with thatched roofs and reed walls. Contact Savannah Trails for bookings.

There are two camps operated under the auspices of the Wildlife Conservation Society of Zambia: the **Wildlife Camp** with *en suite* chalets and a campsite and **Kafunta River Lodge**, comprising eight timber and thatch chalets on stilts.

Marula Lodge is a locally run self-catering lodge near the park.

Wild Zambia Safaris operate fully mobile and walking safaris in the park.

Camping is available close to the main gate outside the park at privately run campsites such as the **Croc Farm** and **Flat Dogs** campsite. For those not in their own vehicles, or if desired, game drives can be arranged. James Schultz's **Likonde Camp** has camping and self-catering chalets, but has been closed for renovation.

The list above is not exhaustive. There are other safari companies building new camps or renovating old ones at a brisk rate, so you are well advised to contact travel agents and the Tour Operators Association for up-to-date information. For further details, bookings and such see chapters 12 and 13.

North Luangwa National Park

This truly magnificent wilderness, surely one of the wildest places left on earth, is something of a special case and entry is restricted to two or three safari companies.

The park lies north of 'South Park' (of course), the major game areas being on the Luangwa and its tributary the Mwaleshi River.

Visitors may only go into the 'North Park' under the auspices of one of the safari companies operating there. Shiwa Safaris and John Coppinger run temporary camps on the Mwaleshi River. Shiwa Safaris access the park from their famed country estate (see Shiwa Ngandu in chapter 10, page 139). John Coppinger drives his guests up from the South Luangwa where he runs Tafika Lodge.

Similar in terms of game and vegetation to the South Luangwa, this park's particular attraction is its remoteness. For the price of limiting access to the companies mentioned above, the park offers an unrivalled exclusivity. Once encamped beneath mahogany and kigelia trees above the glimmering shallow water of the Mwaleshi River, you have 4 636 square kilometres all to yourselves, a superabundance of game and stars. There are lions aplenty and some of the biggest herds of buffalo in Africa. The authors have seen herds of up to 2 000 buffalo here.

There is excellent birdlife as well. Safaris are usually exclusive to one's own party. It is categorically one of the best safari destinations on the continent. The North Luangwa has been brought to the world's attention by Mark and Delia Owens, whose book *The Eye of the Elephant* (or *Survivor's Song* in South Africa) chronicles their struggle to preserve the park from poaching. Although the Owens have now left Zambia, the North Luangwa continues to be managed by a trust under the auspices of the Frankfurt Zoological Society.

Safaris only operate during the dry season, late May to mid-October. The later in the season the better the game viewing. October is extremely hot.

There are no facilities for visitors other than those belonging to the two companies operating in the park. There are only three camps, **Base Camp**, **Buffalo Camp** and **Mwaleshi Camp**, all of which are temporary, 'dry-season-only' camps in the rough-and-ready style of old Zambian hunting camps. The first two are operated by Shiwa Safaris (see Shiwa Ngandu in chapter 10, page 139) the longest-standing operators in the park. They bring visitors from the stately manor house at **Shiwa Ngandu** near Mpika down the Muchinga Escarpment, either on foot or in four-wheel-drive vehicles, to their two simple bush camps on the Mwaleshi River. John Coppinger runs Mwaleshi Camp further downstream and accesses the park from the South Luangwa. These trips are four-wheel-drive journeys that take several hours. However, Shiwa Ngandu is also accessible in a normal vehicle and John Coppinger will arrange transfers from Mfuwe. Transfers by plane or vehicle from Lusaka can be arranged.

These camps are in keeping with traditional bush camps elsewhere. Rebuilt every dry season, they consist of thatch walled and roofed bungalows on earth floors. There are proper beds and linen. Ablution facilities are usually *en suite* but basic, with a pit latrine and bucket showers.

Luambe National Park

This park is just north of the South Luangwa, on the east side of the river.

Proceed north about 80 km from Mfuwe, past the turnoffs to Tena Tena and Chibembe camps. A scout camp and boom across the road mark the beginning of the park.

This is a beautiful park, similar to the South Luangwa but with more spectacular trees, if somewhat less game due to hunting occurring around the park. However it has a greater feeling of remoteness because there are no safari operations in the park. The old lodge is derelict.

The only road is appalling; unbelievably bumpy in the dry season, the black cotton soil becomes a sticky quagmire in the wet. Although maps make the road look prominent, it is in fact just a track and travellers over it may easily think they are lost. Four-wheel-drive is essential.

It is best to visit between May and October. It is likely that the roads will be impassable at any other time.

There are no facilities at present. Check with the NPWS when and whether camping might be allowed.

Lukusuzi National Park

This park is also in the Luangwa Valley but some distance east of the Luangwa River. At the time of writing it has no facilities whatever and due to poaching the state of the game population is uncertain.

There are plans for development, however, and curious visitors should direct enquiries about possible safaris to the **Tour Operators Association of Zambia**, Box 30263, Lusaka, or for private visits, the **National Parks and Wildlife Service**.

The park is situated between the Luangwa River and the Chipata-Lundazi road. Take the Great East Road then proceed past Chipata toward Lundazi for about 110 km. Turn left down a poor dirt road which traverses the park. The condition of the road in the park is uncertain. It is probably suitable for four-wheel-drive vehicles only.

The game status here is uncertain. Big game may be encountered but is likely to be extremely wary due to poaching.

The park is open all year but summer visitors should drive with caution.

There are no facilities at present. Ask the game scouts at the gates for advice.

The Nyika Plateau and National Park

This is also something of a special case because it can only be reached via Malawi.

The Nyika Plateau straddles the border between Malawi and Zambia in the north-east of the country.

The only road up onto the Nyika Plateau is in Malawi, so you must cross over to that country in order to reach the park. There are three possible crossings. You can go directly from Chipata via Lilongwe and Kasungu. Although this is the longest way round on the map, it definitely has the best roads.

Alternatively, from Chipata drive up through Lundazi before crossing the border and proceeding through Mzuzu and then Rumphi. The main road west from Rumphi goes directly to the park gate.

The third alternative, which is the most direct but probably takes the longest, is to remain in Zambia after Lundazi, driving all the way up through some remote countryside to the border gate at Katumbi, which is west of Rumphi and close to the Nyika access road. Note that the Zambian border post at Katumbi can also be reached from Kasama via Isoka. If coming up from Lundazi it is easy to miss the Zambian post because the last junction is on the Malawian side of the boom. Turn left for 100 m at that junction. From the Zambian post it is then eight rough kilometres to the Malawian post.

Both these last-mentioned routes are on poor roads that take a long time to travel and will probably necessitate camping along the way. Remember that you will have to undergo all the usual border formalities, whichever route you take. It is a long way to the Nyika from anywhere in Zambia and you will have to plan carefully, bearing poor roads in mind if you are to make the National Park gates in Malawi before they close at 18:00. Also you will need some local currency to pay the gate fees of 7,5 Malawi kwacha per vehicle and K3 per person per day. There is a bank in Rumphi where you can change dollars, pound or rands into Malawi kwacha. They will not accept Zambian kwacha.

The Nyika Plateau is quite unlike any other place in central Africa. Once you have climbed up the mountain pass, gone through the gate and passed through the broad-leafed wood-land of the lower slopes, you see the plateau opening up into great rolling fields interspersed with patches of thick and deep montane forest. There is no actual border control between Zambia and Malawi once on the plateau, and in fact all internal routes and game drives are in Malawi. Game also tends to stick to Malawi territory, being safe there from Zambian poachers. And the variety is fantastic. Antelope species such as roan, eland and reedbuck are found in large numbers. It is a particularly unusual environment in which to see roan and you are able to do so at close quarters. Other animals that visitors are likely to see include blue monkey, bushbuck, blue duiker, red duiker and leopard. Nyika is said to have the highest concentration of leopard per square kilometre in Africa and visitors have a good chance of seeing one. On the northern side of the plateau lion, elephant and buffalo are apparently also found. The best way to see them is to hire a guide and bearers at Chilanda Camp and take a walking safari over several days to that northern area.

Open all year round, the park offers the best game viewing between November and May although February and March are wet and a four-wheel-drive vehicle is recommended.

The reason Nyika is included in this guide at all is that the **Zambian Rest House** is situated on the Zambian edge of the plateau. With all the unsophisticated grace of a bygone era this is a perfect place to spend a few days far – very far – from the madding crowd. It is now run by **Robin Pope Safaris**, who use it for their own Nyika expeditions, but when not in use it can be booked by other self-catering travellers. You will be expected to hand over your supplies to Mr Gondwe, the manager-cum-chef, who will then cook for you and serve your meals on Federation silver. Starched napkins, spotless sheets on the beds and boiling hot water in the bathrooms all make the Zambian Rest House unforgettable. But if you need cheaper accommodation or camping facilities the main Malawian camp, Chilanda, is not far away.

Walking from the rest house is permissible and one can spend hours hiking in these game-rich dales or trout fishing in the clear streams that run through them.

ROUTE 11
LUSAKA TO SOUTH LUANGWA NATIONAL PARK VIA THE GREAT EAST ROAD TO CHIPATA

DISTANCE: 569 km to Chipata then 120 to the main gate.
TIME: 8 hours **ROAD CONDITIONS:** Fairly good **FUEL:**
Nyimba, Petauke, Katete, Chipata **RECOMMENDED STOPS:**
Mkoma Rock Shelter

The Great East Road begins at Cairo Road's north-end circle and departs Lusaka via the agricultural showgrounds, the University of Zambia and the airport. Between the university and the airport lies the last fuel station, beyond which the next available fuel is likely to be at Nyimba or Petauke, 328 km and 394 km from Lusaka respectively. So fill tanks accordingly. This is one of the better roads in the country, made of tar all the way to Chipata with relatively few potholes. About 100 km out of town the road enters into pretty, undulating country. It is 162 km to Rufunsa. Then the road begins to descend to the Luangwa River.

Beautiful as the bridge and valley is, be careful when taking photographs; there is usually a military roadblock in the vicinity. From Rufunsa it is 65 km to the bridge and then 60 km to Kachalola where fuel may be available. Then it is 42 km to Nyimba and 68 km from there to Petauke. About 12 km before Katete a turnoff left to the Zambia National Service Farm takes one a few kilometres to the national monument site, the **Mkoma Rock Shelter**, where there is a series of stylistic rock paintings dating from the Iron Age. From Katete it is 88 km to Chipata, but travellers proceeding to the South Luangwa should turn left immediately before the independence memorial archway on the outskirts of the town.

From here on the road is a dirt road likely to be very corrugated if it has not been graded recently. It is 67 km to the Chisengu turnoff. Proceed left. The right-hand road, which appears on the map to be a shortcut to Chibembe Lodge, is in very bad condition and therefore not recommended. Thereafter it is 15,7 km to Jumbe, where the road again forks to the left over a bridge. It is almost 17 km to the Mfuwe airport turnoff. Proceed straight on for nearly 6 km to the Catholic church. Here the road forks again. Travellers proceeding to the main gate at Mfuwe and the lodges south of it should keep left then turn right at the T-junction. Travellers proceeding northwards to Tena Tena, Nsefu or Chibembe can take a small short-cut by turning right opposite the church and proceeding over a bridge.

Those going north should be aware that four-wheel-drive may be necessary from here on as several sandy riverbeds need to be crossed. Those proceeding the other way now get back onto tar and the road goes directly to the bridge and gate beyond which it is just a kilometre or so to Mfuwe. Just before the bridge a main road south goes down to Chinzombo, Kapani and Nkwali and opposite there is a signposted turn to the Croc Farm and Flatdogs campsite.

12

WHERE TO STAY

Accommodation in Zambia covers the full budget spectrum from the most luxurious to the positively penal. Top hotels have high standards; there are game lodges that are quite superb; middle-range hotels can be pricey for what they offer; but lodgings of one sort or another can be found in almost every town in the country, although their standards vary wildly. A feature of Zambia is that every town has a rest house run by the district or town council. While some of these have degenerated into brothels or shebeens, they are very cheap and some are quite acceptable with clean sheets and facilities. Travellers on tight budgets would do well to check them out.

Although the following list is as comprehensive as possible, it is restricted to places where tourists might possibly stop and generally excludes the ubiquitous government rest houses and bottom of the market, ungraded establishments. It bears repeating that the tourist industry in Zambia is burgeoning so rapidly that this book cannot hope to be absolutely up to date with developments and travellers should still consult travel agencies. Hotels in Zambia are given a 'star' rating and lodges are graded alphabetically, 'A' being top rated, 'B', 'C', etc., progressively lower graded.

However visitors should not take these ratings entirely seriously, especially where lodges are concerned; having international colour televison in every bungalow is considered more important by Zambians than by visitors dying to get away from it all. So we have dispensed with giving the official rating, simply grading esablishments into upmarket, medium and budget and wherever possible supplemented with a subjective assessment.

Zambia's international dialling code is +260.

Accommodation in and Around Towns and Cities

Lusaka
Area code: 01

Upmarket

Chisamba Safari Lodge, off the Great North Rd, near Chisamba, Tel: 22-6589, Fax: 29-0809, E-mail: chisamba@zamnet.zm.

Holiday Inn, Lusaka Ridgeway, Independence Ave, Box 30666, Lusaka, Tel: 25-1666, Fax: 25-3529, r155, b215. *Centrally located, recently taken over by the Holiday Inn group and revamped with conference facilities, casino, swimming pool.*

Hotel Intercontinental, Haile Selassie Ave, Box 32201, Lusaka, Tel: 22-7911, Fax: 25-1880, Tlx: ZA251880 or ZA41440, r400, b478. *An international-style hotel with most facilities including squash courts, swimming pool and casino, but rather badly in need of a facelift.*

Juls Guesthouse, Plot 5508, Lusiwasi Rd (off Libala Rd), Tel: 29-2979 or 29-3972, Fax: 29-1246, E-mail: julscat@zamnet.zm.

Kaingo Guesthouse, Tel: 26-3231.

Lilayi Lodge, Kafue Rd, Box 30098, Lusaka, Tel: 22-8682, Fax: 22-2906, Tlx: ZA40536, E-mail: lilayi@zamnet.zm, r24, b36. *A pleasant out of town alternative, set on a game farm, but close enough to Lusaka for those with business there. Transfers arranged.*

Pamodzi Hotel, Addis Ababa Dr, Box 35450, Lusaka, Tel: 22-7957/81, Fax: 25-0995, Tlx: ZA44720, r202, b408. *Lusaka's smartest hotel, 2 km from city centre. Banquet rooms, conference facilities, casino, forex, barber and beauty salons, pool, 2 squash courts, 2 tennis courts, a health club, etc.*

Tudor Lodge, Box 31740, Lusaka, Tel: 29-5613, Fax: 29-5614, r3.

Medium

Andrews Motel, Kafue Rd, Box 30475, Lusaka, Tel: 27-2532, Fax: 27-4798, r97, b200. *Rather noisy venue for local socialising, with swimming pool and tennis court.*

Belvedere Lodge, Box 50155, Lusaka, Tel/Fax: 26-3680, r15.

Chainama Hotel, Great East Rd, Box 51033, Lusaka, Tel: 29-2451/7, Fax: 29-0809, r28, b56. *Modern, halfway between city and airport. Pool, function rooms and facilities, rooms have private balconies.*

Fringilla Farm, Great North Rd, Chisambu, Box 31440, Lusaka, Tel: 6-1128, r7, b20. *About an hour north of Lusaka. Tasteful bungalows, good food, and a bustling farm atmosphere, ideal if heading north or on farming business. Clean campsite with bungalows and hot water.*

Garden House Motel, Mumbwa Rd, Box 30815, Lusaka, Tel: 28-9328, Fax: 28-7337, r50, b100. *Reasonably priced, convenient for those intending to visit the Kafue National Park, being 5 km from the city on the Mumbwa Rd.*

The Hillview Hotel, Kafue Rd, Box 30815, Lusaka, Tel: 27-8554, Fax: 22-9074, r8, b12. *A clean, lower budget, small hotel 20 minutes from the city. Take the Kafue Rd and 1 km after Andrews Motel take first tar road right and follow it for about 5 km.*

Lechwe Lodge, Box 31522, Lusaka, Tel: 23-0128, Fax: 22-2684, E-mail: klechwe@zamnet.zm, r4.

Longacres Lodge, Box 50098, Lusaka, Tel: 25-1761, r58.

Lusaka Hotel, Cairo Rd, Box 30044, Lusaka, Tel: 22-9049, Fax: 22-5726, r79, b139. *The only hotel conveniently in the centre of town, it is popular and reasonably priced, but a little claustrophobic, noisy and chaotic.*

Mandala Lodge, Box 34966, Lusaka, Tel/Fax: 29-3883, r5.

Mulungushi Boat Club, off Great North Road, 12 chalets.

Ndeke Hotel, Cnr Haile Selassie & Saddam Hussein, Box 30815, Lusaka, Tel/Fax: 25-2779, r44, b88. *This reasonably priced hotel has a rather charming and vaguely eccentric atmosphere appropriate to a central African capital.*

Zamearth Lodge, Private Bag 107, Lusaka, Tel/Fax: 29-4680, r7.

Budget

The Barn Motel, Great East Rd, Box CH242, Lusaka, Tel: 28-2890/2, Fax: 22-8949, Tlx: ZA48670, r50, b92. *About 20 km from the city centre and 10 km from the airport.*

Fairview Hotel, Church Rd, Box 33200, Lusaka, Tel: 21-2954, Tlx: ZA40572, r30, b64. *All rooms have colour TV – a feature considered by many Zambians to be more important than a new coat of paint.*

Harvey Game Farm Campsite, Tel/Fax: 61-1228, r3.

Parrays Game Farm, located along Mumbwa Rd, camping.

Livingstone
Area code: 03

Upmarket

Chundukwa Tree Lodge, 30 km upriver on Sesheke Rd, Box 61160, Livingstone, Tel: 32-4452, Fax: 32-4006 E-mail: chunduka@zamnet.zm, r4. *This pleasant camp, with chalets built on stilts above the water, is used as a base for Chundukwa Adventure Trails. Pick-ups from town, visits to the falls, canoe and other safaris, including horse safaris, can be arranged.*

The River Club, Tel: 32-3672, r10. *Luxurious evocation of old colonial splendour.*

Royal Chundu, Box 60889, Livingstone, Tel/Fax: 32-1772. *This camp is targeted particularly at fishermen.*

Sindabezi Island Camp, Private Bag 31, Livingstone, Tel: 32-3235, Fax: 32-3224, E-mail: tonga@zamnet.zm, r4. *An island overlooking the falls.*

Songwe Point, Batoka Gorge, Tel: 32-3659, Fax: 3205, E-mail: saflodge@vfsl.gaia.co.zw, r8. *To date one of only two lodges overlooking the Batoka Gorge, this is run and booked through Zambezi Safari Lodge in Victoria Falls.*

Sun International Hotels, with construction only about to commence at the time of writing, readers should refer to the latest travel literature, the website or their travel agents for further information.

Thorntree Lodge, Box 61009, Livingstone, Tel: 32-4273, Fax: 32-1320, E-mail: atd@zamnet.zm, r8.

Tongabezi Lodge, 17 km upriver (take Sesheke Rd), Private Bag 31, Livingstone, Tel: 32-3235, Fax: 32-3224, E-mail: tonga@zamnet.zm, Website: www.tongabezi.com, r12. *An exquisite blend of sophistication and rusticity right on the banks of the Zambezi. Rooms are unique, thatch or tented under thatch. All transfers to and from Livingstone are arranged as well as tours by plane or boat to the falls and tailored safaris. A feature is a picnic on Livingstone Island, literally at the Falls' edge.*

Medium

Chanters Guest Lodge, Lukulu Crescent, in town, Box 60623, Livingstone, Tel: 32-3412, r3. *Bar and restaurant. Rooms are self-contained with satellite TV. Recommended.*

Kubu Cabins & Camping, 35 km upriver, Box 60748, Livingstone, Tel/Fax: 32-4091/3, E-mail: kubu@zamnet.zm, r3. *Timber and thatch 'cabins' offering an extensive package of activities on the river and around the falls. Also camping facilities.*

Ngolide Lodge,110 Mosi-oa-Tunya Rd, Livingstone, Tel: 32-1092, Fax: 32-1113, r16. *A new thatch lodge on the main road as you enter Livingstone. It advertises an ethnic feel. Pleasant looking from outside, but a little cramped within.*

Taita Falcon Lodge, Batoka Gorge, Box 60012, Livingtone, Tel: 32-1850, r8. *Homely comfort perched dizzyingly on the lip of the Batoka Gorge. Recommended.*

Tunya Lodge, Tel: 32-1511.

Wasawange Lodge, close to town on the airport road, Box 60278, Livingstone, Tel: 32-4066, Fax: 32-4067, r19. *More hotel than lodge with conference facilities, air-conditioning, TV, jacuzzi, sauna. Comfortable, but who needs a sauna in the Zambezi Valley?*

Budget

Faulty Towers Bacpackers, Main Rd, in town, Tel: 32-3432, E-mail: ahorizon@zamnet.zm. *A new, hip backpacker's hostel, right where the action is in town. Spotlessly clean and fun.*

Gecko's Guesthouse, in town, two blocks off the main road. Tel/Fax: 32-2267 E-mail: gecko@zamnet.zm. *Backpacker's hostel in a nice old house. Clean bedding, but could use a broom and mosquito nets.*

Grubby's Grotto, Old Governor's House in town.

Hillview Guesthouse, Tel/Fax: 32-3215.

Jollyboys Backpackers, Box 60809, Livingstone, Tel: 32-4229, Fax: 32-4229, E-mail: jboys@zamnet.zm.

Jungle Junction Campsite, about 70 km upstream, Box 60748, Livingstone, Tel: 32-4127, E-mail: jungle@zamnet.zm. *The 'coolest' place to hang out on the Zambezi, exquisitely located on an island in the river about 70 km upstream, or 10 km downstream of Kazungula. Warmly reccommended to campers touring the region, but beware of 'Stevie', the crocodile.*

New Fairmount Hotel, Main Rd, in town, Box 60096, Livingstone, Tel: 32-0726, Fax: 32-1490. *In the centre of Livingstone. Well, it's there if none of the newer and more exciting venues grab your fancy.*

Nyala Lodge, Box 60774, Livingstone, Tel: 32-2446, Fax: 32-1248.

Ndola
Area code: 02

Upmarket

New Savoy Hotel, Buteko Ave, Box 71800, Ndola, Tel: 61-1097/8, Fax: 61-4001, r145. *Centrally located, the hotel boasts the only first-floor swimming pool in the country and a casino.*

Medium

Endesha Guesthouses, Tel: 61-7067, Fax: 61-7250.

Mukuba Hotel, showgrounds, Box 72126, Ndola, Tel: 65-5545/9, Fax: 65-5729, E-mail: mukhotel@zamnet.zm, r50. *Although tricky to find, (follow the signs into the agricultural showgrounds) this hotel has a pleasant atmosphere with a few impala wandering around, well kept gardens and a good restaurant.*

Budget

New Ambassador Hotel, President Ave, Box 71538, Tel: 61-7071, r30. *Basic, but centrally located not far from the bus terminus.*

Kitwe
Area code: 02

Medium

Blue Gate Guest House, Tel: 22-6606.

Eagle Guest House, Tel/Fax: 23-0028 or 22-9748, E-Mail: gayatech@zam-net.com.

Edinburgh Hotel, cnr Independence & Obote Ave, Box 21800, Kitwe, Tel: 21-2188, Fax: 22-5036, r78. *Somewhat run down from former splendour, but there's air-conditioning, a casino and swimming pool.*

Lothian House, Tel: 61-0149.

Mukra Guest House, 26 Mpenzi Ave, Tel/Fax: 22-4266, E-mail: trekaf@zamnet.zm.

Nkana Hotel, Independence Ave, Box 20664, Kitwe, Tel: 22-4166, r63. *Nice looking, set around a pleasant courtyard but slightly run down and apt to be very noisy, especially on weekends.*

Sherbourne Farm Lodge, Tel: 22-1168, Fax: 22-6477.

Budget

Bbuchi Hotel, Box 224957, Kitwe, r17.

Chingola
Area code: 02

Chingola Guest House, Katutwa St, Box 11014, Chingola, Tel: 31-3635, r3.

Lima Motel, Kitwe Rd, Box 10497, Chingola, Tel: 31-1894. *Insalubrious.*

Musunshya Inn, Box 10021, Chingola, Tel: 31-1115.

Nchanga Motel, Box 10024, Chingola, Tel: 31-2148, r30. *Used to be a well-known haunt for certain businesswomen.*

Mufulira
Area code: 02

Kamuchanga Hotel, Box 798, Mufulira, Tel: 41-2377, r25.

Lodge Elizabeth, Tel: 412353, r4.

Mongu
Area code: 07

Lyambai Hotel, Box 910193, Mongu, Tel/Fax: 22-1138, r17. *Don't be deterred by the fact that it is outwardly uninspiring; the hotel is clean and pleasant.*

Ngulu Hotel, Box 910308, Mongu, Tel: 22-1028, r16.

Sir Mwanawina III Motel, Tel: 22-1485, r54. *Run by the district council and located on the Senanga road.*

Tiger Camp, Box 31730, Lusaka, Tel: 26-2810, E-mail: tiger@zamnet.zm.

Senanga (Ngonye Falls area)
Area code: 07

Barotze Lodge, Senanga, Box 30664, Lusaka, Tel: 22-1910.

Maziba Bay, 7 km downstream from Ngonye Falls.

Mutemwa Lodge, 55 km from Kahma Molino.

Senanga Lodge, Box 920077, Senanga, Tel: 23-0156, r16. *Pleasantly sited above the Zambezi. Reasonably comfortable bungalows. OK food. Rather noisy bar terrace.*

Zambelozi Island Lodge, Tel: South Africa (018) 293-0612.

Solwezi
Area code: 08

Changa Changa Motel, Chingola Rd, Box 110248, Solwezi, Tel: 82-1572, r28, b48.

Zambezi
Area code: 08

Zambezi Motel, Box 150001, Zambezi, r28, b48. *The magnificent view is unlikely to make up for less than salubrious facilities.*

Mazabuka
Area code: 032

Mazabuka Hotel, Main Rd, Box 670022, Mazabuka, Tel: 3-0284, r16, b32.

Choma
Area code: 032

Choma Hotel, Main Rd, Box 63050, Choma, Tel: 2-0189, r20, b38.

Kalundu Hotel, Box 630088, Choma, r40, b76.

Kabwe
Area code: 05

Medium

Elephant's Head Hotel, Box 80410, Kabwe, Tel: 22-2522, r35, b70.

Masiye Motel, Box 81210, Kabwe, Tel: 22-3221, r66, b112.

Budget

Mulungushi Motel, Box 80408, Kabwe, Tel: 22-4602, r28, b52. Swimming pool

Horison Hotel, Box 80458, Kabwe, Tel: 22-3398, r18, b31.

Kapiri Mposhi
Area code: 05

Kapiri Motel, GNR, Box 13, Kapiri Mposhi, Tel: 27-1148, r8, b14.

Unity Hotel, Box 59, Kapiri Mposhi, Tel: 27-1350, r36, b52. *Rooms do have separate bathrooms.*

Mansa
Area code: 02

Mansa Hotel, Box 710008, Mansa, Tel: 82-1606, r30, b60. Recently renovated.

Kasama
Area code: 04

Medium

Modern Kwacha Relax Hotel, Box 53, Kasama, Tel: 22-1124, r32, b56.

Budget

Kasama Hotel, Box 165, Kasama, Tel: 22-1188, r16, b30.

Mbala
Area code: 04

Grasshopper Inn, Box 93, Mbala, Tel: 291, r14, b26.

Arms Hotel, Box Mbala, r10, b20.

Mpulungu
Area code: 04

Nkupe Lodge, Private Bag 8, Mpulungu, r4, b7. *Aimed primarily at backpackers this pleasant, downmarket lodge offers chalets and camping to self-catering travellers at very reasonable rates.*

Chipata
Area code: 062

Chipata District Council Motel, Box 20, Chipata, Tel: 2-1288, r30, b60.

Crystal Springs Hotel, Box 510100, Chipata, Tel: 2-1154, r40, b88.

Lundazi
Area code: 064

Lundazi Castle Motel, Box 530100, Lundazi, Tel: 8-0173, r12, b24. *Worth seeing for its sheer eccentricity, a colonial administrator's idea of a Norman castle made to look all the more ridiculous by the trappings of a low budget hotel.*

Chirundu
Area code: 01

Gwabi Lodge, Box 30813, Chirundu, Tel: 25-0772, r6, b12. *Just 11 km east of Chirundu, turn right just after the border post. This simple lodge set in lovely gardens on the Kafue River offers cheap camping with decent ablution facilities or mid-priced chalets all inclusive – certainly the best bet for early and late border crossers. Used by Drifters Canoe Safaris. Will help with minor vehicle repairs.*

Nyambadwe Motel, Box 33573, Lusaka, r12, b12.

St Necktario's, Box 30815, Lusaka, Tel: 25-2779.

Siavonga
Area code: 01

Medium

Lake Kariba Inn, Box 117, Siavonga, Tel: 51-1358 or 51-1269, r35, b70. *Mainly caters for Lusaka's conference trade. An uninspiring appearance belies decent accommodation and dining facilities.*

Manchinchi Bay Lodge, Box 115, Siavonga, Tel: 51-1399, Tlx: ZA70903, r30, b60. *Well-kept gardens at the water's edge. Air-conditioned rooms with en-suite shower/toilet. Exclusive (and expensive) bar.*

Sandy Beach, Box 103, Siavonga, Tel: 51-1353, r5. *Small, tented, personalised lodge 15 km west of Siavonga.*

Zambezi Lodge, Box 30, Siavonga, Tel: 5-1200, r25, b50. *Average facilities at upmarket prices.*

Budget

Eagles Rest Chalets, Box 1, Siavonga (Lusaka), Tel: 51-1168, r12, b50. *Basic but comfortable in a pleasant setting.*

Leisure Bay Motel, Box 4, Siavonga, r14, b28. *Undergoing renovation.*

Sinazongwe & Lake Kariba
Area code: 03

Upmarket

Chete Island Safari Camp, Box 88, Sinazongwe. *This lodge is unique being the only one on a Zambian island in Lake Kariba. Thatch buildings, luxury tents and game viewing on the Zimbabwean side. Also sailing on the lake. For bookings try any of the major agents in Lusaka or UTC in Livingstone.*

Budget

Sinazongwe Lodge and campsite, Box 88 Sinazongwe.

Camps and Game Lodges in and around National Parks

South Luangwa National Park

Big Lagoon Camp, Tel: (01) 22-8683/4, Fax: (01) 22-2906.

Chamilandu Bush Camp, Tel: (01) 22-5976, Fax: (01) 22-6736, *six chalets. Open April to June.*

Chibembe Lodge, Wilderness Trails, Box 35038, Lusaka, Tel: (01) 22-0112/3/4, E-mail: wtrails@zamnet.zm, *six chalets. Open June to October.*

Chinzombo Lodge, Tel: (01) 22-5976, Fax: (01) 22-6736, E-mail: chinzaf@zamnet.zm, *nine chalets. Open April to January.*

Save the Rhino Trust, Box 320169, Lusaka, E-mail: chinsaf@zamnet.zm.

Flatdogs Campsite, Box 100, Mfuwe, E-mail: moondog@zamnet.zm, *four chalets. Open all year.*

Kafunta River Lodge, Box 83, Mfuwe, Fax: (062) 4-5036, E-mail: miles@zamnet.zm.

Kapani Lodge, Norman Carr Safaris, Box 100, Mfuwe Tel: (062) 4-5015, Fax: (062) 4-5025, E-mail: kapani@zamnet.zm. *Open all year.*

Kakuli Camp, see Kapani Lodge for contact details.

Kaingo Camp, Box 810064, Kapiri Mposhi, Tel: (062) 4-5064, Fax: (062) 36-2188, E-mail: shensaf@zamnet.zm, *four chalets.*

Kapamba Trails, Box 70420, Ndola, Tel: (02) 61-2664, Fax: (02) 61-7250, *10 chalets. Open June to October.*

Kuyenda Bush Camp, Tel: (01) 22-5976, Fax: (01) 22-6736, *six chalets. Open April to June.*

Luanfwa Lodge, Box 32540, Lusaka, Tel: (01) 26-1683 or (01) 26-1732, Fax: (01) 26-2438, *eight chalets.*

Luwi Camp, see Kapani Lodge for contact details. *Open June to October.*

Mchenja Camp, Box 37783, Lusaka, Tel: (01) 22-4457, *five chalets. Open June to October.*

Mfuwe Trails, Box 91, Mfuwe, Tel/Fax: (062) 4-5041, *24 chalets. Open all year.*

Mupanduzi River Camp, Wilderness Trails, Box 35038, Lusaka, E-mail: wtrails@zamnet.zm, *six chalets. Open June to October.*

Nkwali Camp, Box 80, Mfuwe, Tel/Fax: (062) 4-5090, *six chalets. Open February to December.*

Nsefu Camp, Wilderness Trails, Box 35038, Lusaka, E-mail: wtrails@zamnet.zm, *six chalets. Open June to October.*

Nsolo Camp, see Kapani Lodge for contact details, *four chalets. Open June to October.*

Tafika Lodge, Box 5, Mfuwe, Tel/Fax: (062) 4-5059, *four chalets. Open May to November.*

Tena Tena Camp, Box 80, Mfuwe, Tel/Fax: (062) 4-5090, E-mail: popesaf@zamnet.zm, *six chalets. Open June to October.*

Tundwe Camp, Busanga Trails, Box 30984, Lusaka, Tel: (01) 22-0897, Fax: (01) 2-2075, *six chalets. Open May to November.*

Wildlife Camp, Box 53, Mfuwe, Tel: (062) 4-5026, *eight chalets. Open all year.*

Kafue National Park

Chunga Camp, Tel: (01) 25-0017, *eight chalets. Open all year.*

David Sherpherd Camp, c/o Masungwa Lodge, Tel: (01) 27-3493, Fax: (01) 27-4233, *three chalets. Open all year.*

Hippo Camp, c/o Bushwackers, Box 320172, Lusaka, Tel: (01) 25-0310, Fax: (01) 25-3869, *seven chalets. Open May to November.*

Kafwala Camp, c/o Steve Blagus, Box 31530, Lusaka, Tel: (01) 22-7739, Fax: (01) 22-7740, E-mail: sblagus@zamnet.zm, *18 chalets. Open April to November.*

Lufupa Lodge, c/o Steve Blagus, Box 31530, Lusaka, Tel: (01) 22-7739, Fax: (01) 22-7740, E-mail: sblagus@zamnet.zm, *14 chalets. Open April to November.*

Lunga River Lodge, c/o Chinzombo Safaris, Box 30106, Lusaka, Tel: (01) 22-5976, Fax: (01) 22-6736, *six chalets, Open May to December.*

Lupemba Camp, Box 25038, Lusaka, Tel: (01) 22-7027, *three chalets. Open May to December.*

Mukambi Lodge, Private Bag E523, Lusaka, Tel/Fax: (01) 22-8184, E-mail: mukambi@zamnet.zm, *10 chalets. Open all year.*

New Kalala Lodge, c/o Acacia Safaris, Box 30475, Lusaka, Tel/Fax: (01) 25-4471, *six chalets. Open all year.*

Puku Pan Lodge, Box 31149, Lusaka, Tel: (01) 26-0134, *eight chalets. Open all year.*

Lower Zambezi National Park

Chiawa Camp, Box 30972, Lusaka, Tel: (01) 26-1588, Fax: (01) 26-2683, E-mail:chiacamp@zamnet.zm, *four chalets. Open March to November.*

Gwabi Lodge, Tel: 51-5062, *five chalets.*

Kayila Lodge, c/o Africa Tour Designers, Box 31802, Lusaka, Tel: (01) 22-4616, Fax: (01) 22-4915, E-mail: std@zamnet.zm, *chalets. Open all year.*

Kingfisher Lodge, Box 36600, Lusaka, Tel: (01) 26-2456, Fax: (01) 26-4794, *three chalets. Open all year.*

Potato Bush Camp, Private Bag 31, Livingstone, Tel: (03) 32-3235, Fax: (03) 32-3224, E-mail: tonga@zamnet.zm, *six chalets. Open March to December.*

Royal Zambezi Lodge, Box 31455, Lusaka, Tel: (01) 22-4334, Fax: (01) 22-3504, E-mail: royalzam@zamnet.zm, *seven chalets. Open March to November.*

Royal Zambezi Camp, Box 31455, Lusaka, Tel: (01) 22-4334, Fax: (01) 22-3504, E-mail: royalzam@zamnet.zm, *five chalets. Open all year.*

Sausage Tree Camp, Private Bag 31, Livingstone, Tel: (03) 32-3235, Fax: (03) 32-3224, E-mail: tonga@zamnet.zm, *six chalets. Open March to December.*

Zambezi River Safaris, PO Box, Lusaka, Tel: (01) 22-4616, Fax: (01) 22-4915, *four chalets. Open all year.*

Kasanka National Park

Luombwa Camp, Box 30974, Lusaka, Tel: (01) 25-3439 or (01) 22-4427, Fax: (01) 25-3427, *seven chalets. Open May to December.*

Wasa Camp, Box 30974, Lusaka, Tel: (01) 25-3439 or (01) 22-4427, Fax: (01) 25-3427. *Open May to December.*

Nsumbu National Park

Kasaba Bay Lodge, c/o Kachelo Travel, Box 30946, Lusaka, Tel/Fax: (01) 26-3973, E-mail: kacelo@zamnet.zm, *eight chalets. Open all year.*

Kalambo Lodge, Tel: (01) 23-3260, *eight chalets. Open all year.*

Ndole Bay Lodge, Box 21033, Kitwe, Tel: (02) 71-1150, Fax: (02) 71-1390, *two chalets. Open all year*

Nkamba Bay Lodge, Gametracker Safaris, Box 33772, Lusaka, Tel: (01) 28-8884, Fax: (01) 28-7677, E-mail: nkamba@zamnet.zm, *nine chalets. Open all year.*

North Luangwa National Park

Buffalo Camp, Private Bag E395, Lusaka, Tel/Fax: (01) 25-2452, *five chalets. Open June to October.*

Mwaleshi Camp, Private Bag E395, Lusaka, Tel/Fax: (01) 22-8682, *12 chalets. Open June to October.*

Kapishya Hot Springs, Private Bag E395, Lusaka, Tel: (01) 22-8682, Fax: (01) 22-2906. *Open June to October*

Sioma Ngwezi National Park

Maziba Bay Safaris, Tel: (01) 22-8682, Fax: (01) 22-2906, or write to Central Reservations, Sunlink International (Pvt) Ltd, Box HG 529, Highlands, Harare, Zimbabwe, *six chalets.*

MISCELLANEOUS INFORMATION

Driving Tips and Spares

Because this book is principally aimed at visitors touring the country in their own vehicles we thought it advisable to include some guidance on appropriate vehicles, what spares to take and some general tips on driving conditions travellers are likely to encounter in Zambia. What follows below is hardly comprehensive, but rather a few tips aimed at the novice intrepid traveller.

As mentioned elsewhere, a four-wheel-drive is not absolutely essential to visit Zambia, but it would significantly extend the range of your travels. In principle, normal sedan cars would be limited to the main tar and hard gravel roads. The main camps in the Kafue, South Luangwa, Kasanka and Lochinvar national parks would be accessible, but more remote camps and national parks would not be. There are not many places that a robust vehicle with reasonably high clearance such as a light pick-up or bakkie could not reach in the dry season, although many of the smaller roads and those in national parks become impassable in the wet season. The smaller roads in western Zambia, which tend to be very sandy, are possibly the only routes where four-wheel-drives are essential in all seasons.

The best option then is a four-wheel-drive and the best makes are strong, simple and popular vehicles for which spare parts and bush mechanics will not be a problem. Any number of different imported vehicle makes are to be found in Zambia. Government officials and those with the money drive spanking new Toyotas, although there are vast numbers of ancient and heavily abused Land Rovers still grinding down Zambian roads under colossal loads. Bear in mind that armed car thieves and hijackers of Lusaka and the northern Copperbelt have a preference for new, white or otherwise anonymous looking pick-ups and four-wheel-drives.

Generally fuel is readily available with diesel and petrol in equal supply. Occasionally whole regions suffer brief shortages, so it is advisable to make regular enquiries. Fuel costs have been rocketing, but at the moment they are about the same as those elsewhere in southern Africa. Travellers should have a fuel capacity of over 100 litres and are well advised always to have one or two jerry cans of spare petrol over and above projected requirements.

It goes without saying that vehicles should be serviced before your trip – preferably weeks before so that ongoing problems can be ironed out. This is especially important in older model Land Rovers in which badly leaking oil seals can prove very irritating. Pack a comprehensive set of tools and spare parts. With regard to tools, a strong wheel spanner and good tyre levers, a puncture repair kit, a set of sockets and spanners ('imperial' for old Land Rovers), several screwdrivers, a tow rope, a strong jack and something broad and firm to stabilise it on soft ground may be considered essential.

In addition, take jump leads, some electrical flex, insulation tape and a lubricating aerosol. If you are going into the bush take pliers, wire cutters and a roll of stout wire. It is quite remarkable what you can make, fix or hold together with good wire. A hammer, hand drill and rivet gun, a wood saw and hacksaw, a shifting spanner and a whole range of self-tapping screws and nuts and bolts may prove useful.

Spares

Definitely pack a litre or two of engine oil, gearbox oil and hydraulic fluid. A condenser and set of points, a spare sparkplug and a coil, coolant hoses, fanbelt and spare tyres and tubes should be considered essential. If doing an extensive trip, a spare distributor cap and rotor are recommended. If the vehicle has an old-style alternator with detachable rectifier, regulator and brushes, take a spare set of these. Potholed roads wear down your undercarriage and a set of shackle bolts and bushes are a good idea (especially for old Land Rovers). Broken springs can usually wait to be replaced in major centres. Most of the listed parts can be found in the bigger towns, but they may prove expensive.

It is desirable to have some mechanical knowledge and you certainly should not venture far from the beaten track in remote areas without it, although in most towns in Zambia you will find a bush mechanic to assist you. Ask at the fuel stations if there are any, otherwise ask at the Zesco offices. But be careful: many such mechanics have an intimate knowledge of car engines, but are not above using your misfortune to line their pockets. Negotiate prices beforehand. They will be extremely reluctant to do this, but you should insist on an hourly rate and knowing the price of parts. It is also advisable to accompany the 'mechanic' when he goes off to fetch a spare part so that you can buy it from its supplier directly.

If despite all your precautions your vehicle still grinds to a halt, don't panic. More often than not the reason will be a simple one. So, if the reason is not apparent go through the possibilities systematically. Do not overlook the obvious.

First decide whether the fault is electrical or mechanical.

Mechanical faults are indicated if the starter motor turns over and there is a spark at the sparkplug leads but the engine won't take. Electrical problems can be more puzzling. Remember that in the electrical system components are connected to the positive terminal of the battery by leads and earthed to the body of the car, as is the negative terminal, thereby completing the circuit. If lights, hooter, etc., are not working, check the major earth leads connecting the battery to the body and the engine or gearbox to the body. If you have been doing a lot of bush driving it is quite likely they may have become disconnected. But if the lights work and the battery remains charged then test systematically back from the sparkplugs to the distributor, coil, solenoid, etc. A spare headlamp makes a good circuit tester.

Tips for four-wheel-driving

The art of four-wheel-driving is simply based on common sense and being gentle with your vehicle. If you have free-wheeling hubs, lock them before going into bad conditions. When it looks as if you are going to get stuck do not try and turn out of your tracks. Change down and try to proceed slowly. If you do stop, try to reverse. Don't over-rev the engine and, especially in old Land Rovers, do not do that and then suddenly release the clutch. That is how you break side-shafts. Try reversing then going forward repeatedly a few times to clear a little running space. Don't push the vehicle to its limits – you will break something. Rather opt for the spades-and-branches routine. When driving off-road be very careful of tree stumps and holes. Go slowly through water and walk through it first to test depth (unless you are in areas where there are crocodiles!). If planning to ford deep water, make sure that the drainage hole at the bottom of the bell housing is plugged and unplug it afterwards.

Many African travellers these days pack hi-lift, jumbo or, as they are referred to in Zambia, Tanganyika jacks. They are extremely useful but also need common sense. If they are not properly greased they will not work. When packing do not secure them to your vehicle where they will get covered with dust and mud. If you do have to transport them on the outside of the vehicle, wrap the working parts tightly to protect them. Check that they can actually be used on your vehicle beforehand. Some modern four-wheel-drive sedans simply have too many fancy fenders and so on to find a purchase. It is even possible to use such a jack as a winch!

Accidents and Emergencies

Road and camping accidents are a hazard that cannot be discounted when adventuring anywhere. And in countries like Zambia, where you might have to be quite self-reliant, being well prepared is important. As we have recommended earlier in this book it is advisable for self-driven travellers to pack a comprehensive medical kit (see pages 32-3) There are books available, such as one published by the St John Ambulance, that give appropriate instruction for the treatment of medical emergencies; and packing such a book along with your kit might be the most sensible advice we can give. Here we can only reiterate the basic principles of dealing with an emergency:

1. Number one: Do not panic. It is necessary that someone takes clear-minded, calm command of the situation. Take the time to make yourself calm now, it will save time later and could save lives. If you have been personally involved, do a thorough personal check first before trying to assist others.

2. Before anything else, assess the situation and determine that the cause of the accident has been dealt with and does not present further immediate danger (for example the dangerous animal is gone or the road accident is over), the road is clear, and an improvised warning system has been established to prevent another accident. (Doing these things will help calm you down and prevent further injury.)

3. Delegate someone to get help.

4. Get your medical kit and **put on rubber gloves**.

5. Differentiate between mildly injured, seriously injured and obviously dead casualties. Then ignore the last category, reassure the first and turn your attention to the middle group. Do not attempt to move the victim unless you absolutely have to, for example in the case of fire.

Now, just as you would with a broken-down car (seriously!), diagnose by a systematic and prioritised assessment. Start with cognition and breathing and then methodically examine the victim from head to toe.

6. Check whether the victim is conscious or unconscious. If they do not respond to your talking to them, use your fingernail to press hard just behind the victim's fingernail. If they do not respond they are unconscious. Then check the victim's pulse and breathing.

7. Pulse: If no pulse, move straight into CPR and mouth to mouth resuscitation. If there is a pulse, no matter how weak, **do not do CPR**.

8. Breathing: If the victim is unconscious there is a danger the victim will choke on their tongue, so open the mouth and sweep the tongue for-

ward with your finger. If your kit has an oral airway, insert the device to keep the air passage open. A bush remedy otherwise is to spike the tongue into the lower lip with a long thorn. (They're unconscious and won't feel a thing!)

9. In the event of a motor accident or serious animal attack, the biggest danger is damage to the spinal cord. Thus do not move the victim, until with assistance you can do so keeping the spinal column, that is the back and neck, absolutely rigid. Always keeping that in mind, lie the victim down on their back or – if vomiting or bleeding from the mouth – on one side with the upper leg crooked forward to stabilise and with supports at the neck to prevent movement. *Don't let the head or neck move.*

10. Continually monitor breathing and pulse. Make that your priority until professional help arrives.

11. In the event of copious blood loss from a wound, staunch with wads of bandage or cloth. Later, if there is no professional help, clean the wound with running water and bandage.

12. Burns: If serious burns are sustained, for goodness sake don't try any of your grandmother's recipes or even paraffin gauze. Rinse the burn with as much clean cold water as is at hand and wrap in clear polythene-like clingwrap.

13. Broken bones: Prioritise, obviously. Spine, head and torso are important, limbs much less so. Remember, you probably cannot tell if there is a spinal injury so keep the spine rigid until professional help is at hand. Seriously broken bones may cause internal injuries. There is almost nothing you can do about this except to monitor and deal with what you can, i.e. make sure the victim can breathe, and when they cannot, assist them with mouth to mouth.

14. Head injuries: Staunch severe bleeding, but do not remove impaled objects. Monitor the victim's cognitive faculties for signs of concussion or brain damage. Bleeding from the ears is a possible sign of serious head injury.

15. If you are carrying a saline drip, now is the time to administer it whatever the injury, even in cases of very severe shock. If you are carrying one but do not know how to administer it, do as follows: take one of the sterile packed needles from the kit and open it. Take the victim's forearm and squeeze the veins in the wrist. This will make the veins stand out in the middle of the forearm. Slide the needle at a shallow angle towards the elbow, into the most prominent vein. You will know you have scored a direct hit when blood drips from the back of the needle. If not try again. When the needle taps blood from the vein,

check there is no air in the tube of the drip by releasing some of the fluid and connect it to the needle. Then ease open the tap and secure the bag above the patient.

16. Now look to the victim's comfort. If it is hot, get them in the shade, or if you cannot move them (remember spinal injuries) get shade over them. Similarly make sure they are warm if it is cold. Especially in hot conditions make sure the patient is getting enough fluids. Now you can administer appropriate pain killers and deal with more minor symptoms. If injuries are serious, just keep going through the monitoring examination outlined above until help is at hand.

Remember your role is to keep the victim alive, not to treat them. Get proper medical help as quickly as possible.

The above guidance is based on what we have experienced or been taught, but we must advise you that we are fellow travellers, not doctors. There is professional advice out there. Get it.

Directory of Safari Companies and Tour Operators

Acacia Safaris, Box 30475, Lusaka, Tel: (01) 27-2105, Fax: 27-4798.

Africa Bound, Box 31567, Lusaka, Tel: (01) 22-9154.

African Experience Limited, Box 30106, Lusaka, Tel/Fax: (01) 26-4256 or Johannesburg (011) 888-8015, Fax: (011) 888-5435, E-mail: lafex@icon.co.za.

African Extreme, c/o Shearwater, Victoria Falls, Tel: 475-7831.

African Travel and Tours, Box 350036, Chilanga, Tel: (01) 21-5374.

Africa Tour Designers Ltd, Box 131802, Lusaka, Tel: (01) 27-3864, Fax: 27-3865, E-mail: atd@zamnet.zm.

Andrews Travel and Safaris, Box 31993, Lusaka, Tel: (01) 22-3147 or 22-1582, Telex: ZA40104.

Big Five Travel and Tours, Box 35317, Lusaka, Tel: (01) 22-1978 or 22-1098, Telex: ZA40091.

Bonar Travel and Tours, Box 4211, Ndola, Tel: (02) 61-1185 Telex: ZA3410.

Busanga Trails, Box 31322, Lusaka, Tel: (01) 22-1694, Telex: ZA40081.

Busanga Travel and Tours, Box 37538, Lusaka, Tel: (01) 22-0897 or 22-3628 or 22-4971, Fax: 22-1681.

Bushwackers Travel and Tours/Adventure Holidays, Box 320172, Lusaka, Tel/Fax: (01) 25-3869, E-mail: bushwack@zamnet.zm.

Bwaato Adventures, PO Box 60096, Livingstone, Tel/Fax: 32-4227.

Chundukwa Adventure Trails Ltd, Box 61160, Livingstone, Tel/Fax: (03) 32-4452, E-mail: chunduka@zamnet.zm.

Chunga Safaris and Tours, C/o TG Travel, Lusaka, Tel: (01) 22-1867 or 22-6019.

Circuit Safaris, Box 21491, Kitwe, Tel: (02) 21-2277 or 21-4447, Telex: ZA51750.

Discover Business Tours and Travel, Box 86400, Lusaka, Tel: (01) 21-2302 or 21-3127.

Eagle Travel, Box 34530, Lusaka, Tel: (01) 22-9060 or 22-8605, Telex: ZA42670.

Farland Tours and Travel, Tel: 61-5060.

Gwembe Safaris, Box 630067, Choma, Tel: (032) 2-0021 or 2-0169, Fax: 2-0054.

Hunters Limited Africa, Box 33050, Lusaka, Tel: (01) 23-0576 or 23-7748, Telex: ZA40009.

Iain MacDonald Safaris, Box 30684, Lusaka, Tel: (01) 22-8184/5, Telex: ZA40187.

Island Safaris, Box 35943, Lusaka, Tel: (01) 21-4964, Telex: ZA45940.

Jadason Tours and Safaris, Box 31212, Lusaka, Tel: (01) 21-1615, Telex: ZA45380.

Jul's Limited, travel, car hire & tours, Tel: (01) 29-2979 or 29-3972, Fax: 29-1246.

Jungle Safaris, Box 30050, Lusaka, Tel: (01) 28-7748 or 28-6706, Telex: ZA40009.

Kachelo Travel Limited, Tel/Fax: (01) 26-5560 or 26-5569 or 26-3973, E-mail: kachelo@zamnet.zm.

Kafue Boat Tours, Box 30813, Lusaka, Tel: (01) 25-0772, Telex: ZA41390.

Kafue Marina, Box 30743, Lusaka, Tel: (01) 21-4926 or 21-8964, Telex: ZA42830.

Kazuma Safaris, Box 30793, Lusaka, Tel: (01) 21-3983, Telex: ZA40233.

Lake Tanganyika Safaris, Box 20104, Kitwe, Tel: (02) 21-4905.

Linyanti Safaris, Box 60443, Livingstone, Tel: (03) 35-0371.

Luangwa Crocodiles Safaris, Box 37541, Mfuwe, Tel: (062) 21-4672/ 21-7023, Telex: ZA40129.

Lubi Travel and Tours, Box 37782, Lusaka, Tel: (01) 22-3964 or 22-3216.

Lubungu Wildlife, Box 31701, Kafue National Park, Tel: (01) 22-5650 or 22-3216.

Lubungu Wildlife Safaris, Box 21701, Lusaka, Tel: (01) 25-3848, Telex: ZA41530.

Magic Carpet Travel and Tours, Tel: (01) 22-2534.

Mahogany Tours and Car Hire, Box 81349, Lusaka, Tel: (01) 25-1268.

Makora Quest, canoeing safaris, Box 60420, Livingstone, Tel: (03) 32-4253, Fax: 32-0732, E-mail: quest@zamnet.zm.

Mercury Tours and Travel Agency, Box 32674, Lusaka, Tel: (01) 22-8975, Telex: ZA40217.

Mulobezi Safaris, Lusaka, Tel: (01) 28-8298 or 28-9056, Telex: ZA40292.

Musungwa Safaris, Box 20104, Kitwe, Tel: (02) 21-5188, Telex: ZA51390.

National Hotels Development Corporation, Box 33200, Lusaka, Tel: (01)24-9144/8, Fax: 24-8352, Telex: ZA44140.

Nkwazi Africa Tours, South Africa, Tel/Fax: (011) 762-4606.

Norman Carr Safaris, Box 30475, Lusaka or Box 100 Mfuwe, Tel: (062) 4-5015, Telex: ZA63008, E-mail: kapani@zamnet.zm

Owani Safaris, Box 77, Mfuwe, Tel: (062) 4-5017.

Premier Travel and Tours, Box 37012, Lusaka, Tel: (01) 22-2931 or 22-4138 or 22-3324.

Raft Quest, 285 Chitimukulu Rd, Livingstone, Tel: (03) 32-2086, Fax: (03) 32-0732, E-mail: quest@zamnet.zm.

Robin Pope Safaris, Box 320154, Lusaka or Box 80, Mfuwe, Tel: (062) 4-5090, Tel: (062) 4-5051, E-mail: popesaf@zamnet.zm.

Royal Travel and Tours, Box 71853, Ndola, Tel: (02) 61-4838, Telex: ZA33320.

Safariland Limited, Box 33830, Bangweulu, Tel: (04) 3-2164, Fax: 36-2164.

Safari Par Excellence, Tel: (01) 27-3864 or 27-4883, Fax: 27-3865, E-mail: safpar@global.co.za.

Safari Travel Agency, PO Box 60719, Livingstone, Tel: (03) 32-3232, Fax: 32-4434, E-mail: bushtrak@zamnet.zm.

Savannah Trails, Box 37783, Lusaka, Tel: (01) 22-4457 or 22-4427, Fax: 22-4427, Telex: ZA40257.

Shenton Safaris, Tel. (062)4-5064 or (01) 29-0146, E-mail: shensaf@zamnet.zm.

Shiwa Safaris, Box 1, Shiwa Ngandu or Box 1, Chisamba.

Sobek Zambezi Expeditions, Box 60957, Livingstone, Tel: (03) 32-1432, Telex: ZA24018.

South End Travel Agency, Box 60225, Lusaka, Tel: (01) 32-0773, Telex: ZA24027.

Stamul Travel and Tours, Box 31541, Lusaka, Tel: (01) 22-1653, Telex: ZA40510.

Summit Safaris, Lunga Luswishi, Tel: (01) 21-6689 or 21-6318.

Sunrise Travel and Tours, Box 34608, Lusaka, Tel: (01) 21-5903.

Syndicate Safaris Ltd, Box 32904, Lusaka, Tel: (01) 21-6049

TG Travel Ltd, Box 32591, Lusaka, Tel: (01) 22-7807 or 22-6019.

Ticcotravel and Tours, Box 410707, Kasama, Tel: (01) 22-1533.

Tiger Fishing Tours, PO Box 31730, Lusaka, Tel/Fax: (01) 26-2810, E-mail: tiger@zamnet.zm.

Tongabezi Safaris Ltd, Private Bag 31, Livingstone, Tel: (03) 32-3235, Fax: (03) 32-3224, E-mail: tonga@zamnet.zm, Website: www.tongabezi. com.

Top Flight Travel and Tours, Tel: (01) 22-4415, Fax: 22-4436.

Transcat Tours, overland camping adventures, Box 32540, Lusaka, Tel: (01) 26-1683, Fax: 26-2438.

United Touring Company, PO Box 61081 Livingstone Tel: (03) 32-4409, Fax 32-4414.

Voyagers Zambia Ltd, Ndola, Tel: (02) 64-0656 or 64-0241/2, Telex: ZA30078.

Wilderness Trails, Box 30970, Lusaka, Tel: (01) 22-0112/5, Fax: 22-0116, Telex: ZA40143.

Wild Frontiers, South Africa, Tel: (011) 315-4838, Fax: (011) 315-4850.

Zambelina Safaris, Box 36147, Lusaka, Tel: (01) 22-9444, Telex: ZA40143.

Zamtravel Tours, Box 30056, Lusaka, Tel: (01) 22-8681, Fax: 22-1205, Telex: ZA45121.

Car Hire Companies

Airmaster Car Hire, Tel: (01) 22-1708 or 22-6966.

Avis, Headquarters – Cusa House, Cairo Road, Box 35317, Lusaka, Tel: (01) 27-2934, Fax: 22-1978. Lusaka Airport – Tel: (01) 27-1058, Fax: 27-1262.

Car Hire of Zambia Ltd, Box 30083, Lusaka, Tel: (01) 22-2454.

Jul's Car Hire, Tel: (01) 29-39-72, Fax: 29-1246, E-mail: julscat@zamnet.zm.

Omar's Car Hire, Box 30083, Lusaka, Tel: (01) 22-2454/22-1240

Ridgeway Car Hire, Box 30929, Lusaka, Tel: (01) 22-5209.

Taiwo Car Hire, Tel: (01) 29-1283, Fax: 29-1248, E-mail: taiwo@zamnet.zm.

Voyagers Rentals, Lusaka – Tel: (01) 25-3082/3, Fax: 25-3048, E-mail: voyagers@zamnet.zm. Ndola – Tel: (02) 62-0604, Fax: 62-0605, E-mail: voyrent@coppernet.zm.

Zamkar Car Hire Ltd, Box 23420, Kitwe, Tel: (02) 21-2884 or 21-1128.

Zungulila Zambia, Box 31475, Lusaka, Tel: 22-7730, Fax: 22-7729, Telex: ZA40172, E-mail: zung@zamnet.zm.

Air Charter Companies

Airwaves, Tel: (01) 22-4334, Fax: 22-3504, E-mail: airwaves@zamnet.zm.

Anderson Air Charter, Box 22671, Lusaka, Tel: (01) 28-6851, Telex: 43880.

Avocet, Tel: (01) 23-3422, Fax: 22-9261/2, E-mail: avocet@zamnet.zm.

Bushveld Helicopters, Lusaka Airport, Box 35058, Lusaka, Tel: (01) 27-8357.

Del Air, PO Box 60012, Livingstone, Tel (03) 32-0058, Fax: 32-3095.

Eastern Air, Lusaka, Tel: (01) 23-3097 or 22-7739, Fax: 22-5178, E-mail: sblagus@zamnet.zm.

Government Communications Flight, Box 310291, Lusaka, Tel: (01) 27-1374, Fax: 27-1423.

Lodge Hopper Tours Helicopter Travel, Box 2801, Nelspruit 1200, South Africa, Tel: (01311) 58-1103, Fax: (01311) 58-1440.

Proflight, Tel: (01) 26-36-86, Fax: 26-1941, E-mail: proflight@zamnet.zm.

Roan Air, Lusaka Airport, Box 310277, Lusaka, Tel: (01) 27-1066 or 22-8822 or 22-9115, Fax: 22-3227 or 27-1054, E-mail: roanair@zamnet.zm.

Zambia Flying Doctors' Service, Tel: (02) (02) 61-1417/8/9, Fax: (02) 61-4054, E-mail: zfded@zamnet.zm.

Directory of Foreign Diplomatic Missions and Embassies

All based in Lusaka – dialling code 01

Angola
Plot 6660, Mumana Rd
Olympia Park Ext
Tel: 29-1142 or 29-0346

Botswana
Diplomatic Triangle
Tel: 25-0555 or 25-0019
Fax: 25-3895

Brazil
74 Independence Ave
Tel: 25-0400
Fax: 25-1652

Bulgaria
4045 Lukulu Rd
Tel: 26-3295
Tlx: 40351

Canada
5119 United Nations Ave
Tel: 25-0833

China
7430 Haile Selassie Ave
Tel: 273-7770 or 25-2410
Tlx: 41360

Cuba
5574 Magove Rd
Tel: 25-1380 or 25-1308

Democratic Republic of Congo
1124 Parirenytwa Rd
Tel: 21-3343 OR 22-9044/5

Denmark
Ndeke House, Haile Selassie Ave
Tel: 25-4182 or 25-3750
Fax: 25-4618

Egypt
Pandit Nehru Rd
Tel: 25-4149
Tlx: 40021

Finland
74 Independence Ave
Tel: 25-1988 or 25-2026·
Fax: 25-4981
Tlx: 43460
E-mail: finemb@zamnet.zm

France
74 Independence Ave
Tel: 25-1332
Tlx: 41430

Germany
5209 United Nations Ave
Tel: 25-0664
Tlx: 41410

Greece
54 Joseph Mwila Rd,
Rhodes Park
Tlx: 40280

India
Pandit Nehru Rd
Tel: 25-3006
Tlx: 41420

Ireland
6663 Katima Mulilo Rd,
Olympia Park Extension
Tel: 29-0482
Tlx: 43110

Italy
Diplomatic Triangle,
Independence Ave
Tel: 25-0775
Tlx: 43380

Japan
3218 Haile Selassie Ave.
Tel: 25-1555
Tlx: 41470

Kenya
United Nations Ave
Tel: 25-0772

Korea
8237 Nangwenya Rd, Rhodes Park
Tel: 251-2978

Malawi High Commission
Bishops Rd, Kabulonga
Tel: 26-5768

Mozambique
Lufubu Rd, Kalundu
Tel: 29-0411 or 29-1251
Tlx: 45900

Namibia
6968 Kabanga Rd, Rhodes Park
Tel: 25-2250

Netherlands
6717 Chilawamabwe Rd
Tel: 29-2310
Tlx: 40211

Nigeria
Findeco House, Cairo Rd
Tel: 25-3117 or 25-3268

Norway
Plot 245/65 Birdcage Walk,
Haile Selassie Ave
Tel: 25-1199

Portugal
Kudu Rd
Tel: 25-3740
Tlx: 40010

Romania
2 Leopards Hill Road, Kabulonga
Tel: 26-2182

Russia
Plot 6407, Diplomatic Triangle
Tel: 25-2183 or 25-2128
Fax: 25-3582
Tlx: 40341

Saudi Arabia
4896 Los Angeles Blvd
Tel: 25-3266 or 25-3325
Tlx: 45550

Somalia
Plot G3/377A Kabulonga
Tel: 26-2119 or 26-3944
Tlx: 40270

Sweden
Alick Nkatha Ave, Longacres
Tel: 25-1711

Tanzania
Ujaama House,
United Nations Ave
Tel: 25-3320

United Kingdom
Independence Ave
Tel: 25-1133

Zimbabwe
Haile Selassie Ave
Tel: 25-4006/12/18

United States of America
United Nations Ave
Tel: 25-0955

Zambian Missions Abroad

Angola
PO Box 1496, Luanda
Tel: 244-2-30162
Fax: 244-2-393-483
Telex: 998-3439

Belgium
469 Avenue Moliere, Brussels
Tel: 32-2-343-5649
Fax: 32-2-347-4333
Telex: 846-63102

Botswana
PO Box 362, Gaborone
Zambia House, The Mall,
Gaborone
Tel: 267-351-951/2
Fax: 267-353-952
Telex: 991-2416

China
5 Dongsijie, San-Li-Tun,
Beijing (Peking)
Tel: 8610-6532-1554/1778
Fax: 8610-6532-1891
Telex: 716-22388

Democratic Republic of Congo
BP 1144, Kinshasa
Tel: 243-12-23-038
Telex: 969-21209

Egypt
PO Box 253 Mohandessine,
Cairo 12311
10 El-Gumhuriya Muttahada
Square
Tel: 20-2-361-0282/3
Fax: 20-2-361-0833
Telex: 927-2262

Ethiopia
PO Box 1909, Addis Ababa
Old Airport Area
Tel: 251-1-711-302
Telex: 976-21065

Germany
Bad Godesberg, Mittelstrasse
39-5300 Bonn 2
Tel: 49-228-376-811/3
Fax: 49-228-379-536
Telex: 841-88551

India
F-8/22 Vasant Vihar,
New Delhi 110057
Tel: 91-11-687-7681/7848/7862
Telex: 953-66084
E-mail: zambia@nde.ssnl.net.in

Japan
10-2 Ebara 1-Chome, Shinagawa-Ku, Tokyo 142
Tel: 813-34910121
Fax: 813-34910123
E-mail: zamet@crisscross.com

Kenya
City Hall Annex, Box 48741, Nairobi
Tel: 254-2-724-850/796/799
Fax: 254-2-718-494
Telex: 963-22193
E-mail: zambiacom@swiftkenya.com

Malawi
Box 30138, Lilongwe
Plot 40/2 Capital Hill, Lilongwe
Tel: 265-731-911
Fax: 265-784-349
Telex: 988-4181

Mozambique
Avenida Kenneth Kaunda, 1286
CP 4655, Maputo
Tel: 258-1-492-452
Tel: 258-1-049-1893
Telex: 946-6415

Namibia
PO Box 22882,Windhoek
22 Curt von Francois Corner
Republic Road
Tel: 264-61-37-610/1
Fax: 264-61-228-162
Telex: 964-0485

Nigeria
PO Box 6119, Lagos
11 Keffi St, South West Ikoyi
Tel: 234-2-269-0426/7
Telex: 961-22966

Russia
Prospect Mira 52 Moscow
Tel: 7-095-288-5001
Fax: 7-095-975-2056
Telex: 871-413462

South Africa
PO Box 12234, Pretoria 0001
353 Sanlam Building, Festival
Street, Hatfield
Tel: 27-012-342-1541
Fax: 27-012-342-4963
Telex: 320016

Sweden
Box 26013, Stockholm
Engelbrektsgatan 7
Tel: 46-8-679-9040
Fax: 46-8-679-6850
Telex: 854-11890
E-mail: zamembas@algonet.se

Switzerland
17-19 Chemin
Du Champ-D'anier, Geneva
1209 Le Petit Saconnex
Tel: 41-022-788-5330/1
Fax: 41-022-788-5340
Telex: 415200

Tanzania
PO Box 2525
Dar-es-Salaam
Tel: 55-51-27-261/2
Fax: 255-51-46-389
Telex: 975-41059

United Kingdom
2 Palace Gate, Kensington,
London W8 5NG
Tel: 44-171-589-6655
Fax: 44-171-581-1353
Telex: 851-263544

United States of America
237 East 52nd St, NY 10022
Tel: 212-758-1110
Fax: 212-758-1319
Telex: 025-62327

2419 Massachusetts Ave NW,
Washington, DC 20008
Tel: 202-265-9717/8/9
Fax: 202-332-0826
Telex: 025-440247
E-mail: zambia@tmn.com

Zimbabwe
Box 4698, Harare
Zambia House, Union Ave, Harare
Tel: 263-4-790-851/2/3/4/5
Telex: 987-24698

Zambia National Tourist Board Offices

Head Office
Lusaka Square, Cairo Rd, Lusaka
Box 30017, Lusaka
Tel: (01) 22-9087
Fax: (01) 22-5174
Telex: ZA41780
E-mail: zntb@zamnet.zm

Livingstone
Tourist Centre, Livingstone
Box 603432, Livingstone
Tel: (03) 32-1487 or 32-1404/5
Fax: (03) 32-1487

Johannesburg
1st Floor, Finance House, Ernest
Oppenheimer Rd, Bruma
Tel: (011) 622-9206/7
Fax: (011) 622-7424
E-mail: zntbjhb@icon.co.za

London
2 Palace Gate, Kensington, W8
5NG
Tel: (081) 587-6343
   or (0171) 225-3221
Fax: (0171) 581-1353
Telex: 28956

New York
9th Floor, 800 2nd Ave (between
42nd and 43rd st), NY 10017
Tel: (212) 949-0133
Fax: (212) 979-0134
E-mail: eddbo@aol.com

INDEX